BACKPACKER
MAGAZINE'S

GUIDE TO THE
Appalachian Trail

BACKPACKER
MAGAZINE'S

GUIDE TO THE
Appalachian Trail

Second Edition

JIM CHASE

STACKPOLE
BOOKS

Published by
STACKPOLE BOOKS
5067 Ritter Rd.
Mechanicsburg, PA 17055
www.stackpolebooks.com

Printed in the United States of America

10 9 8 7 6 5 4 3 2 1

First Edition

Cover design by Wendy Reynolds
Cover photograph of Denis Clark ascending Moxie Bald, Maine, by Alexandra C. Daley-Clark

Library of Congress Cataloging-in-Publication Data

Chase, Jim.
    Backpacker magazine's guide to the Appalachian trail / Jim Chase.—
2nd ed.
        p. cm.
    Includes bibliographical references and index.
    ISBN 0-8117-3185-5 (alk. paper)
    1. Backpacking—Appalachian Trail. 2. Appalachian Trail—Description
and travel. I. Backpacker. II. Title.

GV199.42.A68C46 2005
796.51—dc22
                                                                    2005002369

Contents

Acknowledgments

FROM THE ACKNOWLEDGMENTS, FIRST EDITION
Acknowledgments must start with my wife, Barbara, for her help and encouragement and for amusing our son, Charles, when I needed to write, as well as for her endless reading of my accounts of places she has never seen and for her superb comments on those accounts. Also to Charles himself, for understanding why Daddy couldn't go bike riding. Thanks, too, to my parents for instilling in me the love of wild places and the urge to preserve them, and especially to my father for teaching me to backpack before it was in fashion. Special thanks to my wonderful mother-in-law, Madeleine L. Collins, for her love, support, and for the countless things she did for me and the rest of the family during the research and writing that went into this work.

ACKNOWLEDGMENTS, SECOND EDITION
Times change, and the writing of the second edition was much different from that of the first. In the place of the many people who communicated with me about their knowledge of the Trail for the First Edition, I thank the many webmasters who made so much information so accessible.

There are always people, however, without whose help things just don't happen. Once again, my wife, Barbara, deserves kudos for support in too many areas to mention here. Then there are the folks who helped by putting feet to sections of the Trail so I could put mine elsewhere. Thanks to my son, Charles, now full-grown, for his ground-level research in North Carolina, Tennessee, Virginia, West Virginia, Maryland, New Jersey, and Maine. Thanks also to his University of Delaware compadres Jimmy Sarakatsannis and Jimmy Vennard ("Blue Hen") for their help in North Carolina, Virginia, West Virginia, and Maryland. Thanks to my other son, Ned ("Alfa"), for his help and company on too many trails to name. These reports from the Trail were invaluable, and Jimmy S's Dixie Chili was a great contribution.

Thanks to the ATC staff once again for timely direction. Michele Miller at the Boiling Springs office in Pennsylvania was particularly informative. As always, I'm grateful to the countless anonymous hikers up and down the trail for their fellowship and conversation. They're an interesting and surprising group. If you'd seen "Shrek" walk into the Speck Pond shelter, you'd know what I mean.

As always, thanks and sincerest homage to Benton MacKaye and Myron Avery for their vision and commitment, and for making it all happen. They left the world a much better place, which can't be said for many people.

Introduction: The World's First Linear Park

BEGINNINGS

> *"The project is one for a series of recreational commu-*
> *nities throughout the Appalachian chain of mountains*
> *from New England to Georgia, these to be connected by*
> *a walking trail."*

Thus wrote Benton MacKaye (pronounced muh-KYE) in 1921, in what was to become the unofficial manifesto of the Appalachian Trail. "Its purpose is to establish a base for a more extensive and systematic development of outdoor community life," he continued. "It is a project in housing and community architecture."

Clearly, this wasn't merely a simple desire to see a long footpath blazed along the crest of the Appalachian Mountains. MacKaye had more in mind—much more.

THE START OF THE TRAIL

I remember that when I was a kid, growing up within a few miles of the Trail route in upstate New York, I assumed that the AT had always been there. In fact, it surprises most people that the Appalachian Trail is not an old footpath of the Native Americans who lived there long before the European immigration. You'd think that at the very least, it was a trade route for the settlers, or a compilation of avenues for pioneers, traders, Revolutionary armies, or what-have-you, tacked together at logical points by dedicated volunteers.

The volunteers part is true enough. And the Trail does in places use byways of our Native American and colonial forebears, although not in any consistent or organized way.

The truth of the matter is, the old routes tended to be in valleys and along riverbanks, for obvious reasons. The Appalachian Trail, on the other hand, is a ridgeline route, traveling for most of its distance along the very highest route available. That places it far from the routes of the settlers or their predecessors. In fact, the Trail as it exists today is a creation whose birth is well within the recollection of many people. It was blazed, and is maintained, by the aforementioned dedicated volunteers, who are the sole reason for its existence.

The Trail was first given life in the mind of a single person: J. Benton MacKaye, a civil servant working for the federal government. MacKaye published his manifesto, "An Appalachian Trail: A Project in Regional Planning," in the October 1921 issue of the *Journal of the American Institute of Architects*. Having long recognized the beneficial effect of trips to the wilderness on increasingly citified Americans, MacKaye was proposing nothing less than a linear park, along the crest of the great Appalachian ranges, from Mt. Mitchell in North Carolina to Mt. Washington in New Hampshire.

WILDERNESS NOSTALGIA

America in 1921 was ready, even eager, for the idea. After 300 years of mortal combat against the "howling wilderness," the last frontiers had been subdued in the previous century. Described by Roderick Nash in his seminal work *Wilderness and the American Mind,* the relationship between Americans and the wildlands around them was positively adversarial.

A change, at first subtle, and then pronounced, had taken place in the American conception of wilderness. Wilderness, with its mystery and danger, had been eaten up by a voracious nation. The Great North Woods had been felled, the plains plowed; the buffalo were gone. The wildlands that had been the very formation of the solid, self-sufficient American character had been tamed. Naturally, they were soon replaced by a romanticism that appeared in the latter nineteenth century. Wilderness was then portrayed not as threatening, but rather as untamed and pure. In the nineteenth-century romantic mind, a new concept emerged: the "noble savage" ideal of James Fenimore Cooper. America in 1921 was in perhaps the heyday of a great nostalgia, heralded a hundred years before in the civilized eastern states by such luminaries as Cooper, Henry David Thoreau, and Ralph Waldo Emerson. It was a yearning for the vanished American frontier—a sentiment that was to produce, among other things, the Wild West show, the Hudson River School of painting, the Boy Scouts and Girl Scouts, the National Parks system, and the cowboy-and-outlaw-romanticizing dime novel.

In 1921, the horrors of World War I had served only to suggest to the war-weary country that perhaps civilization (as represented by the jaded, immoral Old World) wasn't all it was cracked up to be, and that what America needed was a healthy dose of what had made it great in the first place: wilderness, and the people of character who had "tamed" it. "Without parks and outdoor life," exclaimed Colorado mountain guide Enos Mills in 1917, "all that is best in civilization will be smothered."

To the American public of the early '20s, there was plenty of evidence that this was true. The post-war unemployment was at its height; for the first time, population in the cities was exceeding that in the country, and the pace of life in general was accelerating. MacKaye hit upon the idea of wilderness camps as an escape for world-weary workers from the cities, people of all classes.

Then, there was a real problem to be solved. Conflict between labor and management was in many places reaching crisis proportions. Eugene V. Debs, a hero of the infamous Pullman Strike of 1894–95, had run for president the previous year for the Socialist Party, and he had gotten a million votes—while sitting in prison. Urban workers in America and elsewhere were exhibiting an alienation from the workplace that would have been unthinkable just a few years before among their agrarian predecessors. Put simply, they didn't like their jobs.

Faced with a legion of workers who were falling inexorably into the workaday humdrum of industrial age living, MacKaye proposed to put a little adventure into their lives, to give them the chance to prove themselves to themselves, and to nobody else. Rather than live out the rat-race all of their days, they could breathe, function as they wished. They could become the heroes of their own life stories. Nature and wilderness would be their teacher, their foil, their companion— their friend. In wilderness, modern people could, in words found in Clarence Stein's introduction to MacKaye's seminal article, *re-create* themselves. (Stein was a friend of MacKaye's, a member of the Association of Architects, and an early Trail backer.)

Wilderness romanticism had already had its effects in 1921. John Muir had done battle in the West to preserve the wildlands of the Sierra Nevada as a temple of nature. Aldo Leopold had gone far to develop the theories of ecology, beginning the process of educating Americans and the world that there was a natural balance that had to be preserved. Bob Marshall would, just a few years later, burst forth from the Adirondacks to propel—in cahoots with MacKaye and others— thousands of square miles of wilderness into federal protection.

It was into this background that MacKaye dropped, almost casually, his idea for a park that would run the length of the Eastern

The backbone of the Appalachian Trail: volunteers build up the cairn on Katahdin in the 1920s. PHOTOGRAPH COURTESY OF THE APPALACHIAN TRAIL CONFERENCE.

Seaboard. People latched onto his idea with a firmness that surprised even MacKaye, nowhere more strongly than in the industrial areas of the Northeast, and within a couple of years, the first sections were blazed. The volunteer corps that would be the lifeblood and driving force of the Trail had begun forming.

And the Trail as we know it was born.

WHY 2,000 MILES?

In a year's time, the number of people who will hike the entire Trail from end to end will usually number less than five hundred, which represents about twenty percent of the hikers who start at one end or the other with the thought of hiking through. As low as this sounds, it's twice the number that would typically make the journey just ten years ago.

Still, the numbers are low, especially when you compare them with the untold tens of thousands who ramble it for short stretches, and a logical question might be: "What does it matter that the Trail is a 2,000-mile, unbroken link?"

The short answer is: it doesn't. Not a particle. The spirit of the Trail is not a matter of thought and reasoning. With the exceptions of the infrequent times when the ridges and peaks along the Trail allow a longer view, a hiker's normal range of vision can be measured in feet, not miles. There is no good, explainable reason why he or she should get a special feeling knowing that the trail under foot is the AT. It's just that they *do* get that feeling. It's a conviction inside that they're part of something.

There are lots of reasons. As the Georgia Appalachian Trail Club puts it in their motto, it may be the "fellowship of the trail." It's a shared experience, a sense of kinship, a binding of like-minded people together.

It shows in a variety of ways: in the powerful drive of local Appalachian Trail clubs to maintain their sections of the Trail to preserve the unbroken link; in the tendency of hikers to "go for a hike on the AT," when there are other trails around, just as good; and in the sheer pride a community takes in having the great Trail pass within its boundaries. They are all part of something special, a part of the rugged, self-sufficient American character.

ON THRU-HIKERS

Much of the literature devoted to the AT is centered on the thru-hikers. These are the many people (in 2003, it was about two thousand) who, each year, start at one end or the other—usually in Georgia—and hike until they reach the opposite end. About one quarter actually complete the journey. They come from all walks of life, and they hike all kinds of ways.

If you run into thru-hikers on the Trail, you'll quickly realize that they are not there for the same reason the rest of us are. That's not to say that theirs is the better reason, or the more compelling, or even the deeper—although it's a pretty profound experience for most of them. It's just that, where our need for wilderness, be it for renewal, beauty, or sheer physical exertion, can be satisfied in a week or a few hours, theirs can only be satisfied by a total commitment. You see, it takes six months to hike the entire AT, and those without total commitment simply don't make it.

If you meet thru-hikers on the Trail, chances are they will be polite but a bit distant. The fact is, they tend to regard us day hikers as tourists, and themselves as the true natives of the Trail community. Don't let it bother you. It's just that, engaged as they are in such a major undertaking, they tend to be a bit detached from the world the rest of us live in. Where we might be concerned with identifying birds, or finding a nice spot for lunch, they have a schedule to keep. They are concerned with their next food pickup, and where they're going to sleep that night. So why do they do it?

There are probably as many reasons why a person thru-hikes as there are thru-hikers, but among those I've met, some general themes stand out.

The first reminds me eerily of the rite of passage in many cultures around the world that I'll call the Vision Quest. In Native American culture, it would often take the form of a young adult leaving the home for the wilderness in search of enlightenment. He or she would fast for long periods of time, pushing their bodies to the limit, and suffering any number of other privations. Often, visions would come, sometimes powerful ones, ones that might influence their spirits for the rest of their lives. In many cultures, it is accompanied by long periods of meditation and contemplation.

If you want to see what I mean, read the Trail Registers in the shelters along the route, especially in the summer months when most of the thru-hikers are passing by. While many thru-hikers in their entries deal with the weather and cravings for ice cream and steaks, others will pour their souls onto the pages, describing what's going on in their minds and spirits. Many are very much within themselves.

The second motive is the Spirit of Adventure. It's much closer to the reasons we all escape to the wilderness from time to time. Closely allied is the "flow experience." These are not unlike the motivations found in mountaineers, polar explorers, or anyone who embarks upon an intensive personal effort on that order.

The seductive quality of such endeavors lies for many people in the elimination of extraneous stimuli. Gone are the honking car horns, the sticky elevator doors, the demanding bosses. All that's left is the Trail and the necessity of walking it. The challenges, though they may be formidable, are simple. Get up the hill, pitch the tent, get in from the storm—things like that. What you do is all part of a flow, a simpler, more reassuring reality. Your benchmark is the measure of how well you can do it, how comfortable you can be in the storm, how many miles you can put in, how self-sufficient you can make yourself. It's just you and the Trail, with everything else eliminated. Your success is easily measured, your satisfaction easy to enjoy without second thoughts. In describing their flow experience, mountaineers say that they don't really think about danger or glory or anything else. Rather, they think simply about the task at hand, and about overcoming the obstacles in their drive for the summit. That's where they get their satisfaction.

The first of many, Earl Shaffer completed the end-to-end hike of the AT in 1948.
PHOTOGRAPH COURTESY OF THE
APPALACHIAN TRAIL CONFERENCE.

In recent years, I've run into a surprising number of folks who start on the Trail simply as an enjoyable way of losing weight. Many of the weight-loss hikers tend to "thru-hike" intermittently: they'll stop for a few months, pick up next year, whatever works for them. In many other ways, however, they share much with other thru-hikers, and respond to the sense of adventure and the flow experience.

One thing I have *never* encountered: a thru-hiker who walked the Trail for recognition.

Thru-hikers typically embark from the southern terminus at Springer Mountain in the early spring—frequently in March, usually in April. This is to take advantage of the warm southern weather to get a jump on the season as Katahdin is usually rather inhospitable at that time of year. April and May see them through the Carolinas and into Virginia. June and July find them passing Harpers Ferry and the Pennsylvania line. By late July and early August, many will have crossed New Jersey and New York and be headed due north in New England. The rest of the month, they will be in the highlands of Vermont and New Hampshire, fortified for the effort by all the conditioning they've gotten to that point.

Usually in September, they're zeroing in on Katahdin, trying to beat the blasts of winter on their way to the wire. Often, they will crinkle through glassy, fragile ice as they cross the frosty Kennebec River on the hikers' ferry. Once at Katahdin, many will have to wait several days for Pamolo, the spirit of the summit, to decide to let them up and to allow the fall storms to clear. They then make their way up to the Greatest Mountain and the finish. What goes on in their minds has been the subject of countless articles and interviews. I'm not sure I've ever heard what sounded like the whole story. I'm not sure that can be told.

Several of the thru-hikers I've met have gone back a year, or two or three, later to do it all again. Many say, "I'm not going to rush it this time." They declare, "This time is for enjoyment, to look at the scenery." Perhaps that's true. On the other hand, perhaps they'll do it even faster. It doesn't matter. For each one, there's something in the experience that they need almost like a drug. It's a fine addiction.

Again, though, things can change. Maybe it's my imagination, but by my strictly unscientific measure (walking the Trail and talking to other hikers) there seem to be a fair number of north-to-south thru-hikers these days. They're still outnumbered—ATC statistics say by about six to one—but in every shelter I've been in during the right season, you'll find at least one or two. My son and I once hiked Mahoosuc Notch in early August and found quite a few, even that late. It seems they start later than their northbound colleagues, reaching Mt. Washington by September and finishing off in the mild Southern winter. In 2003, several north-to-south people we know had to postpone their finish until spring because of harsh winter storms on the Blue Ridge.

Benton MacKaye, speaking of the Trail in the last years of his life, said, "The ultimate purpose? There are three things: 1) to walk; 2) to see; 3) to see what you see. . . . Some people like to record how speedily they can traverse the length of the trail, but I would give a prize for the ones who took the longest time."

Still, I hate to think that MacKaye would object to the true speedsters, the thru-hikers, keeping up their pace of 11 miles per day—or 14 or 21. They're seeing, too, only for them, it's seeing within. A different wind blows in their faces, but it comes from just another kind of recreation. It's perhaps unlike the one that the rest of us enjoy, that MacKaye intended. But it's one that only the Appalachian Trail can provide.

THE TRAIL GUIDES

The individual trail description chapters follow the divisions of the eleven Trail Guides that are published periodically by the Appalachian Trail Conference and its local member clubs. That's on purpose, so you can read up on a section of Trail, perhaps decide on a destination, and then cross-reference with the Trail Guide for the ground-level information that they give so well. The Trail Guides, in order, cover:

1. Maine
2. Vermont and New Hampshire
3. Massachusetts and Connecticut
4. New York and New Jersey
5. Pennsylvania
6. Maryland and Northern Virginia
7. Shenandoah National Park, Virginia
8. Central Virginia
9. Southwestern Virginia
10. North Carolina and Tennessee (including the Great Smokies)
11. North Carolina and Georgia

Even after all these years, I continue to marvel at the Trail Guides for each section. Some have been revised more recently than others, and these are mostly printed on durable plasticized material, are in color, and have more information. All the guides have features that are unique to them. The Vermont–New Hampshire guide, for example, has the best section on geology of the eleven. The recently redone Maine guide introduces an interesting new concept in Trail Guide layout: rather than including all of the detailed trail information in the book itself, it's printed on the back of the maps. The guidebook itself has the information on the history of the Trail, helpful hints, and general trail mileage listings. This gives the hiker the choice of carrying the whole package out onto the trail, or of leaving the book at home and saving weight by carrying just the appropriate maps. (Despite their obvious usefulness, many if not most of the thru-hikers I've met don't carry the guides—too much weight.)

Information common to all Trail Guides includes:

- How to use the guide
- Topographic maps
- The hiker's responsibilities
- Transportation to the Trail
- Descriptions of shelters and campgrounds
- Advice and precautions about things like weather, pests, getting lost, trail relocations, and so on
- Trail markings
- The Appalachian Trail as a whole, including general information on the route, the Appalachian Trail Conference, and the history of the Trail

- Detailed trail descriptions—where the best views are, what the trail is like, etc.

This last item constitutes the greater part of the information contained in any given guide. It is usually detailed to the point of giving mileage markers to the tenth or even hundredth of a mile, and descriptions on the order of: "At mile 5.83, you will find a potable spring rising behind a large rock." The information is the latest available at press time, collected by the same local people who maintain and watch over that section of the Trail. I have seldom found it to be inaccurate.

Usually, the only time it isn't accurate is when the Trail is relocated for one reason or another. That's why the Trail Guides have to be revised every so often, and it's a major source of frustration to the ATC's publications folks—even as they're going to press on any given edition, they know it may be outdated by the time it hits the stands. The absolutely premier way of keeping up on relocations is to join the Appalachian Trail Conference. Its bimonthly newsletter, the *Appalachian Trailway News,* gives authoritative updates on relocations in addition to a lot of other interesting information.

The only route-finding suggestion I would make, beyond the trail guides, is to get U.S. Geological Survey (USGS) maps for the surrounding areas. If the maps that come with the guides have any flaw—and even this has improved significantly, just in the past ten years—it is that they have a narrow focus. It's often difficult to look at these maps and know quickly just what part of the state you're looking at, and the maps won't tell you what you see from most of the lookouts.

WINTER HIKING

Winter hiking on the AT is a matter of location and, to a certain extent, of timing. There have been confirmed cases over the years of hikers enjoying a carefree day on the Trail in shirtsleeves on snowless paths, even in the more northerly sections. On the other hand, several friends of mine got blown off the route last fall in North Carolina.

Virtually every part of the Trail can be hiked in the middle of winter if the right training and precautions are taken. These include extensive research into proper gear, experience in both winter travel and camping, and time spent with the conveyance of choice, be it skis, snowshoes, crampons, or what have you. In Maine, New Hampshire, and Vermont, care should also be taken with avalanches—they're not just a western thing.

Winter hiking is one of life's little-known pleasures. With proper attention to gear and technique, you can have the hills all to yourself.

The views alone are worth the effort. Here are some suggestions, if you have a mind to try the Trail in winter:

- Get good gear—a solid winter tent (much, much warmer than an open shelter), sleeping bag, camp stove, and outer garments at a minimum. A sleeping pad is also essential, as it keeps the cold ground from freezing you from below. Try your gear out in the backyard on a cold night, just like when you were in grade school.
- Talk to people. There's nothing like talking with an experienced hiker to get the true lowdown on what to expect. This is one of many good reasons to join one of the many trail clubs along the way. It's also a good reason to get to know the ranger staff where you're going to be hiking.
- Learn to use mountaineering skis and climbing skins. Skins are wonderful things, enabling you to walk up even steep trails on top of the snow rather than slogging up knee-deep. Then, when you're at the top, you simply rip the skins off and you're off downhill—you'd be amazed how fast you're back in camp, even if you do a leisurely snowplow all the way. Just don't be afraid to take the skis off and walk if you're frightened by a steep section.

    If you're skiing in the bush, *do not* put your hands through the ski pole straps. If your pole basket catches on the brush, the strap can become a kind of hangman's noose and bust up your thumb. It happened to me in New Hampshire.

    Compared to skis, snowshoes come in a decent second. They'll get you up the hill just as fast, though to my mind they're godawful slow on the descent when a hot dinner beckons.
- Stay within your abilities. Your first winter hike shouldn't be on Katahdin or Washington. Try something simpler first. Go to Mt. Greylock in Massachusetts for a good mid-level shakedown, or just take an afternoon on a scenic ridge somewhere. In the South, you'll have to be ready to go right away when the snows hit, but there are plenty of up-and-back peaks to try on a day hike. I have known excellent skiing in North Carolina. Just don't expect powder.
- Know when to quit. Set a "point of no return," and stick to it.
- Check the weather thoroughly. Remember that big mountains create their own weather, so be prepared to react to bad conditions no matter what the Weather Bureau said. Don't be afraid to turn back.

- Carry a charged cell phone, even if you don't intend to use it. Keep it close to your body to keep it warm: freezing can trash the display, and most batteries lose power when they get cold. Keep the phone off until you need it.
- Make sure your friends and loved ones know where you're going and when you're going to be back, and always, always, always register with rangers and anywhere else you can sign your name. (These are good rules year-round, by the way.) Typically, rangers will check the registers if you turn up missing, and they're usually pretty good at triangulating your location from this information.

  If you get rescued, don't get all huffy about it. You'd be amazed how many times rangers and rescue teams reach missing parties, only to have them get all cranky about being rescued. Some get positively offensive. It's bad enough that you feel like an idiot for getting rescued; you don't have to go and prove it. Thank them politely and sincerely, and ask if the squad accepts donations. That's the classy way to act, even if you're absolutely, positively sure you didn't need to be rescued.
- Become an expert on all things pertaining to hypothermia and frostbite. Prevention is relatively easy if you prepare well.
- Remember Murphy's Law.

CHANGES IN THE 2005 EDITION

A lot has happened since this book was first published, back when there was still a Soviet Union. The world situation has changed radically, and as this book goes to press, the United States has new friends and new enemies, and the term "global warming" has gained new and ominous meaning that I'll discuss further in Chapter 2.

On the other hand, since writing the first edition, my approach to hiking and wilderness has remained much the same. I'm still a day and section hiker, and I still get out when I can. Revising the book was, frankly, an excuse to do more of that. I'm a little slower, I carry a cell phone (it's turned off, but I carry it), and I've become more adept at finding places to sit down, but that's about all. My kids have gotten older and both of them are avid hikers and outdoorsmen. They provide further impetus for me to get out on the Trail, and they often accompany me—until they hike away out of sight. They usually wait for me at the next shelter.

The Trail has fared well in these fifteen years. Its 2,100 miles have remained unbroken, and there have been impressive improvements to the route, especially in Pennsylvania and New Jersey. Again, I cover those in the appropriate chapters. The cooperation with the National Park Service to purchase a mile-wide corridor for the Trail has been startlingly successful in many areas. The results of the hard work of the ATC land managers are truly impressive. There are now relatively few sections left that are in danger of being closed down.

One comment I've had over the years about the book is that people wonder why I don't give more information about thru-hiking. I answer that thru-hiking was never the purpose of the book and that the people I really wanted to talk to were day hikers and other short-term users of the AT. Consequently, I've added more about section hiking, including my current picks for favorite day and section hikes. I really want everyone who reads this book to use the Trail and its surroundings as often as they can, even if it's just for a few hours.

Another point I'd like to make more forcefully is the importance of your participation in the Trail process. Local action remains the single best way for those of us concerned with the environment to make our presence felt. Around the time when I wrote the first edition of this book, I had the opportunity to interview Dave Foreman. Dave was one of the founders of Earth First!, an environmental group that became known for its actions against loggers and developers that included tree spiking (driving metal spikes into trees to damage loggers' chainsaws), sabotaging earth-moving equipment and log skidders, and other acts that have been described as "radical." I was mildly surprised to find Dave to be a rather low-key, logical, and well-spoken fellow. I wonder what I expected.

What I remember most about the interview, and the reason I mention it here, is a thing that Dave said to me. I don't remember his exact words, but the gist of it was that sometimes, the most effective action for preservation of the environment happens at the local level. Other people could spend their time lobbying government, he said, and he was fine with that. But sometimes, the only course was for local people to stand up and do what they could for the environment in their own backyards. It was all part of the principle "Think Globally, Act Locally."

Now, I'm not suggesting that we all go out and spike trees. Far from it—even Earth First! has given up tree spiking. Just keep in mind that in many cases, if local people don't do something, nobody will do anything. Local action can be the most effective, especially in the short term. Get involved. Help maintain a trail, or contribute to the organizations that do. The future of the AT really is in your hands.

A truly unsung heroine, Dr. Jean Stephenson was the founding editor of the Appalachian Trailway News, *the magazine of the Appalachian Trail Conference. As secretary of the ATC, she kept in touch with the many member clubs through the delicate formative years and into the 1960s. Without her tireless efforts, most of the wonderful stories of the early Trail days would have been lost.*
PHOTOGRAPH COURTESY OF THE APPALACHIAN TRAIL CONFERENCE.

A FEW LAST THINGS

"Appalachian Trail" being a long moniker, I have chosen two short-hand references to use on the following pages. The Appalachian Trail is known affectionately to hikers as "the A.T." I will shorten that even further to "AT," both in deference to common usage and as a kind of tribute to the official symbol of the Trail, which features the two letters sharing crossbars, the A over the T. It's a great logo, but not easy to put in type.

You may have noticed the spelling of "thru-hiker." That is the common way to spell it, as opposed to the technically correct "through-hiker." Remember, the name of the game here is to travel light.

In addition, I will capitalize the word "Trail" when referring to the Appalachian Trail and use the lowercase "trail" when referring to other trails or to trails in general.

Got it? Let's go.

Bones of the Appalachians

GENERAL GEOLOGY OF THE AT

The first thing to understand about the AT is its setting. Benton Mac-Kaye intended that the stage upon which he set his refuge for beleaguered urbanites be the long spine of the East Coast of North America. In "An Appalachian Trail: A Project in Regional Planning," he imagined a giant marching south down the central ridges of the Appalachians, and what that giant would see. Everywhere, as he stood high in his wilderness refuge, he would see the nearby cities and industrial centers. There was only one place in the East that this could happen—the Appalachian Range. Only this long cordillera was near enough to the population centers yet offered the wilderness that was necessary.

The geological origins of the Appalachians are important to their place in MacKaye's scheme. When and how these mountains were formed would dictate their character and their history. A mountain range is a combination of many characteristics: its flesh and blood are the forests and fields, the wildlife and weather, and the people who live and work there. But its bones are the very rocks upon which it is founded.

These rocks may have come from deep within the earth, or may once have been laid down on the bottom of a long-vanished sea. But whatever the origins of these rocks, at some point they were hurled high into the air—in geologic time, of course, which is to say very gradually—to form our mountain range. What these rocks are and how they came to be where they are, the way they are, have had a profound effect on the Trail and the hiking experience.

The mountain ranges that are variously classified as "Appalachian" begin in northeast Alabama, run up through Georgia, North Carolina, Tennessee, Virginia, West Virginia, Maryland, Pennsylvania, New Jersey, New York, Connecticut, Massachusetts, Vermont, New Hampshire, and Maine. They continue into Canada, up through Newfoundland. From there, there is a gap to make way for the Atlantic Ocean, until they continue over the Caledonian Highlands of Scotland and the rugged mountains of western Norway, before they finally end (some say) on the arctic islands of Spitsbergen. The distance, all told (minus interruptions for oceans), is over 4,000 miles. The Appalachians form one of the longest mountain cordilleras on record. At one time, they may in places have been nearly 50,000 feet tall—20,000 feet taller than Mt. Everest. Today, the Appalachians are perhaps the most orderly, perfectly formed series of folded mountains in the world.

How did this come about? It's a long story and, to a geologist at least, an interesting and complex one.

Geological time is seldom cast in bronze. Geologists have only glimpses of the whole picture with which to work in creating their ingenious scenarios of what happened a billion years ago, and opinions of actual time will differ from scientist to scientist. So will the various scenarios themselves. In many cases, I've had to interpret among several different theories, and often, my unscientific mind has had to choose which of them seemed least mind-boggling. Nonetheless, the evidence suggests that the range we see today is the result of one of the greatest slow-motion cataclysms since the earth began: the Appalachian Revolution.

Here's what seems to have happened. Around 570 million years ago, in the dim early millennia of life, around the beginning of the Cambrian period, the eastern section of what is now North America was pretty flat. Some geologists say that conditions were much like you'd find in the Gulf Coast area today—low, flat land gradually descending onto an extensive continental shelf. Mountains had existed there before, and their bones lay buried under the flatlands, perhaps rising inland into a gentle mountain range much like what we see today. In what is now New York State, the already ancient Adirondacks lay inland, a mass of low, rolling hills.

To say that these flats existed in eastern North America is perhaps a bit misleading. Nobody really knows for certain what part of the globe these primordial layers of sand and mud occupied; the world is not a very stable place, if you're thinking in geological terms. Some scientists have suggested that the East Coast might actually have run along an east-west axis, near the equator. Many things have changed in all those years. It's safe to say, however, that the climate was temperate, so the land wasn't near either of the poles.

What we do know is that the area where the Appalachian Mountains would eventually rise could be found toward the edge of the forerunner of today's North American Plate. And therein lies the entire tale.

PLATE TECTONICS

It has been a century or more since it was first noticed that the eastern edge of South America seemed to roughly fit the western edge of Africa. The conclusion was easy, if controversial—that the two continents had indeed been welded to each other at some point in the distant past. Perhaps it was *too* simple, because for decades, few people gave the proposition serious thought.

But in the mid-twentieth century, geologists found on reflection that the theory that became known as "plate tectonics" could, in fact, answer many questions. Why, for example, were fossils that could be found in northeastern North America also found in northern Europe—and nowhere else? Why did mountain ranges seem to continue from one continent to another—right down to the structure of the ridges and the composition of the rock? And why were there earthquake zones at the edge of these hypothetical plates?

It also answered more general questions, such as, Why do mountains form in the first place? Addressing questions like this had always been a fatal weakness of conventional geology. Who could seriously believe that the very crust of the earth would buckle and fold or fault without being moved by something? The prevailing theory at the time had to do with large theoretical structures called "geosynclines." When enough stuff got deposited onto the earth's crust, the story went, the crust would be forced down, causing it to buckle, fold, and fracture. It seemed to explain why things might sink, but it left something to be desired in explaining why things would rise.

So, as the twentieth century progressed, a new theory developed and gained what is now nearly universal acceptance. It proposed that the earth's surface is composed almost entirely of "plates"—hardened surfaces that float atop the molten rock below. Thick plates form land masses; thinner plates are covered by ocean. These plates are in constant motion, bumping and grinding against each other in a slow-motion dance. The Pacific coast of North America, for example, has lately (i.e., for the past 100 million years or so) been the scene of a side-swipe maneuver by the Pacific Plate. To the north, another plate has been slowly slipping—or "subducting"—*underneath* the North American Plate. The results are numerous: the San Andreas Fault, where a sizable chunk of Southern California is heading for Northern California; Yosemite National Park, where spectacular rock domes have actually been formed from cooled magma that is released by the descending sea plate and bubbles toward the surface as "plutons"; or the chain of volcanoes in the Cascades.

In the beginning of the Paleozoic Era, the situation in the East was this: the remains of an earlier round of mountain-building had been worn down essentially to nothing. This incomprehensibly ancient mountain-building was the "Grenville Event," an only dimly understood episode that occurred somewhere between 1.4 and 1.1 billion years ago and (after hundreds of millions of years of erosion) left mainly rugged, crystalline rock forming a foundation for what was to come. Remnants of Grenville mountains are still visible today in the Adirondacks and other smaller ranges on the Laurentian Shield, and they survived only because they were rejuvenated by later uplifting. They are easily some of the oldest mountains in the world.

At the start of the Grenville Event, North America was much smaller. It covered perhaps the eastern half to two-thirds of the continent as it exists today and was surrounded by a continental shelf and guarded to the east by volcanic islands, perhaps similar to Japan and the Philippines. The land mass evidently consisted of all three kinds of rock—igneous, sedimentary, and metamorphic. The sediments confirm that the rocks formed and molded by the Grenville Event were composed in part of the eroded remains of even older rocks from mountain-building that we may never know anything about, its history lost forever.

The Grenville Event began with plates closing in together. Some other continental mass—thought to have been Europe and Africa, but maybe not—moved in on the east coast, and the North American Plate began to crumple. By the time the two continents crashed into each other, around 1.3 billion years ago, a range of mountains had formed that probably resembled the present-day Appalachians.

It wasn't until perhaps 700 million years ago that the two plates began to part. As they did, a new round of volcano activity began, filling in around and in some cases over the remains of the Grenville mountains—by that time worn down to stumps seldom over a thousand feet tall. As is typical when continents separate, the volcanoes emitted basalt, a hard, flowing form of lava much different from the more explosive, ash-pumice types found where continents come together. A present-day example of the former would be the fast-flowing lava of Hawaii or Iceland; an example of the latter would be the ashy, cindery spume of Mt. Saint Helens. The basalt of these eruptions, which metamorphosed during the uplift of the present-day Appalachians, is visible today as the greenstone atop the Blue Ridge in Shenandoah National Park. Original Grenville rock can also be encountered in certain sections of the Trail, where it has been raised and uncovered. In fact, the changes to the landscape that the Event unleashed (those we can still identify) form some of the most interesting sections of the Trail.

Also accompanying the separation of the plates was the formation the proto-Atlantic Ocean, called Iapetus by some scientists. Around 570 million years ago, Iapetus—which had been getting wider for millions of years—was finally reaching its widest point. (Geologists disagree as to how wide—thousands of kilometers, or merely hundreds.) As it expanded, lava flowing up in the middle of the ocean formed a thin ocean plate between shores. From there, the ocean started to contract again.

All was quiet 570 million years ago. The proto-Atlantic Ocean, which some geologists call Iapetus, was at its widest point, and the North American coast (on the left) consisted of a coastal plain, a continental shelf, and the remains of old mountains, perhaps the Adirondacks, built during the Grenville Event 1.1 billion years ago.

As other plates (Europe and Africa) homed in on North America, the thinner ocean floor began to dive under the edge of the North American Plate. This was not unusual, as thinner plates often went under thicker ones, to be remelted into magma. Offshore, volcanic islands formed. By 450 million years ago, the stage was set for the first great uplift in the formation of the Appalachian Range—the Taconic Orogeny. As the ocean floor dove beneath the continent, mountains began to be uplifted near the outer edge of the continental shelf, forming the Green Mountains of Vermont, the Berkshires of Massachusetts, the Taconics of New York, the Hudson Highlands, and the Reading Prong through northern New Jersey into Pennsylvania. Inland, as the coastline uplifted, a shallow sea extended in places all the way to Minnesota, rimmed to the "east" (whichever direction it really was is open to conjecture) by mountains. Offshore, a deep ocean-floor trench was probably formed at the point of the ocean plate's subduction.

Continents approach, and the first round of mountain-building, the Taconic Orogeny, begins 450 million years ago. As Europe and/or Africa moves closer, one scenario has the North American side of the ocean floor diving beneath the Eurafrican side. This shovels ocean sediment, spurs volcanic activity, and creates mountains. These mountains will later become the Green Mountains of Vermont, the Taconics, the Hudson Highlands, and the Reading Prong. An arc of volcanic islands (not shown) forms offshore, and an inland sea forms to the left of the new mountains.

Then, for 100 million years, things quieted down. The European and African plates were still approaching, but instead of the sea floor being forced under North America, it was diving under Africa, relieving the pressure on the North American coast.

The second great episode, the Acadian Orogeny, happened 100 million years later, as northern Europe swept across the ocean floor, crashing into the northeast corner of North America. ("Crashing," of course, is a relative term in geological parlance.) At the time, the coast in New England ran roughly down the Connecticut River Valley.

As Europe approached, it pushed the ocean floor ahead of it, crushing volcanic islands and pushing sediment onto the North American coast, in many cases thrusting the material right over the top of the existing landmass. Today there is an entire zone of "metavolcanics," including a number of identifiable volcanic island formations, up and down the Connecticut Valley. Swamps formed on either side of the suture line (the line where the continents were welded together), leaving coal deposits from Pennsylvania to Wales and beyond.

This went on until around 230 million years ago. The situation at that time was this: Europe and North America had welded together down to around the Connecticut–New York border. Below that, the diminished Iapetus was still open. That set the stage for the final cataclysm.

And what a crunch it was! Until about 450 million years ago, the African Plate had been rubbing up against Antarctica and other land plates off to the side somewhere—some say this formed a super-continent known as Gondwanaland. At that point, however, the plate

The two plates collide, 350 million years ago. The result is the uplifting of the Blue Ridge and related ranges, and the welding of the offshore volcanic islands into the center of New England. The shallow inland sea, filled with eroded sediment of the new mountains, survives this collision, known as the Acadian Orogeny. However, it will be uplifted 80 to 100 million years later in the Alleghany Orogeny, when the African Plate plows into the lower East Coast.

started a long march to join Europe and America. It arrived 230 million years ago, bulldozing enormous amounts of ocean floor right up over the existing land formations. So great was the impact of this event—the Alleghany Orogeny—that it uplifted all the sediment that had been accumulating in the inland sea for millions of years, and then folded these inland lowlands into washboard mountains, forming first the Allegheny Plateau and the Catskill Plateau and then the Allegheny Mountains and the side ranges in Virginia and the lower Appalachians.

The more general result of this collision was the vast super-continent that geologists call Pangaea. But for every action, there is an equal and opposite reaction. Geologic history since then is said to consist mostly of the breakup of Pangaea—no sooner had these land-masses merged than Europe and Africa headed back across the newly reopened Atlantic. (To this day, the Atlantic is still widening, the new ocean plate expanding from the middle as lava oozes out at the Mid-Atlantic Ridge.) This breakup occured in the early to mid-Jurassic period. It, too, was a cataclysmic event that changed landmasses and climates and, some paleontologists say, caused the dinosaurs to become much more diverse and much, much bigger than they had been before.

As the European and African plates inched away, though, an exchange was taking place. Parts of Newfoundland and lands north were broken off and became parts of the British Isles, northern Europe, and Scandinavia. Parts of western Europe stayed, becoming eastern New England, east of the former coast at the Connecticut River Valley. Prior to the Alleghany Orogeny, the Appalachian Trail would have been stopped by the ocean near Norwich, Vermont.

To treat mountain-building as an isolated event is misleading. Even as mountains are rising, erosion is wearing them down. This is,

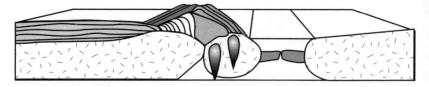

The continents separated 200 million years ago, and the Atlantic Ocean was reborn. Some geologists say that a portion of the European Plate (center) remained welded to the North American Plate to become eastern New England. Plutonic activity bubbled near the surface, especially in the White Mountains of New Hampshire.

after all, a slow process in human terms, and even the most violent and rapid uplift takes millions of years. The Appalachians were no exception, and the weathering of the mountains was equal to the forces lifting them up. Once Europe and Africa had reversed field and started pulling away again, the Appalachian story was entirely one of wearing away.

Some rocks don't resist weathering very well; others hold up through most anything. Niagara Falls is a famous example of the latter. We find a precipitous drop rather than rubble and rapids because a capping layer of extra-hard dolomite wears away much more slowly than the softer rock underneath. Likewise, the Grand Canyon has sheer vertical walls because of a hard caprock layer of dolomite.

A typical model of Appalachian weathering starts with an enormous folded ridge—some geologists say the size of Mt. Everest, while most will only commit to a minimum of 15,000 feet. As the rock weathers away, erosion eats down through the layers. Depending on the hardness of the various layers, a number of things can happen. If the inner layers are soft and the outer ones hard, the center of the ridge will be worn away, leaving two lower ridges, held up by the harder layers. If, on the other hand, it is the inner rock that is the harder, the outer layers will strip away, leaving the harder core, often composed of igneous or hard metamorphic rock.

There are, in places, variations. For example, where the Trail crosses the Hudson River, the rocks are exceedingly old. Some of the rounded summits that hikers see there are billion-year-old plutons—bubbles of molten rock that melted their way up through the strata above until they came close enough to the surface to harden and were eventually exposed by weathering. Old Rag Mountain, in Shenandoah National Park, is also a very old, Precambrian pluton, one that once lay underneath sedimentary layers but was tilted up by folding. It is totally different in structure from the rest of the ridge. The white Barre granite in eastern Vermont is of more recent plutonic origin, forming during the Appalachian Revolution.

A NOTE ON METAMORPHISM

Whenever there is vigorous mountain-building, as there was during the various orogenies that formed the Appalachians, the rock strata that are uplifted are likely to undergo metamorphism—they change into a different form of rock. This happens because of the crushing, bending, and extreme heat that usually accompany geologic activity of this sort.

Heat is especially likely to make changes. As rocks cool, the minerals within them tend to separate and harden into recognizable crystals. The faster the rock hardens, the smaller the crystals will be; conversely, the slower the cooling process, the larger the crystals. Sedimentary rocks have no chance at all to form crystals, since they are formed with pressure rather than heat. Add heat to existing rocks, though, and the process of crystallization can begin again. What was once merely sandstone, for example, can reorganize itself into translucent, crystalline quartzite. Even shale can form crystals and become a glittering, mica-laden schist. And, in some cases, the rock may melt again altogether, and harden as something igneous.

In many—if not most—areas through which the Trail passes, the vast majority—if not all—of the rocks will have been metamorphosed by the forces that created the mountains. It's one reason the mountains have endured for up to 450 million years in some places: metamorphic rocks tend to be harder than the sedimentary ones from which they are often formed.

THE SHAPE OF THE RANGE

The Appalachians are so orderly that some features persist for hundreds of miles. In fact, the range can be divided into just three basic provinces:

1. The eastern ranges, from Maine down through the White Mountains of New Hampshire and the Green Mountains of Vermont, the Taconics and Hudson Highlands of New York, and the Reading Prong into central Pennsylvania, down to South Mountain in Maryland, which becomes the Blue Ridge of Virginia, North Carolina, and Georgia.
2. The Great Valley, extending from southern Vermont, across central New York, down through the Susquehanna and Cumberland Valleys, through the famous Shenandoah Valley all the way to Tennessee.

3. The western ridges, mostly designated as the Alleghenies, extending from the Shawangunks in eastern New York down through the Kittatinnies of New Jersy, Blue Mountain in Pennsylvania, and on through West Virginia and Kentucky into Tennessee.

Each ridge and mountain has its own story, within the context of the dramatic origins of the Appalachian Ranges. These are better left for later, when we're discussing individual sections of the Trail. But be aware, as you walk, that you're on some of the most interesting ground on earth—ground where continents once collided.

GEOLOGIC GLOSSARY

Anticline: An upward fold in the rock strata.

Appalachian Revolution: The sequence of mountain-building episodes, or orogenies, that formed the Appalachians.

Basalt: Hardened lava.

Batholith: A large mass—at least 40 square miles—of coarse-grained, intrusive igneous rock that has been exposed by erosion.

Clastic sediments: Deposits formed of broken up bits of older rock.

Cordillera: A chain of mountains, usually spanning an entire continent.

Dolomite: A calcium and magnesium carbonate deposited in shallow seas.

Equigranular: Composed of different kinds of mineral crystals that are of approximately the same size.

Fault: A break in the rock strata.

Fold: A bending of rock strata caused by pressure.

Geosyncline: A huge basin in the earth's crust within which vast amounts of sediments accumulate.

Gneiss: Rock, frequently metamorphosed from granite, often characterized by a banded appearance.

Granite: A crystalline, igneous rock composed chiefly of quartz and feldspar.

Graywacke: A very common form of "dirty" sandstone, composed of sand mixed with rock fragments and often with clay.

Grenville Event: The original uplift of the eastern edge of the North American Plate, which occurred between 1.3 billion and 950 million years ago. Crystalline Grenville rocks lie under virtually the entire Appalachian Range. Except for the Adirondacks, Grenville mountains were probably eroded away completely when the existing ranges were uplifted. Named for Grenville, Ontario.

Iapetus Ocean: Name used by some geologists to refer to the proto-Atlantic Ocean that existed prior to the Appalachian Revolution and the formation of Pangaea.

Igneous rock: Hardened molten rock.

Klippe: A part of a thrust slab isolated later by erosion. Plural: klippen.

Limestone: A sedimentary rock composed mostly of the mineral calcite.

Marble: Metamorphosed limestone or dolomite.

Metamorphic rock: Sedimentary or igneous rock, the composition of which has been changed by extreme heat and pressure.

Moraine: A buildup of sand, gravel, and rounded boulders left by a glacier.

Orogeny: An episode of mountain-building.

Pangaea: Supercontinent formed by the collision of Europe, Africa, and the Americas during the Acadian and Alleghany Orogenies.

Plate: A hardened section of the earth's crust, floating on the molten rock below.

Pluton: A large blob of igneous rock formed by a bubble of molten rock rising toward the surface through the strata until it cools.

Quartzite: Metamorphosed sandstone or conglomerate that is very hard.

Sandstone: A sedimentary rock composed of sand that has cemented together.

Schist: A metamorphic rock that can be formed from anything from shale to basalt. Characterized by a crystalline structure (indicative of a greater degree of heat and pressure) and often distinct fracture layers.

Sedimentary rock: Hardened layers of material deposited on the surface or under water.

Shale: A sedimentary rock composed of hardened mud.

Slate: Metamorphosed shale. Characterized by sharply defined horizontal fracturing.

Strata: A series of rock layers.

Subduction: The process, during the impact of two plates, of one plate descending beneath the other to be melted in the magma beneath.

Syncline: A downward fold in the rock strata.

Thrust slab: Folded layers of bedrock, resembling a rug bunched up over itself.

Water gap: A sharp division through a ridge, through which a river flows. Often, the ridge was uplifted under the river, which wore down its passage through the rock as the uplift occurred.

Geologic time			Age in millions of years
C E N O Z O I C	Quaternary Period	Present	
		Holocene Epoch	.01
		(Last Ice Age) Pleistocene Epoch	2
E R A	Tertiary Period	Pliocene Epoch	5
		Miocene Epoch	24
		Oligocene Epoch	38
		Eocene Epoch	55
		Paleocene Epoch	63
M E S O Z O I C	Cretaceous Period	(Late Cretaceous Epoch)	96
		(Early Cretaceous Epoch)	138
	Jurassic Period	(Pangaea Breaks Up)	205
	Triassic Period		~240
P A L E O Z O I C	Permian Period	(Alleghany Orogeny)	290
	Carboniferous Periods	(Pennsylvanian Period)	~330
		(Mississippian Period; Acadian Orogeny)	360
	Devonian Period		410
	Silurian Period		435
E R A	Ordovician Period	(Taconic Orogeny)	500
	Cambrian Period		~570
P R E C A M B R I A N	Breakup of Grenville continent—volcanic activity forms lava flows		700
	PROTEROZOIC ERA	(Grenville Event)	1200
			2500
	ARCHAEOZOIC ERA		3600

2 | Appalachian Forests

It is said that when the European settlers arrived in North America four hundred years ago, a highly motivated squirrel could have traveled from the Gulf of Mexico to the Canadian border—and beyond— without once touching its feet to the ground. That's how great the forest coverage in the Appalachian ranges was at the time.

The woodlands through which the Appalachian Trail passes today are the remnants of forests that once had a profound effect on the lives and minds of those settlers. On the positive side, they provided a seemingly unlimited source of fuel and building materials. Indeed, the frame and post-and-beam structures familiar in American architecture were relatively unknown in Europe outside Scandinavia. (The log cabin in America was perfected by Swedish settlers in Maryland and Virginia.)

To this day, while we Americans blithely raise our roofs on walls of wood, Europeans regard such methods as foolishness—inefficient and expensive beyond reason. For their own situations, they're right. But here, wood made perfect sense, at least at first. It was not simply that it was easily and cheaply available; though it may seem strange to outdoorspeople today, the forest was considered an adversary for the first three centuries of European rule in America. It presented real challenges. Trees had to be chopped laboriously and their stumps pulled before there was a field to be plowed. The endless woods blocked expansion by their ruggedness and sheer size.

This perceived conflict took on symbolic form over the years. The wilderness evolved in the imaginations of the American people until it took on unreal proportions. Settlers and city dwellers alike began to believe that the forests harbored danger in the form of hostile animals—and people. It was especially bad in the East, where there were no great mountain ranges above treeline and it was difficult to get an overview of where you were. A traveler easily became lost; one valley looked much like another, especially when the most you could see was at ground level, within about fifty yards. The woods were no place to be. They had to be tamed.

Small wonder that early European-Americans became positively fixated on the idea of the "howling wilderness." For better or worse, European domination of North America was founded in large part on a preoccupation with taming the wilderness to make it useful to humanity. And thus was born the idea of "harvesting" the forests and using the "resources" of the earth. Anyone who has ever walked through the clearcuts of the Carolinas or the strip mines of Pennsylvania knows the rest.

By its location on the very ridgeline of the East, the Appalachian Trail passes through the best of what remains of that incomprehensibly vast forest—in its day perhaps the greatest forest in the world. Fortunately, attitudes changed just in time to save this stretch of America's heritage, a development covered in the next chapter.

LIFE ZONES

Forests are divided into categories that are in turn based on climate—largely how cold it is, i.e., how long the growing season is. The entire range is found in the space, be it narrow or wide, between the tropics and the treeline.

The treeline is that magical division beyond which no tree can grow. The conditions become too harsh—the temperature is too cold, the growing season too short. It is dictated by one or both of two factors: latitude and elevation. In the southern Appalachians, there is no treeline. Because both the latitude and the elevation are too low, there is literally nowhere in the entire region where tree growth is ruled out by harsh conditions (though some experts theorize that the famous "balds" of the southern ranges might be semi-alpine remnants of the summit tundra left by the Ice Age). You have to travel hundreds of miles north—and then climb up into the mountains—for that.

As you travel north, up out of the Gulf plain, the first zone through which you pass is the Southern Pineland. As you climb uphill to where the Trail is, the pines gradually mix with hardwoods until you reach the southern Appalachian forest. As you pass through the lower zones where the logging of centuries past has altered the interaction of the various species, you approach the real thing: the world-famous woods where hundreds of species vie with each other to be the most magnificent.

Between the lowest and highest levels of the southern Appalachians rises a mile of mountain. By the time a hiker reaches the summits above 6,000 feet, most of the life zones in the East have been traversed, up to the boreal forests that are the stunted last stop before virtual tundra—the treeline.

As the Trail moves north, it runs through numerous types of forest, from the spruce summits of the High Smokies to the more open oak and hickory woods as it goes through North Carolina and Virginia. As it winds through the northern states, the route travels the hard, shattered, Precambrian rock stripped bare by the last Ice Age, which retreated a mere 10,000 years ago. Here, summits are increasingly boreal, full of hardy conifers and weather-resistant hardwoods like birch, aspen, and red oak. In the valleys, you pass through northern transition forest—home to the giant sugar maples and beeches that turn to flame every fall. By the end of the Trail, the boreal forest has taken over completely, except for the summits of the White Mountains. These summits are true tundra, home only to grasses, lichens, mosses, and the small bushes and flowers that can handle hurricane winds and a short growing season. Beyond Katahdin—itself an alpine summit— the life zones span out across the face of the continent until the ultimate treeline is reached—the point where the tundra extends right down to sea level and all the way up to the arctic sea.

Although the largest and most vigorous forest is found in the more southern parts of the AT, all sections of the Trail contribute to its environmental diversity, which is part of its appeal. Each zone has its own story, its own charm.

Alpine Summits

This is life at a minimum. Plants that thrive here do so by rigid adherence to a single axiom: Waste not, want not. Nothing grows very tall, partly to avoid the cold and wind and to offer less surface area for evaporation of precious water, and partly in recognition of the fact that there isn't very much soil in which to grow. Flowers have mastered the trick of sprouting, blossoming, and going to seed in a matter of a few weeks, which is about all the growing season they get. Dominant species are lichens and mosses, many of which can be found at lower elevations only if you go hundreds and thousands of miles to the north.

Boreal Forest

The dominant species here share one thing with the alpine varieties and with each other: they're survivors.

Conifers predominate simply because they're efficient. Their needles give them two advantages: they allow less evaporation than broad leaves, and they don't waste the tree's energy and nutrients by falling off each year. The most common deciduous trees are the hardy birches and aspens. These are the first to grow after fire or landslide (or chainsaw) has destroyed the lower transition forest, and they are the first to appear higher up, mixed with the boreal evergreens where the maples and beeches refuse to grow. Farther down, oaks and tamaracks blend in.

Another characteristic feature of boreal forests is the bog. When glaciers recede, they typically leave a wide band of sub-arctic forest covered largely by lakes and streams. As a lake fills in with soil and vegetable matter, a bog is formed.

Bogs are notable for a wide variety of specialized plants like sedges and water lilies. As the tangle of tree roots and plants crowds in around the edges, a living mat of plants may form, creating a "quaking bog," a seemingly solid surface that is actually floating over water. Spruces may figure in this mat; their easily accessible roots were commonly used to lace up birch-bark canoes.

One may find other, even stranger plants atop a bog. The nitrogen-poorness of bogs often opens a niche for unusual species that take nitrogen from other sources—like animals. Carniverous pitcher plants and sundews are common in northern bogs.

Boreal forests strike a delicate balance. Lately, they have been particularly susceptible to pollution—the thin soil offers much less protection from harsh chemicals than the deeper soils of the lowlands, and the mists and rains of higher elevations bring more pollution with them as they descend. Acid deposition (i.e., "acid rain") has in recent years decimated the red spruce and balsam fir on Eastern mountaintops, and the destruction may abate only when the trees are all gone or the pollution is stopped.

Boreal forest, which covers the landscape through much of Canada and the northern United States, continues southward at gradually higher elevations. A forest type that is universal at 2,500 feet in New Hampshire might be pushed up to above 4,000 feet in North Carolina, but it's still there.

Maples and Beeches

As the Trail moves out of the true boreal forest, it gradually enters the northern reaches of mixed deciduous forest. Unlike the forests of the West, where the dividing lines are sharply defined, the change in the East is gradual, probably due to increased moisture acting as a buffer against extreme shifts in temperature.

As the forest moves into the Northern lowlands, the forest type is increasingly dominated by maples and beeches. They are by no means the only species, however. Even this far north, the great variety of the Appalachian deciduous forest is evident. Interspersed with the maples are pines and hemlocks. (The latter are especially fond of moist stream valleys.) Hikers in the Northern Lowlands will encounter oak-hickory forests in places. By the time the Trail reaches the Hudson Valley, these ecosystems will be the rule.

The stately American chestnut, once a major presence in these parts, is gone, destroyed by a fungus blight introduced by accident in New York City in 1904. They are represented only by spindly shoots that grow from the roots, only to die when they reach a diameter of two or three inches. In some places along the Trail, huge, rot-resistant chestnut logs have lain throughout the woods like jackstraws for a half-century or more.

Recently, however, efforts have accelerated toward a blight-resistant strain of the American chestnut. One effort centers around selective breeding of resistant trees; others are trying to create a new strain via genetic modification. In either case, the reappearance of the commercially valuable chestnuts in Northeastern forests could be quite interesting. Stay tuned.

Southern Appalachian Forest

Beneath the boreal and transitional forests of the southern Blue Ridge and the Great Smokies in North Carolina, Tennessee, and Georgia, one finds not the maple-beech forests that dominate in the North but a spectacular, rich forest type found nowhere else. Growing on terrain that has never been stripped bare by glaciers, the incredibly diverse and vigorous southern forests offer a greater variety of plant life than anywhere else on the continent.

The reasons are many. Not only has the soil not been carried away by millennia of glaciation, but the climate is milder and moister than in the North. Then, too, this area was a "periglacial" region in previous eras. In the frequent warming and cooling trends of the lands in the shadow of the great ice sheets to the north, a variety of species were able to take hold.

Southern Appalachian forests, which lie between the coastal low-lands and the boreal forests above 4,000 feet, are dominated only by diversity. Huge tulip trees (yellow poplar), sugar maples, yellow birch, hickory, and oak stand side by side, with redbud, dogwood, and mountain laurel underneath. As the forest progresses uphill, it becomes more and more open, tending toward oaks and red maples with yellow and white pines mixed in. The richness of the plant life is incredible. Water trickles everywhere, moss and lichens cover the rocks, and hem-locks and firs crowd into protected, wet stream gullies.

It is said that a short car drive from the lowlands to the high-elevation boreal forest is the same in botanical terms as a drive of sev-eral days from the American South up into Canada. In a way, that's true. You pass through a similar number of forest types, into a boreal forest not unlike those you'd find up north. But the forests aren't just shaped by the climate. History and geology do their part, too. In the Southern Appalachian forests, the characteristics of the forests you see today have as much to do with humans and their axes, as well as the fact that the glaciers gave the region a miss, as they do with the weather.

ACID RAIN

Professor Hubert Vogelmann of the University of Vermont, one of the foremost experts on the effects of pollution on plant life, once said, "To say that acid deposition kills trees is kind of like saying that cigarettes cause cancer. Scientifically speaking, you can't say either."

He's not suggesting that there's no harm in acid rain. What he means is that it's not within the realm of scientific inquiry to prove empirically that the obvious tree death in the forests of the East is due to pollution. You can't actually see it happening.

Which leaves us with an argument. Even scientists who are terri-fied by what's happening to our forests won't say for sure that it's pol-lution from Ohio Valley power plants or auto exhaust that's doing it—even though the preponderance of evidence points that way. There still remains the possibility that it's something else. True, most scien-tists don't believe that, but the scientific method isn't majority rule.

What they can say is that trees are dying, as are fish in mountain ponds, lakes, and streams. They can also say that the rain, snow, and mists, especially at high elevations, are becoming increasingly acidic. They know, too, that tree rings show that growth in trees has slowed down since the late '50s—just about the time that the amount of sulfur dioxide emissions from Ohio Valley power plants underwent a sharp increase. They know that in lab conditions, trees that are subjected to acid typical of pollution conditions tend to die quickly, in just the ways they're dying in the wild.

From there, it's speculation. Does the acid get into the tree itself and kill it outright? Or does it release heavy metals like aluminum from the rocks and soil, and let them do the job? Does acid damage the root hairs of the plants, causing them to die of thirst? Which does the actual damage: power plant emission or auto exhaust? If it's a combination of the two, which is worse? Exactly what happens?

Faced with obvious damage, scientists offer a dozen or more possible reasons—most, if not all, caused by pollution—but won't take the last step of concluding that acid deposition is the culprit after all. It's not wrong—it's just the way they work.

Unfortunately, it opens the door for special interest groups who oppose acid deposition control to block any action to solve the problem. As long as scientists are unwilling to draw ironclad conclusions, opponents of action can always call for more studies. In 1984, one Ohio congressman, whose district enjoys some of the lowest electical power rates in the East, blocked an acid rain control bill in the House of Representatives. Two years later, an industry group supported by industrial coal users launched a million-dollar campaign of disinformation and letter writing and succeeded in defeating another acid rain bill. Recently, several Eastern states have banded together to sue Midwestern power companies for their pollution.

But the trees and the fish keep dying. You'll see the results from Maine to Georgia. If you want to do something, the first step is to get hold of your senators and representatives.

GLOBAL WARMING

If you think that acid rain action is frustrating, try global warming. Nowhere have political and commercial interests tied the scientific community in knots more effectively.

What is known and agreed upon is that the world climate is getting warmer. Contrary to what some politicians say, there is actually no disagreement on that point. By some measures, we've warmed a full degree in the past fifty years, if not more.

Where the disagreement comes in is on the cause. Most, but not all, scientists believe that human activity, especially in the area of carbon dioxide emissions, has caused or at least exacerbated the problem of warming by increasing the amount of carbon dioxide in the atmosphere, which prevents heat from escaping into space. This is commonly called the "greenhouse effect." A few researchers say they're not sure. Global warming, they say, may be caused by natural processes and normal climatic swings.

This latter group has been embraced by industrial and political interests to prevent any action on carbon dioxide emissions. Often, researchers who raise doubts about the greenhouse effect explanation of global warming are in the employ of these groups to begin with.

The effects of global warming, however, should alarm AT hikers. One of these is greater climatic shift. We see more drought-flood cycles, and temperature shifts can be more extreme. Of the other possible results, we should focus on the hilltops. (The anticipated rise in the ocean levels, while alarming, will not directly affect ridgetop hiking.)

The key problem we might face in this regard has to do with high-elevation environmental zones. Mountains that provide us with alpine tundra zones or high-elevation boreal forest often represent ecological islands. Once, when the glaciers covered the Northeast, this biozone extended right down to sea level, as it does today in northern Canada. As the glaciers receded and the climate warmed, the lowlands were gradually invaded by warmer-climate species, which drove the alpine zones uphill. Eventually, we came to the present situation, in which alpine tundra zones are confined to the highest mountaintops, completely separated from each other.

If the climate continues to warm, we face the possible extermination of these zones. Plant species from warmer zones will increasingly invade the higher habitats until the more delicate alpine species are crowded out completely. Anyone who has walked an alpine summit and seen its beauty can tell you what a tragedy that would be.

Carbon dioxide emissions present an even greater problem than acid rain. To make meaningful progress in its control would require significant changes in our uses of power, and especially in our use of the automobile. However, the sooner we begin, the easier the process will be along the way.

I hope you'll consider this another item on your list when you contact your representatives.

3 History Along the Trail

As I walk along the Trail, I've always enjoyed looking out over the hills and the valleys below and wondering who had walked there before me. The crowds one finds at historical sites suggest that most people feel a bit of kinship for their American forebears when they stand on the spot where something important happened in history.

For example, go to the middle of the Bear Mountain Bridge span in New York—it's right on the Trail—and look out over the valley. The scene before you was one of so much struggle during the American Revolution and before. Or check out the French Broad River at Hot Springs, North Carolina, and pretend that you're there in 1540, watching DeSoto and his train of hundreds of Spanish warriors—and literally thousands of pigs—crossing the gap, looking for gold. Or walk up South Mountain in Maryland and back into the 1850s, guiding slaves along the Underground Railroad to Canada and freedom. In each of the section chapters in this book, I will offer some of the history that happened along the Trail route. Here, though, are some of the events and trends of national—and at times continental or even hemispheric—importance.

NATIVE AMERICANS
Anyone who has had the misfortune to mention the "discovery" of America in the company of a Native American can probably tell you that the land was occupied long before the Europeans arrived to settle it. Unfortunately, those Europeans were far more intent upon settlement and acquisition of property than they were on the history of their

new home. It is often very difficult to fix exactly where a given tribe or nation might have lived prior to European settlement. Even the most authoritative works on the subject have to plead a certain amount of uncertainty about where the boundaries actually were.

There are several reasons for this. First, even as European settlers moved in, they were pushing Native American peoples off their traditional lands. It is hard, then, to know where the nations originally lived, since by the time Europeans got close to them, they may already have moved. Also, in places, the arrival of white people was preceded by their diseases, which in some cases had already nearly exterminated whole villages before the settlers got there. These maladies may have been brought by traders or fishermen who stopped along the coast. One famous example confronted the Pilgrims. When they reached Plymouth in 1620, Chief Massasoit's Wampanoags, some of whom already spoke English, had been decimated by some plague, brought by traders or explorers, which had run rampant through the peoples of the Massachusetts coast around 1617. They may have lost as many as two-thirds to three-quarters of their number. No wonder Massasoit was so friendly—he had no warriors left with which to fight.

Then, too, tribes tended to move about, whether to get to an area where living was better or the land not depleted, or to vacate an area where a more powerful enemy was pushing in. The Iroquois, for example, having finally banded together in the early 1600s to prevent powerful neighbors from bullying them, managed to push the Mahikans out of eastern New York State, into Vermont and Massachusetts. Things got so rough for the Mahikans that one whole division moved out, muscled into Connecticut and Rhode Island between neighboring tribes, and became known as the Pequots. The Pequots, in turn, having bullied their way into their new home, became so hated that the Puritans, possibly egged on by neighboring tribes, eventually exterminated them (though in the late twentieth century, their few descendants regained recognition as a tribe and went on to open one of the largest casinos in the country, in Ledyard, Connecticut). Before that happened, though, another group, known as the Mohegans, had split off due to an internal dispute. Under the leadership of their chief, Uncas, they would later become one of the inspirations for James Fenimore Cooper's famous novel, *The Last of the Mohicans*.

Finally, territorial limits are hard to pinpoint simply because Native Americans were not in the habit of setting them formally. They had their villages, which many nations would move from time to time;

they had their hunting territories, which they would hold against their neighbors by a combination of peaceful agreement, implied threat, and, on occasion, out-and-out warfare; and there were lands that were not really within anyone's sphere. Native Americans did not conceive of land as something that could be owned. It simply was. Another factor was the sparseness of the Native population. In the entire region traversed by what is today the Appalachian Trail, there were probably fewer than 175,000 people. In all that great, big land, you could walk a far piece without seeing a soul. That made it very hard to figure who the proprietors were in any given place.

We do know certain things. For example, we know that the route that became known to white settlers as the Great War Path ran practically the length of the Great Valley of the Appalachians, from Pennsylvania or even from up in New York all the way to Tennessee and Alabama. It was one of the major avenues of the day for both raiding and trading, a preferred trail of the Iroquois Confederacy for regular attacks on their favorite targets, the Creeks and the Catawbas of the South. For extra-secretive passages, war parties of any stripe may have taken to the ridgelines to avoid detection, running along the actual route of the AT. So, for a sizable part of its length, the AT runs parallel to an actual historical long path.

Additionally, oral accounts are sometimes used by scholars to fix the location of territorial boundaries that no longer exist. Regarding the AT, we have a certain amount of oral tradition to reckon with (the accuracy of oral accounts is being taken more and more seriously). The Iroquois Nations, for example, have stories of the days when they came east from the Mississippi Valley—how many hundreds or even thousands of years ago, we can only guess.

But, for purposes of this book, turf limits must in many cases be approximate. In most events, this will take the form of a description of who lived there when the European settlers arrived. In other cases, such as Cherokee territory, Native Americans did establish formal borders when faced by European expansion. In still others, like the Shenandoah Valley, there is for some reason no record of tribes living there when the white settlers first took notice of the area.

EUROPEANS IN THE APPALACHIANS

The role of the Appalachian Ranges in European settlement is better known, simply because those who participated in it kept written records. For settlers, the mountains constituted a barrier, the limits of the known world. Territory beyond the Appalachians was largely unknown and unmapped—the dense forests, the unknown and presumably hostile peoples, and the maze of ridges and mountains made the prospect of crossing the range daunting to say the least.

The early history of the North American continent was in great measure controlled by anyone who could control the passages through the Appalachians. Along similar lines, the growth of cities was determined by the Way West. New York City, for example, not only had a fine harbor but also stood at the mouth of the vast Hudson-Mohawk River basin, which led deep into the western reaches of what today is New York State. This was already fueling expansion by the 1700s, but once this route hooked up with Lake Erie via the Erie Canal in the 1820s, it constituted the finest passage west in the United States, which assured the growth and prosperity of New York. Similarly, Philadelphia and Baltimore stood at the beginnings of fine water routes which gave access to the rich interior valleys of the Susquehanna and the Delaware Rivers.

But even the Hudson was not the most influential passage in the early centuries of European settlement. The St. Lawrence was. It was inevitable that the first explorers in the West would come not from the territory that is now the United States, but rather from whoever controlled the great waterways of the St. Lawrence and the Great Lakes. That privilege belonged to the French, and they had the honor of exploring the Lakes, the Ohio and Mississippi basins, and the beginnings of the Great American West. It was only later, when the English had defeated the French and Indians in the 1760s, that they and their descendants finally made their way across the Appalachians.

Subsequently, many areas around the route of the AT became battle sites in various wars. This was especially true where there were rivers—the Potomac, for example, was hotly contested in the American Civil War. The Hudson, first the football of the English and Dutch, then the French and English, and later the English and Continentals, was the focus of more battles than practically any other waterway in America.

Since that time, the situation of the great coastal cities has become a mixed blessing. Placed as they were along the transportation routes inland, they were the natural sites for the Industrial Revolution to take hold. Raw materials could move down from the heartland, and they did: timber was cut for charcoal, iron ore was mined from the ground, and both were shipped to the cities for smelting; fields were cleared and the crops grown on them taken to urban markets; coal and oil were unearthed and used to power industrial cities. Because the cities were on the coast, finished products could then be loaded on ships for trade, and they grew and developed into the envy of the industrial world.

Once again, the Appalachians acted as a kind of barrier. Immigrants arrived and stayed in the coastal areas. For years, few ventured away from the oceanfront to the inland areas. By the early twentieth century, industrial workers finally outnumbered farmers along the coast, while the mountains remained mostly wild. The result was the opportunity that Benton MacKaye would address with his proposal of an Appalachian Trail: a wilderness mountain range within a day's travel of half the people in America, ideal for the respite from city life that modern industrial workers so desperately needed.

HOW THE APPALACHIAN TRAIL CAME TO BE

The creation of the Trail is one of those special events that can be traced to a moment in time—in this case, October of 1921. It was then that J. Benton MacKaye published an article entitled "An Appalachian Trail: A Project in Regional Planning" in the *Journal of the American Institute of Architects.*

MacKaye's whole idea was not just to create a trail. He was a thinker, an idea-man, and a trail was just the method he proposed for doing a larger, greater job. During his years in government service, first with the Forest Service in its early years, and later with the Department of Labor, he had become concerned with the impact of industrialization on workers, and he explored ways in which government and human resources could be marshalled to ease the stresses of the industrialized world and thus improve people's lives. Like many outdoorsmen, he had become convinced that recreation time in the wilderness was a surefire way of restoring the spirits and energy of people working and living in the cities.

Earlier in 1921, he had contacted Clarence Stein, chairman of a committee on community planning in the American Institute of Architects. At first, it may seem surprising that he communicated with an architectural association rather than the Park Service or some recreational administration. To MacKaye, though, it made sense. He viewed his scheme as one of regional planning rather than recreation or con-

When these two men first met, the history of the nation was changed. Benton Mac-Kaye (right) reminisces with Clarence Stein, who arranged the publication of Mac-Kaye's revolutionary article, "An Appalachian Trail: A Project in Regional Planning," in 1921. PHOTOGRAPH COURTESY OF THE APPALACHIAN TRAIL CONFERENCE.

servation—he was setting out to improve people's lives, not help them pass the time. In the words of Clarence Stein, in his introduction to MacKaye's article,

> *We need the big sweep of hills or sea as a tonic for jaded nerves—And so Mr. Benton MacKaye offers us a new theme in regional planning. It is not a plan for more efficient labor, but a plan of escape. He would as far as practicable conserve the whole stretch of the Appalachian Mountains for recreation. Recreation in the biggest sense—the re-creation of the spirit that is being crushed by the machinery of the modern industrial city—the spirit of fellowship and cooperation. . . . To all of those whom community or regional planning means more than the opening up of new roads for the acquisition of wealth, this project of Mr. MacKaye's must appeal. It is a plan for the conservation not of things—machines and land—but of men and their love of freedom and fellowship.*

In "An Appalachian Trail," MacKaye made his case deliberately. He first stated his overall point, that modern workers need escape from the workplace and the living situations that it enforces on them. He then proceeded to illustrate why he felt his plan would suit those needs. Why the Appalachians, for example? "These mountains," he explained, "in several ways rivaling the western scenery, are within a day's ride from centers containing more than half the population of the United States."

MacKaye recognized the radical aspects of his proposals. He was by this point known for his broad-mindedness, having, in the late 'teens, proposed cooperative farms as a solution to labor and farm production problems. In his article, he suggested that if the United States were to take on a project like the AT, it would require a "new deal in our agricultural system," as well as a "new deal" in our forestry methods. One wonders if FDR ever read this.

In any case, the original proposal went far beyond the simple blazing of a trail. In order for industry, as he said, to "come to be seen in its true perspective—as a means in life and not as an end in itself," he was planning a vast wilderness complex, complete with recreational "community camps" throughout the range; "shelter camps," not unlike many of the hut-to-hut systems in place today; and "food and farm camps," in which workers would go "back to the land" to provide "the food and crops consumed in the outdoor living."

The trail itself was proposed to be much like the AT as it exists today. The route was to run from Mt. Washington in New Hampshire to Mt. Mitchell in North Carolina, with side trails suggested in a variety of places. Among these was a side route west from the AT in southern Virginia to the Allegheny Range, then south to the Great Smokies, and on into Georgia; another led up from Mt. Washington to Katahdin in Maine. Both are actually part of the main route today. Another proposed side branch departed the AT in the area of Shenandoah National Park and ran north through western Maryland and into Pennsylvania, just like the Big Blue–Tuscarora—only in MacKaye's plan, it doesn't rejoin the AT. MacKaye also clearly marked the cities that would be served by the Trail, as well as the railroad lines that would link them to the route.

In his final call to action, MacKaye invoked memories of the still-recent Great War: "Indeed the lure of the scouting life can be made the most formidable enemy of the lure of militarism (a thing with which this country is menaced along with all others). It comes the nearest perhaps, of things thus far projected, to supplying what Professor [William] James once called a 'moral equivalent of war.' It appeals to the primal instincts of a fighting heroism, of volunteer service and of work in a common cause."

It's not that the idea of a through-trail over long distances was a new one. At the time, the Long Trail was well along, blazed by the Green Mountain Club across the length of Vermont, from the Massachusetts line to Canada, across some of the finest terrain the Greens had to offer. The New England Trail Conference (NETC) had already debated the possibility of creating a trail that would run from New York City up the Hudson River Highlands and over the mountains of western New England to Quebec. In places, this probably would have been very close to the route of the AT today. There were other plans to extend the proposed Long Trail down the western New England route, across the Hudson River, and down the west Hudson Highlands to connect with a series of trails already under development in New Jersey—again, very much like the current route of the Appalachian Trail. As Allen Chamberlain of the NETC wrote in May of 1922, "Whoever was privileged to see that plan [MacKaye's] recognized it at once as a logical extension of the New England Trail System."

Yet it took Benton MacKaye to set the actual 2,000-mile Trail in motion. This has puzzled some people. In many ways, MacKaye was a total outsider, not connected with any of the major trail clubs, and not party to the discussions and plans that were already in motion when he published his article. How could he, a dreamer and planner without the practical drive possessed by other men and women involved in the trail projects, inspire such action?

The answer is that his vision tied together the plans and dreams and longings of all those others who had embarked on smaller projects. It explained their ambitions, giving them coherent and far-reaching form. It spoke to the reasons why people wanted trails in the first place.

As discussed in the Introduction to this book, America was at this time in the throes of a love affair with the wilderness that it didn't quite understand, but that it was powerless to resist. Already feeling themselves exploited by the advance of the Industrial Age, people longed for a return to simpler times, to a way of finding again the simpler virtues of the pioneers, the virtues that made the United States the

James P. Taylor provided the impetus for the Long Trail in Vermont, a major forerunner of the AT. PHOTOGRAPH COURTESY OF THE VERMONT HISTORICAL SOCIETY.

new superpower. Put another way, adventure had gone from their lives, and they had to find it.

Possibly the greatest adventurer of all time, polar explorer and Nobel Peace Prize laureate Dr. Fridtjof Nansen of Norway, used to assert that the spirit of adventure was a human imperative equal to—and at times greater than—the drive for survival. It was, he said, like a blank page that needed to be written upon. MacKaye also grasped this notion, that there was some inexplicable need within people that could be satisfied by time well spent in the wilderness, and it was this that made him distinct from other trail advocates. While everyone else was being driven by this modern need to re-create themselves in the wilderness, MacKaye actually understood it. When he proposed a linear park to run the length of the entire Appalachian Range, he wasn't merely responding to an urge that he felt but couldn't pin down. He knew why the urge was there, and what would satisfy it. And he had a plan.

When MacKaye published his plan in October of 1921, people recognized the rightness of it—although agreement wasn't always unanimous, causing NETC Chairman Albert M. Turner to lament, "There are some people so hard-headed that the sudden impact of a vivid and iridescent idea makes no particular impact on 'em." Overwhelmingly, though, it was as if trail-builders breathed a collective sigh of relief and said, "Of course! That's it." Someone had finally explained why they felt the way they did, and had given them a plan and a goal.

So they went to work. The beauty of the MacKaye plan was that it operated on several levels. Its purpose wasn't really to see a trail established, nor was it to provide simple recreation. In MacKaye's own words, it was a case of priorities. He wanted a way, through careful regional planning, to reduce the industrialized city to "a means in life and not an end in itself." Working at the factory was to be a way to an end, which in MacKaye's mind was nothing less than a better life for the worker. You worked because you needed money to survive. The rest of your time was spent improving your life, and the Trail and its parks and camps were intended to aid in this improvement.

Work on the Trail progressed quickly in the early years, leading Albert Turner to declare, "Maybe this Maine to Georgia stuff is all a dream; I don't know; but the part east of the New York line is all in a day's work—we're at it." Within eighteen months, the proposed route was on paper in more than one way. Newspaper articles appeared in New York and Boston, written by early Trail luminaries: Raymond H. Torrey, who built the New York–New Jersey Trail Conference out of the old Palisades Park Trail Conference, and Allen Chamberlain, who was among the participants in the New England Trail Conference's earlier plans. Soon, things were also underway on the ground level, so to speak. By the fall of 1923, the first trail miles had been blazed in Bear Mountain State Park, forty miles north of New York City. Further plans were made to link up the lower sections of the Long Trail in Vermont with some of the Dartmouth Outing Club's trails, and from there, lead into the Appalachian Mountain Club's White Mountains system. All of this would already yield the better part of three hundred miles of trail.

The stories have it that the early years of the Trail were high on enthusiasm and low on production, and that it really took the appearance a few years later of people like Judge Arthur Perkins and Myron Avery to get things off the ground. They took over the leadership of the Appalachian Trail Conference in the late '20s, when momentum began to flag. They are among the heroes of the Appalachian Trail, second only to MacKaye himself, and it is often said these days that the effort to create the AT didn't really take off until they arrived.

This is both true and untrue. It is untrue in the sense that in point of fact, many things actually did happen in the early years. A core of the route was put together in the upper Mid-Atlantic states and New England, and the notion of the Trail was promulgated strongly in some quarters. The overall route was also largely mapped out during this period (although in places, the precise route—and how it was to be put in—remained a mystery). And most important of all, the Appalachian Trail Conference was founded, with Major William A. Welch, the guiding light of the Palisades Interstate Park Commission and the newly formed NY-NJTC, as its first chairman. All this tended to be forgotten in later years, after Myron Avery formed the Potomac Appalachian Trail Club and later ascended to the chairmanship of the ATC. The histories were written by contemporaries of Avery and give the impression that not much happened until they got there.

On another level, though, it's true that certain things were not done early on. While the ATC did succeed in putting in hundreds of miles of trail, these largely constituted the "easy miles." These were the parts of the AT route near urban areas where the need for the Trail was so keenly felt, even before MacKaye's proposal. But in other areas, like Maine and the whole southern end of the proposed route, "tramping" hadn't caught on as a pleasurable pastime. Support for the Trail idea couldn't be marshalled by a few newspaper articles. At times, the organization could be downright discouraging. Charlie Elliott, a founder of the Georgia ATC, recalls that Forest Service official Everett "Eddie" Stone "said to me, 'I want you to organize the Georgia Appalachian Trail Club.' Just like that. Just like I could go out into the street and round up fifty people who would walk with me up the summit of a mountain. Most of the folks I knew had never seen a mountain." Elliott did have his troubles. At the first meeting he called, he was "the only living individual who stepped across the threshold." The second time, things were little better: "I was not alone. That night the janitor kept me company."

Support for the Appalachian Trail in such places had to be earned and nurtured. That took organization. Fortunately, organization arrived in the person of Judge Arthur Perkins of Connecticut. Filling a vacancy on the ATC's executive committee in 1926, he brought the organizational and leadership ability to the Conference that it needed. When, early the following year, Major Welch regretfully stepped down from the chairmanship of the ATC, Perkins was the obvious choice. The time for the thinkers was past; people of action were now needed.

With Perkins came Myron Avery, a Mainer by birth, who was just beginning his law career with Perkins's firm. Soon, he would move to Washington, D.C., and a whole new chapter of the Appalachian Trail would begin.

The transfer of leadership that heralded the exciting, but all-too-brief, Perkins era occurred at the annual meeting of the NETC, and MacKaye was the invited speaker. He took the opportunity to give one of his finer speeches. Called "Outdoor Culture: The Philosophy of Through Trails," it might better have been called the "Barbarian Utopia" speech. It was one of the finest expressions ever made of the belief in wilderness as a cure for the ills of civilization. MacKaye had come, he said, "to organize a barbarian invasion. . . . This crest line should be captured—and no time lost about it. . . . The Appalachian Range should be placed in public hands and become the site of a Barbarian Utopia."

His reasoning was disarmingly simple. Civilization was as "unthinking" and "ruthless" as a glacier. He cited ancient Rome as an example, theorizing that overcivilization was the cause of its downfall and that the barbarian invasions lent a cleansing influence. By embracing the barbarian ethic—the free, human spirit—common people, no longer dependent on fake heroes like cinema stars (MacKaye mentioned Douglas Fairbanks), could become heroes in their own lives.

Later at that meeting, Major Welch, all but overwhelmed by his responsibilities at the Palisades Interstate Park Commission, resigned as ATC chairman and Perkins assumed the job. What followed was a whirlwind of activity. In 1927, Avery—by then an attorney with the U.S. Maritime Commission—formed the Potomac Appalachian Trail Club along with H. C. Anderson, P. L. Ricker, the Joseph W. Coxes (Sr. and Jr.), and Frank Schairer (who would go on to be the PATC's trail supervisor for many years). These are names that are encountered again and again in Trail history. The PATC began blazing south of Harpers Ferry soon after. They put in a whopping half mile their first trip—due, they said, to dull axes.

That same year, Perkins and Raymond Torrey spoke at a meeting of the Blue Mountain Eagles Climbing Club, an organization that would become very important to the Trail in Pennsylvania. The next year, Torrey met with the new Pennsylvania Trail Conference. With the Northeast (except for Maine) in good hands, Avery and the PATC turned their attention to the South, becoming, in MacKaye's words, a "maker of clubs." Contacts were made, little by little, in critical areas like Georgia, where the GATC was finally founded in 1930 by Everett Stone of the Forest Service, Roy Ozmer of the ATC, and Stone's resolute assistant, Charlie Elliott. With Perkins at the helm of the ATC, things were beginning to happen again. MacKaye, as active as ever, nevertheless was becoming more of a spiritual leader than an administrator.

Around this time, the route was finalized, with protected public land utilized wherever possible. One of the first problems was the choosing of a southern terminus. Several options were discussed. MacKaye's proposed ending spots were Mt. Mitchell and Mt. Washington, and they had their charms—Mitchell was the highest mountain in the South, Washington the highest in the North. But the two peaks were very quickly bypassed in favor of Maine's Katahdin in the North and "someplace in northern Georgia" in the South.

Just where was still a mystery. At first, MacKaye's side trail past Mitchell to Georgia was considered, but at the insistence of the only existing hiking club in that part of the country—the Smoky Mountains Hiking Club, centered around Knoxville, Tennessee—a more westerly route through the Great Smokies gained support. From there, several options were available, including Cohutta Mountain in northwest Georgia and Mt. Oglethorpe farther east. The Smoky Mountain club favored Cohutta, since that destination would allow the Trail to go all the way through Great Smoky Mountains National Park; Roy Ozmer of the GATC preferred Oglethorpe, as it was closer to the actual southernmost point of the Blue Ridge on Springer Mountain. It was only after a compromise, allowing greater routing through the Smokies, and then a kind of backtrack through the Nantahalas to Oglethorpe, that everyone was satisfied.

Things putted right along, and 1,700 miles of Trail were complete by 1932. There were small gaps here and there—six miles in eastern Pennsylvania; twenty in North Carolina; ten in Connecticut; and, of course, the entire length of Maine.

Arthur Perkins, the dedicated, practical, and diplomatic man who had in a few short years given the ATC the organization it would need to extend the Trail into the remoter reaches of its route, died after an illness that had forced his resignation in 1930. Myron Avery had taken over the chairmanship upon Perkins's departure, and the ATC continued without breaking stride. Avery would put his stamp on the organization during the nearly twenty years he was to be chairman, and subsequent accounts would describe his influence in almost biblical terms. Sadly, Perkins's contributions to fixing the route and organizing the all-important clubs tend to go by the boards, relegated to a footnote in some histories of the Trail.

Avery could best be described as the Irresistible Force. He hopscotched across the country, meeting with prospective club organizers, inspecting potential routes, and re-inspecting trail already blazed. When the rest of the ATC cried out for the problematic Maine route—of which practically none had been blazed—to be abandoned, he personally went there (it was his home state) and organized the Maine Appalachian Trail Club in 1935. He would wear the additional hat of MATC trail supervisor until 1949, and then serve as the club's president until his death in 1952.

Under Avery's leadership—described by those less than fond of him as a kind of bullying—the Trail was essentially completed by 1936, except for a mile in Tennessee and two miles in Maine. In his single-mindedness, though, Avery had actually left two trails. One was on the ground, blazed with metal markers and rectangles of white paint. The other was a trail of bruised egos and hurt feelings. The niceties of tact were not said to be his strong suit.

One of his real strengths, though, was his simple attention to detail. He was kind of like a ball player who could play every position and then find time to take tickets at the gate. One example was something as simple as the Appalachian Trail blaze.

From Maine to Georgia, the Appalachian Trail is marked by white painted blazes, two inches wide by six inches high. This method of marking came into style back in the '30s. The design was personally evaluated and approved by Myron Avery himself. "These dimensions," he later wrote, "are not the result of an accident. They were very definitely determined. A blaze of this size is in keeping with the shape of the tree, and hence creates an impression of proportion which is lacking in a blaze of other dimensions."

Before the painted blazes became standard, metal AT signs were nailed up at key sections of the Trail. They were the descendants of the copper squares that Major Welch developed for the initial sections in Harriman State Park in the '20s. The square was followed by a diamond shape, but there were problems. The first replacements were galvanized diamonds with the AT insignia printed on them. Unfortunately, they had a tendency to fade. They were for a time in 1933 replaced by galvanized diamonds with a Bakelite varnish, but this peeled. Finally, the ATC settled on a metal diamond that was anodized—the part surrounding the insignia was immersed in chemicals that permanently gave the surface a whitish cast, while the insignia itself was protected from the chemicals and thus didn't become discolored.

These lasted longer, but the metal markers were still expensive to make, and they were frequently stolen—hence the popularity of the painted marker. As hikers walk down the Trail today, the sight of the blazes acts as yet another reminder of the size of the project in which they are participating. This selfsame blaze adorns everything from scruffy ridgetop balsam firs up in Maine to giant yellow poplars in the Great Smoky Mountains. It is placed on the footpath at prescribed distances, sometimes in pairs to denote a major change in Trail direction. It is not placed at random, but as part of a plan that was so well thought out that even its size was a deliberate decision at the highest organizational levels. It's typical of the way Myron Avery operated. No task was too large—or too small—to warrant his attention.

(By the way, if you run across one of the metal blazes and you're tempted to take it as a souvenir, please desist. You can buy one from the ATC in Harpers Ferry for practically nothing.)

A logical question might be whether Avery, who was so task-oriented, had any real feel for the spirit of what the ATC was attempting to do beyond the mechanics of its day-to-day problems. In actuality, he did understand what had been accomplished—who better? Not only had he run the project with almost superhuman vision and endurance, he had also walked every inch of it, literally—in 1936, he became the first to walk the entire route (some of which was not yet even blazed). In 1937, in a statement delivered a couple of months before an MATC trail crew completed the final two miles on Maine's Spaulding Mountain, he said, "To say that the Trail is completed would be a complete misnomer. Those of us who have physically worked on the Trail know that the Trail, as such, will never be completed." These were not the words of a man whose single-mindedness was simply aimed at drawing a line on a map. They were spoken by someone who actually understood the Trail in spiritual terms—who understood that it was a living, changing thing.

Since that day in 1937, the story of the Appalachian Trail has been one of preserving what has been gained. At first, less than half of the AT route crossed publicly owned land. The rest passed over private land where the simplest dispute between a landowner and a hiker could break the 2,000-mile chain. Much of the public land (875 miles) was National Forest, and the Forest Service isn't in the Agriculture

Department for nothing—its priorities have always been more on the side of timber cutting than on preservation.

But if the official role of the Forest Service was at odds with the Trail's mission, the hearts and minds of many of its staff were not. The first victory in the effort to preserve the route of the Trail came quickly, on October 15, 1938. The Forest Service agreed to protect a zone on either side of the Trail for one mile. Timber cutting would be prohibited within two hundred feet of the Trail. This was significant, though not as far-reaching as the ATC would later deem necessary to secure the route.The Forest Service, in spite of its mission to promote timber harvesting, seemed to take on the AT as a project near to its heart. Perhaps it was the fact that MacKaye had been one of them: to this day, in USFS literature, he is referred to as "Forester Benton MacKaye."

For whatever reason, wherever I have traveled on the AT, local club members seem quite fond of their local Forest Service and proud of their working relationship. For their part, Forest Service staff seem exceptionally proud of their sections of the Appalachian Trail. The route is always included prominently on Forest Service maps (which are frequently among the best available for hikers).

With the Forest Service holding the line over a third of the route, there then began a campaign to give the Trail itself a legal status. It began in 1945, with congressional efforts to establish a national system of footpaths, and wouldn't end until the late '60s and mid-'70s, with the passage and subsequent funding of the National Trails System Act of 1968. Introduced by the great environmentalist Senator Gaylord Nelson of Wisconsin, the act established the status of National Scenic Trail as a legal one, carrying certain protections, and designated two trails in that category: the Pacific Crest Trail and the Appalachian Trail. The act mandated that the Park Service take certain measures to protect the route and acquire up to twenty-five acres per mile to maintain the wilderness spirit of the Trail.

The Forest Service responded by setting aside land along the Trail as it passed through National Forest land. But on the Park Service side, things lagged. The trouble was, Congress had mandated the protection of the Trail and acquisition of land for that purpose but had not yet provided any funds to do it with. That would come with the Appalachian Trail Act of 1978. It appropriated $90 million to be doled out over a period of time and upped the mandate for the Trailway to up to 125 acres per mile. Within a year, the Park Service had successfully negotiated its first land purchase, at Nuclear Lake in eastern New York State.

One more victory remained, and it came in 1984. On January 26 of that year, the National Park Service signed over management of the lands acquired for the Appalachian Trail, and responsibility for maintaining the Trail itself, to the Appalachian Trail Conference. It was the first time in history that responsibility for public lands had been placed in private hands. After the enormous hue and cry on the part of many for the "privatization" of federal lands, it is interesting that this is the only major example of it happening. Considering the high caliber of the ATC staff and volunteers, this is certainly not a situation over which we need to lose any sleep.

Benton MacKaye lived until 1975 and died peacefully just before he would have turned ninety-seven. Following a dispute with Myron Avery (described in more detail in the Central Virginia chapter), he was for some time not associated with the ATC or the Trail he inspired and worked so hard to see blazed. However, in the early '60s, he reconciled with the Conference and spent part of his last years meeting with members, corresponding with the leadership, and writing and speaking about the early days of the Trail. (In the interim, he had been involved in the formation of the Wilderness Society, becoming its president and working with environmental giants like Bob Marshall and Aldo Leopold, who considered him their peer.) It's appropriate that his should be the final word on what the Trail was all about, since it was his vision that set the whole thing in motion, more than eighty years ago: "The ultimate purpose? There are three things: 1) to walk; 2) to see; 3) to *see* what you see."

New Brunswick

Québec

Baxter
State Park

Katahdin
Abol Bridge
Millinocket

Gulf Hagas
Chairback Mtn.
Barren Mtn.

Monson
Moxie Bald Mtn.
Pleasant Pond Mtn.

Bigelow
Mtn.

Crocker
Mtn.

Saddleback
Mtn.

Sugarloaf Mtn.
Spaulding Mtn.

Grafton Notch

Baldpate Mtn.

Mahoosuc Notch

Old Speck Mtn.

Moose Eye
Mtn.

100-Mile Wilderness

Penobscot River

Mahoosuc Range

Kennebec River

New
Hampshire

Atlantic Ocean

MAINE

4 Maine

Trail Distance:
Katahdin to the Maine–New Hampshire
State Line .... 281.4 miles
Maintaining Club:
Maine Appalachian Trail Club: Katahdin to Grafton Notch

INTRODUCTION

Katahdin is an appropriate northern terminus for the Trail, and not just because it stands in one of the finest wilderness areas in the Northeast. "The Greatest Mountain" stands alone in Maine, a rugged sentinel surrounded by lowland bogs and lesser peaks and ridges.

It was once so remote that for the first three hundred years of European settlement in North America it was climbed by only a handful of people. The local people, the Penobscots, had in their oral history enough stories of hunters disappearing in the rugged region to keep the curious away. They believed Katahdin to be the home of the evil deity "Bumole," who was said to kidnap hunters and warriors who ventured too close, and then hold them captive beneath the mountain. During their captivity, he would often marry them to one of his sisters or daughters. The warrior would then be sent back to his people, with the stern admonition never to marry or have relations with another woman. Those who ignored the warning would disappear beneath the mountain forever. Even Henry David Thoreau, the great American Transcendentalist, on failing to climb Katahdin in 1846, departed from his benign view of nature long enough to wonder if the mountain hadn't been out to get him.

Of all the many sections of the Appalachian Trail, Maine stands as the most remote. Farther south, the Trail crosses roads and runs within a few hundred yards of tract housing. In Maine it remains for the most part in woods so deep that city dwellers' minds may begin playing tricks on them. Those travelers whose skills are not yet fully developed should think twice about attempting some of these sections of the Trail. For skilled hikers, however, the AT in Maine is a must.

Special note must be taken of the Maine Appalachian Trail Club. Its far-flung membership maintains the longest segment of Trail of any of the ATC's member organizations, through the ruggedest, remotest country on the entire route. What's more, there is less of the Trail protected from development in Maine than anywhere else, which leads to more rerouting as land is purchased or as landowners change their minds and demand the removal of the AT from their domain. Though they won't brag about the job they do (or about anything else, for that matter), the Maine Club members deserve our admiration—and our thanks. The native Mainers' get-it-done attitude is what keeps the Trail alive up there.

GEOLOGY ALONG THE TRAIL

Maine was formed in the middle phases of the Appalachian Revolution, around 350 million years ago, as the European and African continents crashed into North America to form Pangaea. As the continents approached, they plowed up sediments and rock from the deep ocean floor and pushed them up and onto the continental shelf, crushing the band of offshore volcanic islands against the North American coastline. Eastern Maine may actually have been formed originally on one of the other continents—probably Europe—and left on North America after Pangaea began to break up some 200 million years ago, just as the first dinosaurs emerged.

The mountains of Maine from Katahdin through the Mahoosucs were formed east of the suture line between the North American continental plate and the Eurafrican. They are variously composed of deep sea sediments and granitic plutons and batholiths.

Katahdin itself was formed in much the same way that the Presidentials were in New Hampshire. It is a granite monadnock—a solitary peak thrust up among dissimilar structures, usually standing higher than the surrounding countryside. (Mt. Greylock in Massachusetts is another monadnock that the Trail will cross on its way south.) Katahdin was originally molten rock that melted its way up through the deep bedrock. As it approached the surface, it began to cool slowly, forming a giant mass of granite that was eventually exposed by millions of years of erosion. No one knows for sure what the mountains above looked like when the granite finally cooled. Katahdin as it appears today is the product of erosion; its boulder-covered appearance prompted one geologist to say that it has been "buried under its own ruins."

The other ridges and ranges for the most part follow the northeast-southwest tendency of the whole Appalachian province. The rocks they contain vary, depending on how far inland they are, and how much of the original mountain has been weathered away. Many are, like Katahdin, granite mounds that bubbled up some 200 million years ago as the Eurafrican continental plates began to drift away. The Ice Ages scoured these mountaintops completely, removing much of their original mass. Many of the rocks exposed these days are deep ocean sediments that have been metamorphosed, such as the slates that one finds in many parts of Maine. Many of the deep notches in Maine have been made more spectacular by vertical layers of slate jutting toward the sky, and these have in places been dotted and criss-crossed by intrusions like basalt dikes and granite plutons. The roughness of the Maine coast bears witness to the variable geology of the Maine bedrock, as well as to the sculpting effect of the glaciers.

NATURAL HISTORY ALONG THE TRAIL

Maine's lowlands are dotted with ponds and lakes, another legacy of glacial activity. Many of these are "kettle" lakes, formed by huge chunks of ice left buried as the glacier retreated. When the ice melted, a pond, often without an outlet, was left. Additionally, moraines, the huge piles of boulders and gravel left by a glacier at its terminus, altered and impeded the flow of water, forming huge lakes and wetlands. Many of Maine's lowlands were formed in glacially scooped basins kept wet by moraines.

Ponds and lakes are frequently surrounded by bogs. The city dweller might think of this as a drawback—city swamps tend to be the homes of rats and junked cars. But in reality, a good bog is one of the most beautiful, fascinating ecosystems imaginable. Wetlands are among the most fertile life zones on earth, and the Maine bogs are home to countless waterfowl, fish, moose, deer, bears, raccoons, weasels, minks, otters, fishers, martens—you name it. You can find a variety of carnivorous plants growing on the interlaced plant life that flourishes out over the water on the edge of a pond or lake: the pitcher plant *(Sarracenia purpurea)* and the sundew *(Drosophyllum rotundifolia)* are common.

Cold streams are home to brook trout *(Salvelinus fontinalis)*, which is actually not a trout at all but a variety of char, and Atlantic salmon

(Salmo salar), which is present only if the stream has access to the ocean. Deep lakes contain hidden, hard-to-reach populations of a fish for which Maine is famous among anglers: the togue or lake trout *(Salvelinus namaycush,* another char), as well as populations of Atlantic salmon whose ancestors were landlocked by the retreating glaciers. Moosehead Lake, along the route, is famous for both.

Another kind of Maine wildlife is also notable: insects. Be aware of the worst seasons for mosquitoes and black flies, and always carry strong insect repellent.

Maine's lowlands are surrounded by the boreal and transitional deciduous forests of the North. At Maine's higher latitudes, you don't have to go as far up on the mountain to reach treeline, and spruce-fir forests appear even in some lowlands.

HISTORY ALONG THE TRAIL

When the colonists arrived from Europe, the entire region that is now Maine was the domain of the various Abnaki tribes. These Algonkian peoples had organized into a loose confederacy in response to the threat presented from the east by the Iroquois Confederacy, in particular the Mohawks of eastern New York.

The two main tribes that populated Maine were the Passamaquoddies and the Penobscots. They were the archetypal eastern woodlands people, traveling in skillfully crafted birchbark canoes, hunting for most of their food, and growing the rest. Unlike their more southern counterparts in lower New England, they were relatively unharmed by the European settlement in the seventeenth century, but in the early eighteenth century they became embroiled in the ongoing conflicts between the English and the French (with whom they sided, as did most Algonkian peoples). By the 1730s, they had suffered several brutal defeats at the hands of the British and had begun to retreat up into Canada, where many of them are today. The rest live largely on state reservations in Maine. Old Town, Maine, known today for its canoes, has long been a Penobscot community and a source of Abnaki hunting guides. In lawsuits brought by the Penobscots against the state in the 1970s, however, they won back large tracts of their old domain.

Notwithstanding Scandinavian claims of a Viking landing in the tenth century, Maine's coastline was the first to be populated by European immigrants, starting early in the seventeenth century. Old Castine, near Acadia National Park, was first fortified by the French in 1607, thirteen years before the Plymouth Rock landing.

Things were a bit difficult for settlement for quite some time. The French and the British were engaged in skirmishes in the area until around 1675 and in all-out war that lasted into the eighteenth century. When settlers finally did begin to arrive, they moved up the river valleys in search of farmland and timber. These have remained two of the mainstays of the state's economy ever since.

So remote was the Maine interior that a documented ascent of Katahdin wasn't made until 1804, by Charles Turner, Jr. By 1846, when Henry David Thoreau made his attempt, only a handful of others had done the climb, mostly surveyors trying to map the features of the state. When Thoreau traveled to Katahdin, it was through totally uninhabited country. To this day, there are whole sections of the Appalachian Trail in central Maine where the only access is by barely passable logging roads, and then only occasionally.

HISTORY OF THE APPALACHIAN TRAIL IN MAINE

"Nail it up," Myron Avery said.

It was "probably the shortest dedicatory speech on record," someone who was there at the time recalled later. The date was August 19, 1933, and the place was the summit of Katahdin. The occasion was the symbolic claiming of the spot by the Appalachian Trail Conference as the northern terminus of the Appalachian Trail. Avery ordered one of his colleagues to nail the sign marking the terminus onto a white spruce post they had hauled to the summit and embedded in a rock cairn.

It was a far more important occasion than the "speech" might indicate. Katahdin almost lost its chance to be on the Trail at all. When Benton MacKaye first proposed the Appalachian Trail, his choice for the northern terminus was Mt. Washington in New Hampshire. Once the idea took off, though, that was very quickly changed to Katahdin. It was also a switch that the ATC would very nearly come to regret.

In 1932, after Myron Avery had become the guiding spirit and goad to the Appalachian Trail Conference, workers started laying down trail like the Union Pacific racing to lay the golden spike. By that October, the *Appalachian Trailway News* could report that 1,700 of the proposed 2,056 miles of Trail had been completed. It then listed the gaps in the route: Smith Gap to Little Gap in eastern Pennsylvania (six miles), Tennessee's Nolichucky River to Devil's Fork Gap on the North Carolina–Tennessee border (twenty miles) . . . and the entire state of Maine, comprising more than 250 miles.

Staking their claim to the northern terminus, Myron Avery (center), with Albert Jackman (left) and Frank Schairer (right), started from Katahdin on August 19, 1933, to blaze the Trail in Maine. Their companion, Shailer S. Philbrick, took the photo. PHOTOGRAPH COURTESY OF THE APPALACHIAN TRAIL CONFERENCE.

The trouble was that unlike the other regions through which the AT was to travel, there were few existing trails in Maine, and no hiking clubs to take up the effort. Considering that the area was also remote and diabolically rugged, the task was monumental.

The *Trailway News* article also reported that "Eight months ago, the seeming hopelessness of the Maine situation led to suggestions of its abandonment and a substitute of some White Mountain Peak for Katahdin as the northern terminus of the Trail." The anonymous peak was the majestic Mt. Washington. Nonetheless, Maine-born Myron Avery was damned if his Maine terminus was going to be taken away by New Hampshire or anybody else. The article went on to say that Avery had developed "exhaustive data" on the 175-mile region between Dead River and Katahdin, to go along with the exploration of Arthur C. Comey from Grafton Notch in the Mahoosucs to Dead River. In other words, they had looked over the region and had an idea of how the Trail might be routed using existing trails, roads, and mountain routes.

But it was both Avery and "a Broadway actor and Maine guide" who finally gave successful impetus to the efforts in Maine. The latter was Walter D. Greene, an actor with a summer home in Maine. He had for years roamed out from his cabin on Sebec Lake to blaze trails in the remote areas, especially the terrifically rugged section in the Barren-Chairback Range, which he blazed in the spring of 1933.

The ATC expedition in the summer of 1933 that took Avery to the summit of Katahdin was more than just symbolic. He and his companions (Shailer S. Philbrick, Albert H. "Jack" Jackman, and the redoubtable J. Frank Schairer, trail supervisor of the Potomac Appalachian Trail Club) intended to blaze the Trail off of Katahdin to Monson. And that's what they did. Coming down off of Katahdin, painting the now-familiar white blazes all the way, they followed logging roads, old trails, and the Barren-Chairback route already blazed by Greene and Philbrick, all the way to Monson—a distance that measured 118.7 miles on Avery's measuring wheel. (The wheel itself is now famous for having been in so many pictures with its owner.)

Philbrick then went right back at it, blazing another 54.8 miles from Blanchard, near Monson, to Mt. Bigelow, bringing the total for the summer to 173.5 miles. With less than a hundred miles to go, there could be no further question that the AT would indeed go all the way to Katahdin.

Perhaps the most famous wheel since Ezekiel's, in the hands of the man who rolled it the entire length of the AT—Myron Avery, who leads the way, as usual. PHOTOGRAPH COURTESY OF THE APPALACHIAN TRAIL CONFERENCE.

The ATC scored two major coups in 1935: the founding of the Maine Appalachian Trail Club, with Greene as its first president and Avery (who was already chairman of the ATC and president of the Potomac ATC) as its first supervisor of trails; and the agreement of the Civilian Conservation Corps to take on the blazing of the rest of the Trail as one of its projects. These accomplishments virtually assured that the project would succeed, which it did when a CCC crew blazed the last two miles on August 14, 1937, on the slopes of Spaulding Mountain. It was the last link in the entire Appalachian Trail route. Like Avery's terse dedication on Katahdin, it was done without fanfare—the crew simply finished the job and moved on down the Trail to another assignment.

Hikers on the AT will run across frequent reminders of the contribution of the CCC, especially in National Parks and National Forests. These take the form of anything from cabins and bridges to graded trailbeds. In the South, where the AT was displaced in the '30s by the Skyline Drive and the Blue Ridge Highway, the relocations were made by the CCC.

In the years following the completion of the Trail, the Maine section has had a history similar to many other sections, including neglect during the Second World War and efforts by the maintaining club in cooperation with the ATC to protect the route from development. The difference in Maine is that most of the route was across private land. The MATC never had the advantage of the long stretches of National Forest that the southern reaches had.

According to the latest Maine Appalachian Trail Guide, the MATC has relocated over 170 of its 277 miles since the early 1970s in an almost superhuman effort to secure the route on protected land. Although that effort is now nearing completion, it is farther from the finish in Maine than it is anywhere else. Hikers should remember as they cross any private land in Maine that the MATC doesn't need any irate landowners to make that job any harder.

But in typical Maine fashion, the job will be finished, and it will be finished without a lot of fuss, the way it has always been done.

THE TRAIL IN MAINE
Katahdin

Katahdin isn't so much a mountain summit as it is an assembly of summits. The highest point, also the highest in the state of Maine, is Baxter Peak.

Henry David Thoreau's account of his attempt in 1846 to climb Katahdin (or "Ktaadn," as he spelled it) has given us perhaps our best view of what the countryside was once like. After hiring Penobscot guides at Old Town, Thoreau approached Katahdin by bateau up the West Branch of the Penobscot. It is said he camped on a point of land within sight of Abol Bridge, and that he and his companions caught many fine brook trout on the spot. From there, they headed north, crossing Abol Stream and continuing up a tributary toward Katahdin.

There were, of course, no trails in those days, and the going was exceedingly rough. The forests were thick, and no routes had yet been discovered around the many boulders and blowdown thickets. For the most part, ascents of remote mountains were made up streambeds or slides.

Thoreau and company set up a base camp at the base of Rum Mountain (another peak in the Katahdin group), and Henry climbed it. From their base, they continued up the stream until it petered out at its source. Thoreau, mistaking South Peak for the highest point, had intended to continue from there on a compass bearing (all other parties had taken the easier climb up the 1816 slide, which is the route of the Abol Trail). He reached his high point perhaps somewhere below the Table Land, or maybe farther east near the base of South Peak. Due to clouds, he wasn't sure exactly where he was, and his party gave up the climb 1,200 feet below the summit. He makes no mention of, and did not see, the spring that lies below the summit and bears his name. In spite of the tendency to say that Thoreau "climbed the mountain," he didn't make it that far.

Hikers today need not worry about losing their way: the various trails to the summit are mostly very well marked. Myron Avery would later write, "If, on a clear day, the Trail across the Table Land seems overmarked, we would ask our critics to defer judgment until they attempt to cross the Table Land in a dense fog. Then, undoubtedly, they will find the paint blazes too far apart. For, in the fog, the real source of danger on Katahdin is the numerous misleading lines of cairns."

The Trail leads steeply off the summit of Baxter Peak to the southwest, soon reaching the comparatively level terrain at Table Land. Crossing that, a distance of nearly a mile, it reaches the Gateway, at which point it begins to descend stiffly once again, down a heavily bouldered route toward the treeline, 1,750 feet below the summit. Once at the treeline, it passes by the Cave, a space beneath a large boulder that can be used as a refuge in an emergency.

Upon reaching Katahdin Stream, which it will follow down to the bottom, the Trail passes by some beautiful fifty-foot waterfalls and finally reaches Katahdin Stream Campground just over five miles from the summit. This completes one of the most rugged descents along the Trail's entire length—over 4,000 feet in those five miles.

One of the most popular ways to access Katahdin is via the surrounding campgrounds. Run by Baxter State Park, the Katahdin Stream, Daicey Pond, and Abol campgrounds offer a place to set up a base camp or leave your car. However, you need reservations in advance to do either. Also nearby is Abol Bridge Campground, which is privately operated. None of these sites has a phone, and at Baxter, you often get an answering machine. I have at times found it a bit of a challenge to make arrangements.

Some people assume that the park is essentially closed in the winter, but this isn't true. There are still rangers on duty, and they enforce a number of rather commonsense rules for those wanting to climb above treeline. They include:

- "A minimum party size of four (which may consist of separate teams of two) is required for winter mountain hiking and climbing or ski-mountaineering or snowboarding above treeline."
- "A minimum party size of three is required for overnight activities below treeline at roadside campgrounds and campsites. A minimum size of four is required for camping at Chimney Pond or Russell Pond."
- "The maximum winter party size is ten."

Now in the lowlands, the Trail has reached the wet regions of Maine. In "The Maine Woods," Thoreau described what followed his Katahdin hike: "The primitive wood is always and everywhere damp and mossy, so that I travelled constantly with the impression that I was in a swamp." From here, the Trail will weave its way among the thousands of lakes and ponds, which the ATC Trail Guide describes as looking from the summit of Katahdin "as if a mirror had been broken and scattered over the mantle of dark green spruce and fir forest cover, with the myriad lakes reflecting the sun's light to the observer."

Passing by two impressive waterfalls (accessible by short side trails), the AT then descends into the valley of the West Branch of the Penobscot. The West Branch is a wild river that features some of the best whitewater in the Northeast. There are a number of rafting and guiding operations in Millinocket that can take you down.

The 100-Mile Wilderness

After descending into the valley, the Trail crosses the Abol Bridge (Abol is short for Aboljackamegassic, which is recorded as meaning "bare ground" in Abnaki, or, in the case of Abol Falls, Aboljacarmegus, or "smooth ledge falls"). It then approaches the entrance to what is known as the 100-Mile Wilderness. Actually, it's about 98 miles, and it's nothing to be taken lightly. This most remote of all AT sections is crossed by primitive timber roads in only a few locations, and it's no easy walk out on any of them.

If you're an Easterner who has been frustrated by an inability to really get out on your own, far from civilization, this is your chance. If you want to attempt the crossing, allow eight to ten days, and be sure to make arrangements with the Great Northern Paper Company's gatekeeper to leave your car at the Control Gate at the site. Or, better yet, get somebody to drop you off and leave your car in Monson. That's where you're going to end up.

As it enters the Wilderness, the Trail heads first for Rainbow Ledges and Rainbow Lake. It was there in 1954 that "Grandma" Emma Gatewood's first attempt to thru-hike the AT failed. She got lost, and after spending the night out in the bush, made her way back to Rainbow Lake to find her rescuers pitching horseshoes. They had given up on her.

They might have saved themselves the trouble entirely, because Grandma could take care of herself. The following year, 1955, she set out from Mt. Oglethorpe in Georgia, and by September she had become, at age sixty-seven, the first woman to thru-hike the AT. She then did it two more times, and hiked the Long Trail, the Oregon Trail, and a number of others in the bargain. She was only the sixteenth person to hike the entire AT, and the eighth to thru-hike the entire route, but she stands as perhaps the best known and best loved of them all. She died in 1973 at eighty-five after a short illness. To this day, along the route, people will tell you that "Grandma Gatewood slept here."

The Trail proceeds generally uphill toward Rainbow Ledges from the West Branch. These are part of a relatively steep, unwooded knob overlooking Rainbow Lake from the east. The ledges are bare because of a forest fire in 1903 that was evidently hot enough to kill the trees and burn the ground cover away completely.

The Rainbow Lake area is uninhabited except for some private camps. Hikers should stay away from them except in emergencies. The

Trail follows the south shore of the lake to near its outlet, and then follows Rainbow Stream down toward Nesuntabunt ("three heads") Mountain and Nahmakanta Lake. On the way, it crosses a logging road that leads out toward Millinocket. The Trail climbs Nesuntabunt (a short, steep pitch with good views toward Katahdin from a ledge down a side trail), and then goes down steeply to Nahmakanta Lake. This lake, with its sandy beach and fabulous views, is worth a long weekend all by itself, especially to that extent that its name—"Plenty of Fish"—still holds true.

The Trail then takes off to the southeast, passing by several other beautiful lakes (Pemadumcook and Jo-Mary, the latter named for a Penobscot guide) and some low-lying, boggy country on its way to the White Cap Mountains and nearby Gulf Hagas, the "Grand Canyon of the East."

The White Cap Range

White Cap and its neighbors run in the 2,750- to 3,500-foot range. White Cap, the first that the Trail reaches, is 3,644 feet high and has an open summit noted for its spectacular view. Nearby Hay Mountain (3,244 feet) and Gulf Hagas Mountain (2,683 feet) offer less in the way of views. The range is accessible on either end via very rough logging roads, which are described on the MATC trail guide map. They involve passing by control gates operated by the paper companies, so check in advance for any arrangements you may need to make; the Maine trail guide lists which logging company controls which logging road access.

Gulf Hagas and The Hermitage

At the southern end of the White Cap Range, the Trail passes near Gulf Hagas. Access to it is from the Hermitage, a stand of 130-foot-tall white pines owned by the Nature Conservancy. (Camping and fires are prohibited.) The trails into the Gulf area were blazed by Walter Greene in 1934.

The Gulf itself is a 2.5-mile-long gorge cut down into tilted layers of slate—the remnants of deep-ocean sediment pushed inland by the Acadian Orogeny 350 million years ago. The West Branch of the Pleasant River cascades down over a series of falls until it reaches still or "dead" water near the Hermitage. Gulf Hagas Brook also enters here, with the spectacular Screw Auger Falls just above the confluence.

Access to this section of the Trail is through the Katahdin Iron

Works, an old smelting operation that is now a museum. It is off of Route 11 near Brownville Junction. It's a 7.4-mile walk from the Iron Works to The Hermitage, but you can drive in as long as you park out of the way of the logging trucks.

The Barren-Chairback Range

Next, as the 100-Mile Wilderness closes in on Monson, it enters one of its true highlights: the Barren-Chairback Range. It was blazed by Walter Greene in the spring of 1933, in anticipation of Myron Avery's arrival, to prove that the Trail could be blazed in Maine.

The AT enters the range from the Chairback side, climbing up the cliffs from which it got its name—it seems they reminded somebody of a ladderback chair. The range is noted for its steep ups and downs. Even though the mountains are only in the 2,200- to 2,600-foot range, they are exceedingly rugged, and there are open summits on a few— Chairback and Barren (with its abandoned fire tower) being notable.

The range is a favorite overnight section hike and is suitable for a long weekend. There are two shelters high in the range that can afford a lot of privacy if you're not there in the height of the season.

The Trail comes down off Barren Mountain steeply and heads once again into a low knob-and-valley region, climbing over a series of parallel ridges as it heads southwest into Monson. Some of the streams don't have easy crossings—there aren't always bridges over bodies of water in Maine the way there are farther south. If you don't believe it, wait until you get to the Kennebec River.

Moxie Bald and Pleasant Pond Mountain

Through this section, a lightweight fly rod and a Maine fishing license are required equipment. I, anyway, can't bear to pass by clear streams like this without dropping a line at least once or twice.

The Trail, by the way, doesn't actually go into Monson—it hits the shore of Lake Hebron a couple of miles up the road and moves away to the west.

Passing by the lake to the west, the AT enters another lowland wilderness, the slate canyon of the West Branch of the Piscataquis River. The route goes through the canyon for 5.3 miles. There is good swimming in the pools, if you don't bother the fishermen.

Once through the canyon, the Trail fords the Piscataquis and follows the Bald Mountain Stream up toward the boggy northern end of Bald Mountain Pond. Following this is a steep climb up Moxie Bald

Mountain, a 2,630-foot peak with, as you'd expect from the name, a bald summit. Then, it's a quick down-and-up again to the top of 2,477-foot Pleasant Pond Mountain, with views to be had from ledges around the summit.

Naturally, Pleasant Pond is not far away. A fast descent off of Pleasant Pond Mountain brings you to this moderately developed lake, with road access to the small village of Caratunk, on the Kennebec River.

Crossing the Kennebec

The Kennebec is big trouble for thru-hikers. Day hikers don't worry so much, because they can simply start or finish their hike on either side, using their car to get around the ford. But on occasion, even short-term users come face to face with the problems of crossing this wilderness stream.

Bridgeless and 150 feet wide, the Kennebec's fording situation is complicated by a power station upstream that regularly releases large amounts of water. If you're on the water when the wave comes, you stand to be in deep trouble—what was knee-deep when you started crossing can quickly go over your head and wash you away. The MATC and the ATC have jointly been providing ferry service to avoid accidents, and they highly recommend that you use it. Get hold of one or the other to find out the ferry schedule.

In the first edition of this guide, we gave advice on fording the Kennebec and avoiding the releases. These days, however, the MATC quite adamantly instructs hikers not to do it. We won't second-guess them.

Carry Pond Country

Once across the Kennebec, the AT heads immediately into the low-lying terrain around the three Carry Ponds—East, Middle, and West. It was through this wet, marshy section that Benedict Arnold—not yet a traitor—passed in November of 1775 on his way to an unsuccessful surprise assault on Quebec. The Arnold Trail was reopened in the '30s, and the AT follows the route for a couple miles between Middle Carry and West Carry Ponds. The Arnold Trail then heads to Flagstaff Lake, which is actually the dammed-up Dead River, up which Arnold traveled toward the St. Lawrence.

The hardships endured by Arnold and his seven hundred men would seem to give little advance warning of his later betrayal. How could a man willing to undertake such an expedition become a turn-coat? By some accounts, after putting forth so much effort, Arnold would later feel unappreciated when he was passed over for promotion. Perhaps if the expedition had succeeded. . . . But it didn't, and the result will be described in the New York section.

After leaving the Carry Pond region and the Arnold Trail, the AT heads for the Bigelow Range. The Trail rounds the south end of Flagstaff Lake and then starts climbing.

The Bigelow Range

This high range is known for its spectacular views and its brutal up-and-down. From Flagstaff Lake, the AT will climb nearly 3,000 feet, dropping and rising sharply several times on its traverse through the range.

Bigelow Mountain is the fourth highest mountain on the AT in Maine, after Katahdin, Crocker Mountain, and Old Speck. It consists of West Peak (its highest, at 4,150 feet), Myron Avery Peak (4,088 feet), and several other smaller summits in the 3,000- to 3,500-foot range. Both Avery and West Peaks feature open, alpine summits that contain fragile ecosystems with rare plant and animal life. An abandoned fire tower on Avery Peak helps Bigelow lay claim to some of the finest views in the entire state, rivaling even Katahdin.

The entire range makes for a popular backpacking trip, a short but strenuous 17.8 miles. A number of the campsites—such as Myron Avery Memorial Lean-to, in the shallow notch between Avery and West Peaks—offer memorable accommodations, being among the highest in the North. Also, don't forget Horns Pond, with a couple of lean-tos on a classic tarn lake. It's perched at 3,100 feet at the base of South Horn, a 3,831-foot beauty with an open summit.

The Bigelow Range Trail continues west toward Stratton, Maine, while the AT cuts sharply south a couple miles down the trail from Horns Pond.

Crocker, Spaulding, and Saddleback Mountains

The thirty-mile section from Stratton Brook at the base of the Bigelow Range to Sandy River at the southwest end of the Saddlebacks is among the ruggedest sections of the entire AT. The combined up-and-down in either direction is around 10,000 feet.

In the first five and a half miles, the route climbs nearly 3,000 feet to its second highest point in Maine, the North Peak of Crocker Mountain, at 4,168 feet. The Trail used to include the summit of nearby Sugarloaf Mountain, which at 4,237 feet is the second highest point in all of Maine, but it had to be taken off the route in the early '70s due to widespread ski area development on the mountain. Continued building still threatens to force more relocation even now.

Once past the two main peaks of Crocker Mountain (North and South), the AT descends sharply into the valley of the South Branch of the Carrabassett River, through which a dirt logging road passes that can usually be used as an access for day hikers. It then climbs up the flank of Sugarloaf Mountain to a point on the ridge about three-quarters of a mile and 700 vertical feet below the summit (which is accessible via a side trail). Hikers passing by this point on their way to neighboring Spaulding Mountain should keep in mind that it was this section, blazed on August 14, 1937, that formed the final link in the 2,000-mile route of the Appalachian Trail.

Once past Spaulding Mountain (3,988 feet), the AT takes a sawtooth descent into the steep valley of Orbeton Stream and then immediately ascends sharply into the Saddlebacks. This section is characterized by open summits and a traverse of more than three miles—from the east side of The Horn to just west of the summit of Saddleback Mountain—over bare granite, alpine ridges and peaks. Bad weather can brew quickly, so be prepared in case you get caught out on this section.

From the 4,116-foot summit of Saddleback, the fourth highest on the AT in Maine, the Trail drops drastically again, bottoming out in the Sandy River Valley at around 1,500 feet five miles later. Saddleback was recently a bone of contention as the ATC worked to protect the Trail from ski area development. The result was a compromise solution in 2000 that managed to protect the route and its immediate surroundings and to prevent use of a wilderness lake as a source of water for snowmaking.

The Saddlebacks are among the best short hike and day hike destinations in Maine. Ambitious climbers can do a day hike of Saddleback, hiking out to the Saddleback Ski Area to the north if desired. Relatively frequent road access at various points adds numerous dimensions to hiking in these still-wild hills.

Sandy River to Bemis Valley

For those with a naturalist's bent, the next section won't seem like a letdown. Mountaineers might give it a pass (unless they're on their way to the Bemis Range and don't mind a few miles to stretch their legs), but anybody interested in the ponds and bogs of Maine's lowlands will adore it. This section passes by a half dozen wilderness ponds, each more pristine than the last, and crosses a number of wild streams and sphagnum bogs.

The MATC recommends hiking this section from north to south, to take advantage of the sandy beach and swimming on Long Pond near the southern end. I'd avoid it in June, though. New Yorkers such as myself are fond of touting our Adirondack black flies as the most ferocious on earth, but I wouldn't want to try to prove the point in these bogs at the height of the black fly season.

The Bemis Range
Crossing the Bemis Stream, the AT begins a fairly gradual ascent toward 3,592-foot Bemis Mountain. This is an area of open summits, with a series of rocky knobs that don't require a whole lot of descent in between. The entire range covers around a dozen miles and has four main peaks, including 3,762-foot Elephant Mountain, just off the Trail, and Old Blue Mountain, 3,600 feet, which is on it. The MATC advises hikers to carry water, as this is a dry area.

Dunn Notch and the Baldpates
After passing by Wyman Mountain and several lower ridges and intervening notches, the AT reaches Dunn Notch, a deep cleft in the ridgeline cut by the West Branch of the Ellis River. There are a number of cascades and waterfalls there. The Trail then ascends steeply into the West and East Peaks of the Baldpates. Both are open summits and afford fine views of the Mahoosucs to the south. If you can leave your car at either end, this makes a fine 10.1-mile day hike.

Dropping down off of West Peak, the Trail heads into Grafton Notch. This spectacular, 1,000-foot-deep valley marks the end of the Maine Appalachian Trail Club's responsibilities. From the Notch, day hikers can range out over quite a variety of trails, most up into the Mahoosucs to the south. The Baldpates make a good up-and-back ascent.

The Mahoosuc Range and the Ruggedest Mile
on the Whole Durned AT
Maine was just bound to go out with a bang. The wild Mahoosuc Range is many a thru-hiker's choice as the roughest, toughest section

along the entire AT. The only rival is said to be the Nantahalas, the last range on the route before it heads into Georgia and the finish at Springer Mountain. There are those who say that trail builders and maintainers in North Carolina have done such a good job on the Nantahalas that it has lost some of its flash and bash. Decide for yourself, if you get the chance. My choice is the Mahoosucs, and especially the mile or so through the Notch.

The Mahoosucs are truly something special. Uncrossed by roads for its entire length, the Trail here features open peaks and boulder-scrambled glacial valleys that require the skills of a human fly to cross.

Out of Grafton Notch, where there is parking, the Trail first climbs up the flank of Old Speck Mountain—at 4,180 feet, the third highest mountain in Maine. The hiker is presented with a choice: taking the southern route around the Eyebrow Cliffs, or taking the Eyebrow Trail to the north, traversing the top of the escarpment.

The AT then heads up a ridge leading south to the West Ridge of Old Speck, approaching to within about a third of a mile. A side trail completes the ascent. There has been work in recent seasons to open the summit for better views, especially to the north, although there is also a short tower. The East Spur Trail off the other side leads to an alternative return route to Grafton Notch.

After descending the southern slopes of Old Speck, the AT passes by Speck Pond and its shelter, and climbs over the open summit of Mahoosuc Arm, a 3,777-foot knob. It's then a steep descent into Mahoosuc Notch. A real steep descent.

It's with aching knees and shoulders that you arrive at the bottom, to be confronted almost immediately by the ruggedest mile on the entire AT. The Notch itself is a glacially carved valley, featuring exceptionally steep walls and strewn with huge boulders. The Trail clambers up and over, down and under, and—when possible—between them. Allow lots of extra time for the passage. Mahoosuc Notch is listed on the National Register of Natural Landmarks.

As hikers approach Mahoosuc Notch, they tend to ask hikers going the other way things like "Are we in the Notch yet?" Trust me on this: you'll know when you're there. Last time I went through the Notch, it was in a driving rainstorm. The good news is that the Notch is high enough in the hills that the water in the stream that runs through it didn't really rise all that much, but as any backpacker knows, heavy rain brings misery enough. The rocks get slick and treacherous, and you may as well give up any idea of staying dry.

The best advice I can give is first to be sure of your routing. There are plenty of blind alleys and side trails that end atop crags you can't fly off. I also found trekking poles invaluable. Finally, be prepared to take your pack off when necessary. There will be times when you need every bit of your balance, and there is at least one narrow point that simply can't be passed without passing your pack through separately. Carry dry clothing and remember that Full Goose Shelter is just up the hill on the other side a few miles.

The last six miles of the AT in Maine climb up into the Filling Mill Mountain–Goose Eye Mountain section of the Mahoosucs. After the scramble through the Notch, you may find this section almost idyllic, walking under the sky through high country meadows on the wooden walkways so thoughtfully provided by the Maine trail crews. These are largely open-summited peaks interspersed by high-elevation bogs that feature interesting—and rare—plant life. Goose Eye is perhaps the most impressive peak in the Mahoosucs, even though it's only 3,794 feet high.

From near the summit of Goose Eye, the Goose Eye Trail leads three miles down to the Success Pond Road, meeting it at the same point at which the Carlo Col Trail sets off on a 2.6-mile ascent of neighboring Mt. Carlo. The two trails can be linked up with the AT for a fine day hike that takes in both mountains.

The last peak the AT crosses in Maine is 3,562-foot Mt. Carlo, with an open summit that offers fine views of what's ahead and behind. The Mahoosuc Range continues into New Hampshire, with the border 0.9 mile southwest of the summit. You'll know when you get there by the yellow blazes.

AUTHOR'S CHOICE

There are a couple of classics in Maine. First is Katahdin itself. For the literary-minded, a quick read of Henry David Thoreau's account of his 1846 climb is a required prelude to a long day's climb up the beginning of the Appalachian Trail.

My favorite spot in Maine, though, has to be Mahoosuc Notch. This is an ideal long weekend section hike; in addition to the stone maze of the Notch itself, you get to cross Old Speck, Goose Eye, and several other high peaks with mountain meadows and great views. The shelters are comfortable, the ATC staff friendly, and the experience memorable in general.

Québec

Vermont

White Mtn.
Natl. Forest

Mt. Washington

Crawford Notch

Mt. Lafayette

New York

Kinsman Notch

Mt. Moosilauke

Pico Peak

Killington Peak

Bromley Mtn.

Stratton Mtn.

Green Mtn. Natl. Forest

Glastenbury Mtn.

Mt.
Madison

Mt.
Jefferson

Mahoosuc Range

Mt. Moriah

Carter Dome

Pinkham Notch

Mt.
Guyot

Franconia
Notch

Maine

Cube Mtn.

Smarts
Mtn.

Connecticut River

New Hampshire

Massachusetts

**VERMONT AND
NEW HAMPSHIRE**

5 New Hampshire and Vermont

Trail Distances:
Maine–New Hampshire State Line to
New Hampshire–Vermont State Line .... 157.9 miles
New Hampshire–Vermont State Line to
Vermont-Massachusetts State Line .... 137.0 miles
Total Distance .... 294.9 miles

Maintaining Clubs:
Appalachian Mountain Club:
Grafton Notch, Maine, to Kinsman Notch,
New Hampshire .... 118.8 miles
(Maine miles: 14.4)
Dartmouth Outing Club:
Kinsman Notch, New Hampshire, to Vermont Rt. 12 ...... 75.5 miles
Green Mountain Club:
Vermont Rt. 12 to Vermont-Massachusetts State Line ..... 115.0 miles

INTRODUCTION
Maine almost lost out. When Benton MacKaye first envisioned the
Appalachian Trail, the immediate choice for the northern terminus was
New Hampshire's Mt. Washington. At 6,288 feet, it is easily the most
impressive mountain in the entire Northeast. Called "Agiocochook,"
or "Home of the Great Spirit," by the local tribes, it is, even in the
defaced commercialization of these later years, a mountain to be reck-
oned with. The highest wind speed ever recorded—231 miles per
hour—was clocked on its summit, and its winter temperatures can
quickly drop to levels that are unusual outside a cryogenics lab. Its
soaring peak perches a full thousand feet above treeline, making its
slopes the longest open running on the entire Appalachian Trail.

As a hiker and environmentalist, I always find the roads and
railways and souvenir stands on Mt. Washington to be troubling on
several levels. In addition to the environmental damage that has neces-

sitated heroic efforts in recent years to preserve the fragile alpine ecosystem atop Washington, and in addition to the lost solitude that might have rewarded the rather significant effort required to walk up the thing, there is the hiker's sense that all those people up there simply didn't earn their way up. It goes against our very reason for being there.

As hikers, though, we always have ways to mitigate the damage. True, it's a shame that it had to be the Home of the Great Spirit that drew the attention of the developers. The Adirondacks, in contrast, sacrificed Whiteface, the sixth tallest in the range, to the tourist trade, and left the top five peaks roadless and remote. But even Mt. Washington itself is mostly wild. It's the great secret that all hikers know, the inspiration for Benton MacKaye's whole concept: all you need to do to get away from the plastic and the glitter is to put your boots on and walk for about half an hour. Soon, the gum wrappers and soda cans that bloom in the shadow of the snack bar are replaced by sedge and rare cinquefoil; the croaking of ravens and the song of winter wrens take the place of screaming kids and the inane conversations of people who got to the top the easy way.

Besides, once the developers built their road and their cog railway up Mt. Washington, they left most of the other peaks alone. The New Hampshire–Vermont region is otherwise a wild, wonderful area, all the way from the Mahoosucs to the Berkshires.

GEOLOGY ALONG THE TRAIL

The geological history of New Hampshire and Vermont is about as complex as you'd expect of two areas that were originally formed on separate continents. As the Trail continues in a generally southeasterly direction, it nears the old continental boundary, which crosses near Norwich, Vermont, in the Connecticut River Valley.

Before that, though, it crosses a complex series of formations, ranging from plutons to dike structures to metamorphosed volcanics. A lot happened in this narrow strip of land. Huge basaltic dikes pushed through the rock strata, later to be eroded out by rivers into spectacular flumes through which icy streams cascade. Glacial meltoff, milky with powdered rock, scoured out immense potholes and channels through the bedrock.

In the beginning, 600 million years ago, the eastern areas of New Hampshire, like those in Maine, lay either on the western edge of the Eurafrican Plate or on the bottom of the ocean. As the European Plate neared the North American across Iapetus and the uplifts began on the continental shelf and on into Vermont and down the eastern coast, volcanic islands formed out in the ocean. Eventually, these islands, the sea floor, and the continental shelf were all squished up onto the new Taconic and Berkshire Mountains that awaited them. When the impact occurred 350 million years ago, the result was a huge continent, Pangaea. Its two halves were joined at the present Connecticut River Valley, with the volcanic band squashed in at the suture line.

The great crunch in New Hampshire and Vermont did much the same kind of thing as it did elsewhere: rocks that were once deep under the ocean were plowed up onto the land, folded, compressed, and bulldozed over the often younger bedrock farther west. Sediments were so crushed and heated that they either turned into advanced metamorphic structures or remelted entirely into granite. As the remelted rock bubbled up through the earth's crust toward the surface, vast plutons welled up, and widespread volcanic activity sprang up everywhere.

In that way, the structure of New Hampshire bears some similarity to Yosemite National Park in California. Many of the mountains are the remains of ancient granite plutons that melted up through the rock and hardened as they reached the surface. It's the basic geological story of New Hampshire—reason enough to call it the Granite State.

One characteristic of New Hampshire is the "ring dike." These were formed when overlying bedrock sank into a magma chamber beneath, opening cracks around the edges for magma to squeeze up toward the surface. The result is a dike in the form of a ring, rather than the more typical linear dike formed when magma forces its way up cracks in the bedrock.

After passing over the volcanic band left by the pre-collision islands that were welded into the fabric of the North American continent, the Trail passes into Vermont and a whole different situation. The Vermont structures bear more resemblance to the ridges that will later be encountered in Virginia and North Carolina. Mostly the remnants of the sea floor and continental shelf that were thrust over the edge of the ancient Grenville continent, these folded and faulted ridges are in places eroded all the way down to the core Grenville rock. You find absolutely no Grenville rock anywhere in Maine or New Hampshire, since these areas were formed elsewhere.

To the north and east of where the Trail crosses into Vermont, the plutons that formed the commercially important Barre granite pushed their way up through thick layers of rock strata. The sheath rocks sur-rounding the plutons themselves are composed of metamorphic rocks that some geologists theorize must have been formed by pressure that would be present only beneath 39,000 to 49,000 feet of overlying rock. This would mean that the mountains formed along the northern end of the Vermont–New Hampshire border could have been nearly 50,000 feet high, half again as high as Mt. Everest! It would also mean that mountaineers have missed the golden age of New England alpinism by only a few hundred million years.

NATURAL HISTORY ALONG THE TRAIL

When Henry David Thoreau first climbed Mt. Washington in 1839, he spent much of his time observing the plant life, trying to determine its relation to his increased elevation, and from there, to the equivalent increase in latitude. He figured at the time that every four hundred feet of ascent was equivalent to traveling seventy miles farther north.

The many alpine summits in New Hampshire are the ecological counterpart of the tundra of northern Canada. The scruffy balsams and firs of the boreal forests give way completely to a kind of high-altitude desert—a desert governed by cold and a short growing season, not by lack of moisture. Trees are replaced by grasses and sedges that cling desperately among the boulders, among the true monarchs of the alpine summit, the lichens. The upper limits of the White Mountains are home to quite a variety of species not found below. The White Mountain butterfly *(Oeneis melissa)*, found nowhere else, is a famous example, while the dwarf cinquefoil *(Potentilla Canadensis)*, a viney rel-ative of the rose, grows only on the Madison Flats of Mt. Washington. These are species left over from the last Ice Age; they have survived for more than ten thousand years in isolation from similar environments. As the glaciers retreated, the higher elevations became refuge to species that could not survive in the oncoming warmth.

What resulted was a unique role for the alpine summit: that of island amid a sea of more temperate environments. Similar instances can be found in various parts of the U.S. The Canaan Valley of West Virginia is a sequestered boreal environment more typical of some-thing on the Canadian shield, and several northern species find their southernmost ranges there. The sub-alpine peaks of the Blue Ridge and the Smokies also form islands of boreal fir-spruce forest.

But the few truly alpine summits of the East—Katahdin, the White Mountains, a handful in the Adirondacks—form the most complete islands of all. Their plant varieties are literally hundreds of miles from where they can survive anywhere near sea level. So they remain up there, perched on their ridges. What is disturbing is the potential for global warming to push these species to ever-higher elevations, until they can no longer be supported at all.

HISTORY ALONG THE TRAIL
Native Americans
The hills of New Hampshire were originally the haunts of a number of Algonkian peoples. The largest group, the Pennacooks, lived in central and southern New Hampshire. To the north lived bands of Abnakis, the people who controlled the lion's share of Maine; they extended all the way down into northeastern Vermont.

"Pennacook" apparently meant "At the Bottom of the Hill." This might suggest that they made their homes for the most part outside the mountains, though they may on occasion have hunted there. The White Mountains may have been mostly in the domain of the Abnakis.

In any case, Vermont was apparently divided among the Abnakis to the north, the Pennacooks in the east, the Mahicans in the west, and the Pocumtucs of Massachusetts in the south. The action of *Northwest Passage*, Kenneth Roberts's famous biographical novel of Major Robert Rogers, is concerned with a 1760 British raid through Vermont into southern Quebec against the Algonkian St. Francis tribe, allies of the French—probably the Abnakis.

The Europeans Arrive
In 1630, the first Chases arrived in Massachusetts Bay Colony in the person of William, a ne'er-do-well carpenter and my great-some-odd-grandfather. Never one to take a stand on matters of faith, William soon left Boston and the Puritans to throw in his lot with the Pilgrims on Cape Cod, where he remained in his obscurity, surviving fairly regular scrapes with his neighbors and the authorities, and parenting an equally undistinguished member of my family tree—his son, also a William.

At the same time, two more Chases, brothers named Thomas and Aquila, also arrived in Massachusetts. They soon vacated the premises as well, only in their case, it was for different reasons. They disagreed on some theological point, so off into the howling wilderness of New Hampshire they went. The same hard-headed independence that sent the brothers even farther into the terrifying wilderness on an issue of principle is today evident in everything from the license plates ("Live Free or Die") to the annual town meetings that still control the course of most of the state's townships and constitute one of the last vestiges of pure democracy anywhere in the world.

Although the southern reaches of Vermont and New Hampshire were settled as early as the 1630s, the north remained rather inhospitable until shortly before the American Revolution, especially in Vermont. The mountainous areas became warpaths for marauding French and their Algonkian allies coming down from Quebec. It wasn't until the 1760s that the northern invaders were finally defeated and settlement could proceed north of the lowlands.

One favorite route for the northern raiders went through what was described as "The Notch"—a narrow defile said to be only twenty-two feet across. After the raids ceased, the route was lost until the 1770s, when it was rediscovered by hunters. It probably refers to Crawford Notch. English chronicler John Josselyn, in the 1700s, described the country north of the Notch as "daunting, terrible; being full of rocky hills as thick as mole hills in a meadow, and clothed with infinite thick woods." He went on to give the "rocky hills" a name: the White Mountains.

Once the French were defeated and settlement began in earnest, Vermont became a bone of contention. Claimed by both New Hampshire and New York, the territory was subject to land grants being issued for the same land from two separate authorities. Ethan Allen and his Green Mountain Boys, famous for their action against the British during the Revolution, were originally organized to block by force New York settlers—"Yorkers"—coming into Vermont from the west. These vigorous Yankees, their minds irrevocably made up on many things, were strong patriots during the Revolution and enthusiastic abolitionists before and during the Civil War. They've been a bastion of Republican conservatism ever since. Burlington, of course, remains the exception, voting to send a Socialist to Congress and generally differing from the rest of the state on most matters. But then, as my Vermont friends are fond of saying, the primary advantage of life in Burlington is that "you can get to Vermont real easy from there."

However, even that is changing. Vermont is being developed so fast that it has been rated as one of the most environmentally endangered areas of the country. As Vermont and New Hampshire become more gentrified through immigration from the cities, even political realities are being altered.

HISTORY OF THE APPALACHIAN TRAIL IN
NEW HAMPSHIRE AND VERMONT

Unlike Maine, New Hampshire and Vermont were relatively easy to include in the Appalachian Trail route. Much of the Trail already existed in the form of the Appalachian Mountains Club's White Mountains system, the Dartmouth Outing Club's trails, and the Green Mountain Club's Long Trail and its side routes.

When development of the AT began, in fact, discussions were already underway to link up these trails into a longer route. The various organizations were meeting together under the banner of the New England Trail Conference before Benton MacKaye published his article.

Trail historians Guy and Laura Waterman have pointed out that although there were many trails blazed over the years in recreational hotspots like the Presidentials and the Franconia Notch area, it wasn't until the widespread appearance of the automobile that it became practical—or even desirable—for them to be linked up into longer routes. Once the Tin Lizzie made trailheads more accessible, though, things moved quickly. It's not coincidence, they suggest, that efforts to blaze the Long Trail in Vermont began in 1910, the year Henry Ford took the first step toward putting a car in every garage. It's also not surprising that, in 1933, the Green Mountain Club, like the Appalachian Trail Conference at about the same time down in Virginia and North Carolina, faced efforts by well-intended commerce-boosters to pave a ridgetop road the length of the Green Mountains.

In 1916 and 1917, there was a great deal of debate among the principals of the NETC regarding longer routes. Allen Chamberlain, a columnist with the *Boston Evening Transcript*, proposed extending the Long Trail down the Taconics to New York City. Another plan linked the Long Trail up with Green Mountain Club member Professor Will S. Monroe's existing trails in New Jersey. It's unclear whether these plans were or were not on MacKaye's mind in 1921 when he proposed his Appalachian Trail. He was, however, well acquainted with Allen Chamberlain, and had been since the early 'teens.

Of all the trails then in existence, the Long Trail must stand as notable. Begun in 1910, it was the brainchild of schoolmaster James P. Taylor. The whole idea came to him on Stratton Mountain as he waited for the weather to clear. (Perhaps coincidentally, Benton MacKaye would later claim that the inspiration for the AT came to him on Stratton Mountain—there must be something about the place. Thank goodness that, after an absence of several years, it's back on the route.)

By the time MacKaye published his proposal for the Appalachian Trail, large chunks of the still-incomplete Long Trail were already in existence. When it was finished in September of 1931, flares were lit simultaneously on fourteen mountaintops along its crest. Its southern sections have been incorporated into the route of the AT, and today the two routes run concurrently for nearly a hundred miles.

THE TRAIL IN NEW HAMPSHIRE AND VERMONT
The Mahoosucs to Pinkham Notch

The Trail crosses from Maine to New Hampshire in high style, through the wildest, ruggedest range on its entire length. The Mahoosucs are always near the top of any thru-hiker's list when it's time to tell stories about hardships on the Trail.

Because the thirty-one-mile section through the Mahoosucs is unbroken by roads, this part is often hiked through in its entirety. For that reason, both the Maine and the New Hampshire–Vermont trail guides include the section in Maine from Grafton Notch to the Maine–New Hampshire state line.

The Appalachian Trail crosses the state line in a shallow notch between Mt. Carlo in Maine and Mt. Success in New Hampshire. The spot is marked by yellow blazes. The Trail then climbs up the meadowed summit of 3,565-foot Mt. Success, 1.8 miles to the southwest.

The rest of the way to the Androscoggin River, the AT sticks to the ridgeline, descending into valleys at Gentian Pond, Moss Pond, Dream Lake, and Page Pond. The country is characterized by high-elevation meadows and ledges, many of which give superb views of the other peaks in the Mahoosucs or even the Whites to the southwest.

Like the Maine section of the Mahoosuc Range, the New Hampshire section is accessible by side trails that intersect the AT at regular intervals. These generally offer approaches of somewhere in the neighborhood of three miles. A particularly nice hike ascends from North Road near Shelburne, NH, to Gentian Pond Campsite, with the Dryad Falls Trail available for a pleasant loop past some nice falls. Be prepared, though, because the last quarter mile of ascent to Gentian Pond is exceptionally steep. The Appalachian Mountain Club system trailhead is on Success Pond Road, near Berlin, NH.

The Trail used to continue straight down the ridge from the summit of Mt. Hayes into Gorham's Upper Village. In 1976, it was rerouted south from Mt. Hayes, to cross the Androscoggin nearer to Shelburne. The new section, built on the centennial of the Appalachian Mountain

Club, is called the Centennial Trail. The old section is still open as a side trail. The Androscoggin, by the way, is known as a fine trout stream, especially along its upper reaches, and as an exciting river to paddle.

From its crossing of the Androscoggin, the Trail quickly heads back up into the mountains. In the next five miles, it will ascend nearly 3,000 feet, which foreshadows the radical up-and-down that will characterize it through most of New Hampshire. It soon tops 4,000 feet in Mt. Moriah as it enters the Carter-Moriah Range on its way to the Presidentials.

Most of the Carter-Moriah Range is in the White Mountains National Forest. Fires are prohibited above the treeline (i.e., where trees are less than eight feet high) and near trailheads and shelters. Check with the Forest Service for specifics: White Mountains National Forest, PO Box 638, Laconia, NH 03247, (603) 524-6450.

Another access to the Carter-Moriah Range is over the Carter Moriah Trail out of Gorham. It joins the AT on the summit of Mt. Moriah and continues concurrently with it to Carter Notch Hut. From there, the AT follows the Wildcat Ridge Trail to Pinkham Notch. Throughout the Carter-Moriah Range, the AT remains above 4,000 feet except in the steep-sided notches. Once across Wildcat Mountain, it descends a knee-popping 2,000 feet in under two miles on its way to Pinkham Notch.

The Presidential Range

The Appalachian Mountain Club's mountain facility, Pinkham Notch Camp, is located, appropriately enough, at Pinkham Notch. It is the gateway to the Presidential Range, the highest, most spectacular mountains in the Northeast.

Most guides to the White Mountains begin with long strings of warnings, in capital letters, boldfaced, italicized, in the middle of the page, quoted. We writers are afraid that readers will underestimate these mountains, go off and do something stupid, get themselves killed, and blame it on us.

The Whites *are* deceptively dangerous. Situated in stormy New England, crossroads to several major weather paths, they are also high enough to create their own weather. Storms can blow up quickly, and they can be among the most violent on earth. So here goes—the obligatory (and necessary) warning: When in the Presidentials, ALWAYS PREPARE FOR COLD AND STORM, EVEN IN SUMMER. It's recom-

mended that you follow that dictum in any mountain range, but in the
Whites, it should become your religion.

Just don't be too afraid of the mountains. They can be safely visited without too much fear of death, if you take the proper precautions.
The White Mountains, and especially the Presidentials, have been a
recreational attraction for over a hundred years. The road to the summit was begun as early as the 1850s, with a number of mountain lodges
built in the area to house tourists and hikers. The famous cog railway,
the first of its kind in the world, began operation in 1869.

Human visitation began long before that. The first known ascent
of Mt. Washington is credited to one Darby Field, who explored the
"tops of the white hills" in 1632, possibly looking for gold or gems. He
returned to civilization to report seeing some kind of "shining stone,"
and then retreated into obscurity. Others followed the same year,
apparently looking for the shining stones. One was the deputy governor of Maine, Thomas Gorges, who reported traveling "about seven or
eight miles upon shattered rocks, without tree or grass, very steep
all the way. At the top is a plain about three or four miles over, all
shattered stones, and upon that is another rock or spire [Sugar Loaf],
about a mile in height, and about an acre of ground at the top." In the
1700s, British Major Robert Rogers, of *Northwest Passage* fame, evidently failed in his summit attempt. He reported four or five miles of
thick beech, hemlock, and white pine, followed by six or seven miles
of black spruce covered with "white moss," and beyond that, "scarce
any thing growing." His particular route is not known.

Henry David Thoreau's 1839 route *is* known, as is his path in 1858.
The first instance took place in August and September of 1839, when
he and his brother John began their mountain adventure at Franconia
Notch, approaching Mt. Washington from the west. Once on the sum-
mit, they went back the way they had come to Crawford House in
Crawford Notch, and then back south to Conway.

In 1858, they ascended to the base through Pinkham Notch. Hiring
a local packer, they took the Tuckerman's Ravine route to the summit.
Thoreau himself, not as strong as he had been nineteen years before
(he would die four years later), took a couple of bad falls on the way
up. Their packer let the campfire burn out of control, incinerating a
couple of acres. To this day, many local people attribute the fire to
Thoreau himself: he had been responsible for a bad one in his home-
town of Concord, Massachusetts, several years before.

Once the Trail leaves Pinkham Notch, it takes a long, counter-clockwise arc north, crossing the lowland for about four miles, passing the Mt. Washington auto road and several trail junctions. Once it passes the point where the Madison Gulf Trail branches off, however, it begins a relentless uphill section for the next 2.4 miles, during which it will ascend nearly 2,800 feet to the summit of Mt. Madison. This part of the route climbs up the Osgood Trail, named for B. F. Osgood, who blazed it in 1878. It is the oldest route to the summit of Mt. Madison still in use.

Once the AT passes above the treeline on the southeastern slopes of 5,363-foot Mt. Madison, it stays above it for another 12.7 miles. It won't dip below 5,000 feet for ten miles, when it descends from Mt. Franklin. This is the longest high-elevation distance through unwooded territory on the entire AT. You're totally exposed out there, and you should make intelligent preparations for foul weather.

The alpine ridges and peaks constitute an exceedingly delicate ecosystem. Tiny plants cling to crevices between the rocks, accomplishing their entire year's growth in a matter of weeks. In several places, the AT has been rerouted to avoid particularly fragile areas. Don't leave the Trail if you can avoid it: even walking over the boulders can damage the lichens on their surfaces, and the rocking that your footsteps cause can crush or uproot small plants.

Once above the treeline, the AT arcs around to a more southwesterly direction. Crossing Mts. Adams (5,798 feet), Jefferson (5,715 feet), and Clay (5,532 feet)—all easily reached by side trails—it makes its way toward the giant, Mt. Washington.

Mt. Washington's summit has been easily accessible since the 1850s. There is a concession building there, with souvenirs and a snack bar, as well as toilets, a post office, and public phones. A short ways off is a weather observatory and radio towers. There is even a horse corral. As on Whiteface Mountain in the Adirondacks, hikers work very hard climbing Mt. Washington, only to be confronted by red-faced tourists with their ankles nearly crippled from pressing the accelerator all the way up the mountain.

Frankly, though I do wish all that stuff wasn't on top, it doesn't spoil my climb. The view is much the same, once you turn your back on the development, and for the most part, the tourists don't talk to you, beyond the inevitable few who ask if you really walked all the way up—a dumb but easily answered question. I make a quick trip to the summit, maybe buy a candy bar or something, and then retreat down to a more remote knob along the trail. Some of the tourists probably watch me going down the meadows and wonder where I'm headed. What they don't know doesn't hurt them.

Once off of Mt. Washington, the AT descends sharply to Lakes of the Clouds, where there is an Appalachian Mountain Club (AMC) hut. A short loop to 5,385-foot Mt. Madison branches off the AT nearby. From there, descending gradually, the Trail passes nearby 5,004-foot Mt. Franklin, 4,761-foot Mt. Eisenhower, 4,310-foot Mt. Pierce, 4,052-foot Mt. Jackson, and finally 3,910-foot Mt. Webster (formerly Notch Mountain).

The Presidentials are crisscrossed by too many trails to enumerate here. Far better to get hold of the Appalachian Mountain Club's excellent *White Mountain Guide,* which does for the Whites what the ATC guides do for the Appalachian Trail.

The AT returns to earth in Crawford Notch. Named for the family that lived there, it is the former site of one of the first travelers' hostels, the Willey House, founded by the Willey family in 1825. Their tenure there ended tragically the following year as a freak rock slide wiped out the hostel and the Willeys with it. (Rock slides occur regularly in the mountains; that this one hit anyone is the freakish part.) The site can be seen today, about a mile to the north of where the AT crosses the Saco River Valley.

North of the Notch is the site of the Crawford House, where Thoreau stayed in 1839. Though the last incarnation of the original house burned down in 1976, the AMC has since purchased the land and runs a hostel and information center on the site. There's a shortcut to the hostel from near the summit of Mt. Pierce, where the Crawford Path (the route to the summit of Mt. Washington along which the AT travels, cut in 1819 by Abel Crawford and his son, Ethan Allen Crawford) diverges from the AT. It was Thoreau's route in 1839.

Crawford Notch to Franconia Notch

Traveling west out of Crawford Notch, the Appalachian Trail heads into the longest uninterrupted wild section in New Hampshire or Vermont. It is a rugged, precipitous range, and the Trail will go steeply up and down a great deal.

Climbing over a low shoulder of the 4,300-foot mountain named for the unfortunate Willeys, the Trail goes several miles at about the

1,500-foot level until it reaches Thoreau Falls. There is no evidence that Thoreau ever passed by here.

Following Whitewall Brook, the AT passes up the steep-sided Zealand Notch on the old roadbed of the Zealand Valley Railroad. It was put in there to haul logs out from the timbering operations in the late 1800s.

The path then climbs up 4,560-foot Mt. Guyot—the first of two mountains on the Trail (the other is in the Great Smoky Mountains) named for Arnold Guyot, the famous Swiss geographer of the mid-nineteenth century. It continues to near the summit of 4,902-foot South Twin Mountain (a side trail goes the 1.3 miles to North Twin), and then descends steeply to Galenhead Hut. Then, it's up to visit a mislaid president on 4,488-foot Mt. Garfield, down again, up to 5,249-foot Mt. Lafayette, over to 5,089-foot Mt. Lincoln, and then to 4,459-foot Mt. Liberty. One section between Mt. Lincoln and neighboring Little Haystack is a precipitous knife edge—be careful in windy or slippery weather. Viewed from Franconia Notch, Mt. Liberty resembles a reclining profile, giving rise to one of its traditional names, Washington Lying in State.

You'll be lying in state soon yourself, because your knees won't support you: over the next 2.5 miles, the Trail is going to drop nearly 3,000 feet. If Mahoosuc Arm weren't enough, this section should convince you of the benefit of trekking poles.

What you're dropping into is the famous Franconia Notch. Thoreau did pass by here in 1839, and he marveled at what he saw. The most famous sight used to be the Old Man of the Mountains, a rock formation on the side of Profile Mountain. It was on the west side of the Notch a couple miles north of where the Trail crosses. Despite heroic efforts by the state to stabilize and preserve the Old Man (he is on the New Hampshire quarter and countless other state promotions), nature finally took its course in the winter of 2003–2004, and the rocky icon tumbled into the valley below.

Closer to the Trail is the Flume, a chasm cut by Flume Brook (which has its source on Flume Mountain). It's a vertical-sided canyon—a basalt dike, with the basalt eroded out by stream action—sixty to seventy feet high, eight hundred feet long, and, in places, only twelve to twenty feet wide. There is a fee for admission.

Closer still to the Trail in this area is the Basin, a stream pothole cut twenty-five thousand years ago by the meltwater of the retreating glacier. Thoreau called it "the most remarkable instance of [its] kind. . . the well known Basin on the head waters of this stream—where a mere brook, which may be passed at a stride, falling upon a rock has worn a basin from thirty to forty feet in diameter. . . ." There is another pothole, one hundred feet in diameter and forty feet deep, off a side path near the Flume. Again, admission is charged.

Franconia Notch to Kinsman Notch

The Trail follows Kinsman Ridge most of the way to Kinsman Notch. Ascending gradually (it regains 3,000 feet over seven miles), it crosses the North and South Peaks of Kinsman Mountain (4,293 and 4,358 feet, respectively), just southwest of the backside of Profile Mountain.

After passing by the AMC's Lonesome Lake Hut (which features "dormitory-style lodging"), the Trail joins up with the Fishin' Jimmy Trail, which it follows all the way to Kinsman Pond, 1.8 miles to the west. Fishin' Jimmy (blazed in 1930) and the Kinsman Ridge Trail (1917) were among the original AMC trails that were tied together into the AT in the White Mountains. After hopping over Wolf Mountain and several other knobs, it makes its fairly gradual descent into Kinsman Notch.

The Notch is site of the Lost River—a formation one would be more likely to find in the limestone-rich Great Valley areas of Virginia and Tennessee. It's an underground river. It is not, however, the result of water action dissolving soft limestone. What has happened here is that the Lost River first gouged out a course deep into the bedrock, perhaps along a fracture line, perhaps scouring out a narrow dike of softer volcanic rock. Later, large boulders dropped down over the top of the narrow gorge, effectively burying the river. It gurgles along for about half a mile, underground. You can get down to it via special trails, boardwalks, and ladders.

Kinsman Notch to Glencliff

After leaving Kinsman Notch, the AT enters the region maintained by the Dartmouth Outing Club. The first section begins with another 3,000-foot grunt, up Mt. Moosilauke. This 4,802-foot alpine-summited peak can be done as a day hike from either direction but shouldn't be attempted by the weak of leg (or lung).

The summit of Moosilauke was once topped by the Prospect House, which was served by a five-mile carriage road from the south.

The house burned down in 1942, but its foundation is still visible on the summit. The carriage road is now a hiking trail.

The Trail on the western side of Moosilauke is another case of aggravated assault on your knees: it descends around 3,700 feet in about four miles. (Again, think trekking poles.)

Glencliff to the Connecticut River

This last section in New Hampshire demonstrates vividly how lucky Trail hikers are that the Dartmouth Outing Club already had trails in place when the AT was proposed. Surrounded on all sides by roads, farms, and houses, the Trail nevertheless passes through pleasant wilderness, including a number of cleared fields. For adventurous souls, this is an especially good area for backcountry skiing.

There are two major grunts in this section: Mt. Cube (2,911 feet) and Smarts Mountain (3,240 feet). They are the tallest of some half dozen sawtooth ridges that the AT crosses on its way to Vermont. There are a number of side or alternative trails in the area, making it a grade-A destination for day hikers. The area just east of the Dartmouth Skiway toward Smarts Mountain is especially well served by side trails.

As it approaches the Connecticut River, the Trail enters the zone of the Ammonoosuc volcanics. These are the remains of the volcanic islands that formed out in the proto-Atlantic Ocean, before Eurafrica hit North America. These rock formations are the last stop before leaving what was probably once part of Europe and crossing the ancient coastline of North America.

After passing through the college town of Hanover, New Hampshire (home of Dartmouth College and the Dartmouth Outing Club), the AT crosses into Vermont on the Interstate 91 roadway.

Vermont

The first forty miles inside Vermont are the same sort of broken field running that characterizes the AT in the last sections of New Hampshire. These are former farm fields in the process of reverting to woodlands. They're not the most adventuresome miles on the route, but they make splendid short walks and picnic trails. What the heck—this is Vermont, after all!

After entering Vermont, the Trail heads up into the low hills east of the main Green Mountain chain. The first elevation it attains is on Griggs Mountain, at about 1,570 feet. It's probably named for a Union cavalry commander who shadowed Jeb Stuart (right by my house) in June of 1863, during the Civil War. The Trail then follows Podunk Brook across Interstate 89 to the White River. After crossing the river, it goes into the hills near West Hartford, Vermont. Then it's through the varied country until it reaches Vermont Route 12 north of Woodstock. Here, the responsibilities of the Dartmouth Outing Club end and the Green Mountain Club takes over.

The next eighteen miles are over still more open and closed territory, running between the official boundary between the White Mountains and the Green Mountains. As the Trail passes over the Ottauquechee River near Sherburne Center, it comes within a mile of the Green Mountain Club's Long Trail, which it joins at Gifford Woods State Park. From there, it enters the Green Mountains in earnest, passing by several ski areas on its way to Massachusetts.

The first of these is reached not long after the AT joins the Long Trail, when it climbs over a shoulder of 3,957-foot Pico Peak. It and nearby Killington Peak (at 4,235 feet, the second highest mountain in Vermont after Mansfield, which is not on the route) host major ski resorts.

Pico and Killington have been difficult for Trail organizers to maintain due to heavy ski area development during the '80s and '90s. The ski industry in the Northeast was unable in recent years to keep up with the demand placed on its slopes and facilities. Pico, the first major ski area to appear on the AT, and Killington are among the most popular areas in Vermont, and they have tried to meet the demand of legions of skiers by expanding their slopes and lifts. The Appalachian Trail Conference is currently negotiating with the areas, while at the same time trying to prevent development from infringing on the Trail route. We all hope that some compromise can be reached.

As long as the facilities are there, though, some people may as well derive benefit from them. One possibility is to engage in "downhill mountain climbing"—taking the lift to the summit of one of these peaks, and then walking down, nice and leisurely. It could be a welcome alternative for people with physical problems that prevent them from activities that are too strenuous—like climbing up a 4,000-foot mountain. A lift ride usually costs only a few bucks, and you're soon out of sight of the top station and rotating lift bullwheel. Cross-country skiers do it all the time, riding up and then touring for miles and miles, all downhill.

Besides the chair lifts and gondola, though, Killington is also reached by several trails. There is a shelter, Cooper Lodge, near the summit, and the views of Vermont, New York, and New Hampshire are spectacular. Basing out of a camp somewhere along the route, hikers can spend several days exploring the area.

As the Trail passes through the Coolidge Range (named for dour New Englander and local boy, Silent Cal) it's again time for a lot of up and down. Killington is the last time the Trail will pass above 4,000 feet until Virginia.

The general sequence that the Trail then follows takes it from trailheads in the valleys, through the lower hardwood forests (dominated by the sugar maple that forms such an important part of the Vermont economy), up to the spruce groves on the ridgecrests. Once out of the Coolidge State Forest, the Trail descends into the Mill River Valley near Cuttingsville and Clarendon. The valley, like most in New England, is characterized by fields and young woods. The Trail then climbs up into the Wallingford hills, hopping up and down between 1,500 and 2,000 feet. There are a few crossroads in the middle of the section, and some nice stretches over rocky knobs in hardwood forest with some spruce groves along the ridgelines. At Greenwall Shelter, the Trail enters the Green Mountain National Forest, through which it will pass for the next seventy-three miles. The 5.1-mile Green Mountain Trail runs a nice side loop over the rocky ridge of Green Mountain, which parallels the AT just to the west.

The Minerva Hinchey and Lula Tye shelters draw some comments for their names. They were named for two former secretaries of the Green Mountain Club who, between them, served from the '20s to the late '70s.

After it crosses the Danby-Landgrove Road near Danby, the Trail moves up to the main crest of the Green Mountains, crossing west of the summits of Buckball and South Buckball Peaks on its way to Baker (2,850 feet) and Peru (3,429 feet) Peaks. It then crosses 3,394-foot Styles Peak and 3,260-foot Bromley Mountain before descending once again into the valley at Route 11.

This section has a number of good side trails, including the 5.3-mile Old Job Trail (the former AT), which diverges from the AT near the Danby-Landgrove Road and rejoins it 5.1 miles down the Trail. This creates a loop of over eleven miles that cuts a circuit around the Buckball mountains.

At Route 11, the Trail once again passes by ski areas: Big Bromley and Snow Valley. The Trail actually descends Bromley Mountain on a wide ski trail. Manchester, Vermont, is just a few miles to the west.

The AT leaves Route 11 and climbs gradually up onto the ridge again, reaching Stratton Pond after 10.4 miles. Stratton Pond is the most popular area on the entire Long Trail (as well as the largest body of water), and the Green Mountain Club has taken precautions to minimize impact to the environment. Please obey the caretakers' instructions.

It used to be that the AT veered away from Stratton Mountain at Stratton Pond. The 8.6-mile blue-blazed Stratton Mountain Trail diverged from the main AT at Stratton Pond and came back in again at Black Brook, 3.9 miles down the Trail. Since the late '80s, however, the Trail has once again taken in the summit of Stratton Mountain. Thanks to the Appalachian Trail Conference, the route once again goes to the summit of the mountain on which its birth was first contemplated by Benton MacKaye.

South of the Arlington–West Wardsboro Road, where the new Stratton Mountain section joins the old route, the Trail climbs up to around the 3,000-foot level, crossing over several smaller peaks on its way to 3,748-foot Glastenbury Mountain. There are a number of beaver dams in a couple of the notches near Story Spring Shelter, near the beginning of this section, and they may make the Trail somewhat mucky.

On Glastenbury Mountain, the summit, like most in this region, is wooded, but there is an abandoned, rickety fire tower there that might still be climbed with extreme caution. Its condition is uncertain these days, so it's advisable to check with rangers or recent hikers. If it can still be climbed, it offers impressive views, especially of the famed ski valley of Vermont, home to Haystack Mountain, Mt. Snow, and other ski areas.

Just south of Glastenbury Mountain, the West Ridge Trail diverges. It goes on to traverse the conspicuous ridge visible to the west of the AT, cross the summit of 2,857-foot Bald Mountain at the southern end of the ridge, and travel 7.8 miles to the steep-sided Wallomsac Brook gorge. Hikers can complete a loop of around twenty miles by heading out of Woodford Hollow at the end of the gorge and back up the City Stream valley on Route 9 (about a mile) until it crosses the AT.

The AT itself takes a more easterly route, climbing over knobs such as Little Pond Mountain and Maple Hill on the way. After Route 9, it again ascends into the woods for the last stretch before the Massachusetts border. This part of the route continues to go over small knobs and down into valleys, many damp from beaver activity. Just to the north of Seth Warner Shelter, it crosses its last high point for many miles—a nameless peak of 3,025 feet.

The AT crosses into Massachusetts on a short knob in the woods above Williamstown, Massachusetts.

AUTHOR'S CHOICE

If you're up to it, the traverse above the treeline in the White Mountains is a once-in-a-lifetime experience.

Another favorite is through Zealand Notch. It's a wild hike through a scenic and steep valley, but because the Trail passes over a rail roadbed, it's a fairly easy walk. Leave a car at one end and walk through.

In Vermont, I'd wait until winter and ski. There are sections of the Long Trail that are part of the developing Catamount Ski Trail; get more information at http://www.catamounttrail.org/.

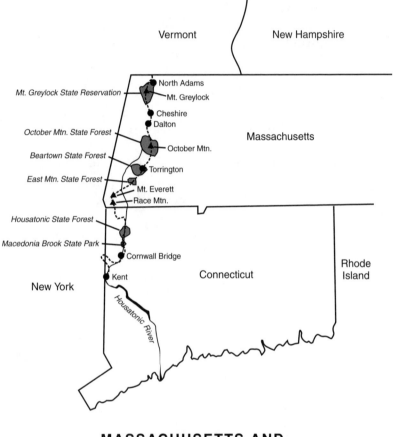

Vermont

New Hampshire

Massachusetts

Mt. Greylock State Reservation

North Adams

Mt. Greylock

Cheshire

Dalton

October Mtn. State Forest

October Mtn.

Beartown State Forest

Torrington

East Mtn. State Forest

Mt. Everett

Race Mtn.

Housatonic State Forest

Macedonia Brook State Park

Cornwall Bridge

Rhode
Island

Kent

Connecticut

New York

Housatonic River

**MASSACHUSETTS AND
CONNECTICUT**

6 | Massachusetts and Connecticut

Trail Distances:

Vermont-Massachusetts State Line to
    Massachusetts-Connecticut State Line . . . . 89.5 miles
Massachusetts-Connecticut State Line to
    Connecticut–New York State Line . . . . 52.3 miles
Total Distance . . . . 141.8 miles

Maintaining Clubs:

Berkshire Chapter, Appalachian Mountain Club:
    Vermont-Massachusetts State Line to Massachusetts-Connecticut
    State Line
Connecticut Chapter, Appalachian Mountain Club:
    Massachusetts-Connecticut State Line to Connecticut–New York
    State Line

INTRODUCTION

As the Appalachian Trail leaves Vermont near Pownal and Stamford, it heads into what has long been called the "Lake Region of America." The name is derived from the Lake District of northern England, a favorite haunt of British ramblers, as hikers there call themselves. Once out of the adventuresome sections of northern New England, the character of the hiking becomes more modest. Multi-day expeditions give way to Sunday afternoon outings to look at the birds, and the Trail gracefully accommodates the change.

This is also the Trail's first foray into the Industrial Belt. Of course, the gentle, rolling Berkshires and Litchfield Hills over which the AT courses for the next 136 miles could hardly be termed urban blight. In fact, they are, in their way, among the most scenic miles of all. As the fall leaves explode into color in western Massachusetts, who would want to be anywhere else? But the roads crisscross frequently. The land surrounding the Trail, and sometimes right underneath it, is largely privately owned, and some valley crossings are hard for the ATC to maintain without running sections over roads. It is this, more than anything, that makes day hikes and section hiking the order of the day in southern New England.

The amateur Trail historian would do well to pause atop 3,491-foot Mt. Greylock—one of the most frequently climbed peaks in the world, as it happens—and give some thought to what lies to the south. For the next 850 miles, the most heavily populated, problem-plagued, sprawling, dirty, and (to me, at least) ugly band of industrial wasteland in North America lies within a hundred miles of the Trail. Plastered to the East Coast like old paint, this is Megalopolis—the hectic beehive of human activity that Benton MacKaye had in mind when he developed his idea for an Appalachian Trail. Here is where the people live who are in such desperate need for Clarence Stein's beguiling vision of re-creation, for an escape from the noise and dirt and tension of their everyday lives. It's the region in which I've lived most of my life.

Standing on Greylock, the hiker should feel a powerful sense of awe—and not just for the spectacular scenery of the place. A greater awe should be reserved for the mere thought that in this hard-driving region, such a place as the Trail could exist at all, and be built entirely by volunteer effort.

Thanks to those volunteers, past and present, the Appalachian Trail will pass by the cities, within easy striking distance of every last citizen in Megalopolis, and remain green, rocky, sweet-smelling, and harmonious to the ear and eye. Paradise really is just a couple of hours away for anyone with a car, bus fare, or a thumb they're not too proud to stick out on the highway.

GEOLOGY ALONG THE TRAIL

The north-south line formed by the Green Mountains of Vermont, the Berkshires and Taconics of Massachusetts and eastern New York, and the Litchfield Hills of Connecticut represents the very first uplift of the Appalachian Revolution. As such, it is composed of extremely old, crystalline rocks that have been metamorphosed many times.

A half-billion or so years ago, much of this cordillera was part of the sea floor off the continental shelf of the eroding Grenville-era North America. The last mountain-building was at least half an aeon past. Iapetus, the proto-Atlantic Ocean, was at its widest point.

However, as the continental plates began to shift again, and Europe and Africa first headed for their rendezvous with the East Coast, things began to happen. This was to be the Taconic Orogeny, the first round of mountain-building.

The sea floor at first began crashing together at a rift in the relatively thin ocean floor plate, off the North American continental shelf. The European side dove under the North American side, shoving the sea floor up and toward the North American Plate. This was out in the ocean, beyond the limits of the rather wide continental shelf. As the sea floor was pushed toward North America, it was raised up; floor material rose up out of the water, and the volcanism released by the subduction created a series of volcanic islands just to the east.

Once the subduction had managed to push the whole structure—gathered up like a deck of cards off a tabletop—right up against the solid Grenville core of the continent itself (which was at the time the shallow continental shelf on the edges of the continental plate), the relatively thin ocean floor plate began to subduct beneath Europe on the other side of the Iapetus Ocean. This took the pressure off the North American side of the ocean, and mountain-building stopped for the time being.

What was created was a band of land off the North American shore, with a shallow inland sea over the continental shelf that had not yet been uplifted. The main mountain range that was formed was the Green Mountain–Berkshire cordillera. Where slabs of broken, overthrust strata were pushed over the western edge of the Berkshires and into the inland sea, the Taconics were formed.

In the 100 million years before the next impact, erosion, which is always with us, worked its will on the Taconic and Berkshire Ranges that were created. Eroded rock material was washed into the ocean as well as the shallow inland sea, forming new continental shelves and deltas. These would later be uplifted themselves during the building of the Appalachian Ranges.

As the Taconics eroded, layer upon layer of the original Paleozoic ocean floor material wore away. In some places, Grenville rocks were thrust up and over the more recent Paleozoic layers; this can be seen along the western New England cordillera of the Greens, Berkshires, Taconics, and Litchfield Hills. Much of the more recent rock remained, though—the limestones and siltstones of the Precambrian ocean floor that would be metamorphosed into the famous Vermont marble when Europe finally arrived.

The cordillera wore away further during the two major ice ages of the Cenozoic Era, finally emerging as the low, rounded, rolling hills we recognize today. As the glaciers retreated, leaving behind lakes and the huge, erratic boulders seen in every farmer's field in New England, the mastodons and other bizarre animals moved in—along with people.

HISTORY ALONG THE TRAIL

At the time of the first European settlement of North America, the region through which the AT travels in northern Massachusetts was the territory of the then-powerful Mahican tribes. Their name means "Wolves," and the French referred to them that way, calling them "Loups." And ferocious they must have been, too, for in the early 1600s, when the first Europeans (the Dutch, in this case) met them, they were at war with the mighty Mohawk Nation.

They weren't tough enough, it seems. In 1664, the Mohawks, members of the newly formed Iroquois Confederacy, had gained enough power of their own to force the Mahicans to leave a part of their territory near Albany, New York, and settle in the area of Stockbridge, Massachusetts. As outlying clans migrated away from the increasing European settlement, selling their lands and disappearing, the core group—by then known as the Stockbridge Indians—stayed in Massachusetts, gradually decreasing in numbers and selling off their land to survive. Eventually, they packed up and moved to Wisconsin.

In the Northeast, it is sometimes difficult to determine exactly where certain tribes actually lived. Always in motion through wars and migrations, things deteriorated quickly for the Native American nations once the white settlers arrived. All we have in most places is a snapshot of their lives acquired at the time the first Europeans met them. It is pretty certain, though, that this part of the Trail was Mahican turf, though nobody knows for certain how long this had been the case. To the east was the territory of the Pocumtucs, the Mahicans' cousins. Prior to 1664, when the Iroquois forced the Mahicans eastward, the Pocumtucs may have hunted in the Berkshires as well. It is known that the Mahicans extended down into Connecticut: a band called the Wawyachtonocs was known to have lived in the northwest corner of the state, where the Trail crosses the state line.

It's somewhat surprising that colonial history doesn't play a greater part in the area crossed by the Appalachian Trail in Massachusetts and Connecticut. But by quirks of fate and geography, the western portions of the two states remained relatively free from the conflict that usually spells "historical interest." During the early colonial days, these areas lay outside of both the major areas of colonization. They were too far to the south for much beyond an occasional raid arising out of the conflict between England and France over control of Vermont and New Hampshire. They were separated from their parent colonies at Massachusetts Bay by the Connecticut River. Though today it doesn't appear to be too much of a geographic hurdle, the river evidently did present a cultural barrier between east and west. Evidence for this division can be found to this day in language patterns: the Connecticut is the division between the Boston-based "pahk the cah in Hahvahd Yahd" dialect and more Mid-Atlantic pronunciations.

Originally an agricultural area, western New England gradually went fallow as the country's production was dominated by the huge farms to the west. Its recent history has been one of increasing development as bedroom communities for nearby urban areas continue to spring up, especially in Connecticut.

HISTORY OF THE APPALACHIAN TRAIL IN MASSACHUSETTS AND CONNECTICUT

There is probably less to tell about the blazing of the Trail in western New England than there is about keeping those blazes put. When the first enthusiasm was sparked across New England in 1921 and 1922 for a trail that was to link the entire Eastern Seaboard, action in this part of the country was swift. Albert Turner of the New England Trail Conference declared that other parts of the country might have trouble getting their sections of the Trail together, but east of the Hudson they were already "at it."

As a matter of fact, the New England Trail Conference had already been discussing just this kind of thing for years. The plan—and that's all it was at the time, just a plan—was to link up the Green Mountain Club's Long Trail with existing trails in New York and New Jersey via other trails down the Berkshires and Taconics. Many of these already existed, too.

The blazing of the trail in western New England was the bailiwick of the Appalachian Mountain Club, one of the oldest hiking clubs in America. A major player in the NETC, it was already nearing its half-century mark when things began in the '20s. They had many other trails through New England, including those along the ridges of the Taconics and Berkshires.

Keeping the Trail in this area has been an ongoing effort. When it was first blazed, the AT in Massachusetts and Connecticut crossed over much farmland. Better yet, it was unused farmland. But as the Industrial Revolution expanded outward from New York, Albany,

Providence, New Haven, and Boston, more and more people came to live in these hills.

The ridgelines remained relatively wild. More difficult were the valley crossings, where residential areas would frequently pop up. The Nature Conservancy had holdings in these areas, which helped, but in many areas, road walking became more and more the norm.

The solution hasn't been anything earth-shattering. Trail supervisors and workers from the AMC have simply met each challenge, made each rerouting, plotted, and planned until the route in New England is now mostly secure. The state of Connecticut and commonwealth of Massachusetts have been helpful by establishing several state parks and forests along the ridges, and the Scenic Trails Act gave a boost to the efforts, but on the main, it has been a simple case of hard work that has preserved the Trail's unbroken route. That's the New England Way.

THE TRAIL IN MASSACHUSETTS

The Trail enters Massachusetts in the shadow of the Dome and Pine Cobble, two knobs in the southern Green Mountain chain, each in the neighborhood of 2,000 feet tall. It enters near Williamstown, Massachusetts, a small, scenic town that is home to Williams College. (It only *seems* that every small town in Massachusetts is home to some institution of higher learning or other.) After descending about 1,500 feet into the Hoosic River Valley (a major tributary of what becomes the Housatonic), it immediately ascends sharply onto the flanks of Mt. Greylock.

At 3,491 feet, Greylock is the highest peak in Massachusetts and one of a number of monadnocks scattered around New England. Greylock's name is of unknown origin; it is perhaps a reference to the peak's frequent cloud cover. Some claim that it came from an eighteenth-century chief of the Waranoke tribe.

A monadnock is essentially a core of harder igneous rock that remained long after the surrounding strata had eroded away. The word comes from an Abnaki word that means "mountain stands alone," which is how most monadnocks appear, and was first applied to a similar lone peak in southwestern New Hampshire. Both these lonely mountains are counted among the many peaks climbed by Henry David Thoreau in his various ramblings, and his description of his ascent of Mt. Greylock makes an interesting prelude to a walk up the peak.

The Mt. Greylock State Reservation, though very popular, still makes a fine destination. The 11,500-acre reserve hosts over ten miles of the AT and more than fifty miles of trail total. The stated emphasis of the reservation management is "hiking." There are thirty-five camp-sites and a visitors' center. The Mt. Greylock Reservation contains, besides Greylock itself, several other of the highest mountains in Massachusetts. There are many ski trails, and it makes a great getaway for cross-country skiing enthusiasts. You can find more information at http://www.mass.gov/dem/parks/mgry.htm.

Also in the area is the Taconic Crest Trail and the Taconic Skyline Trail. These don't hook up with the AT, but they run for 26.4 and 20 miles apiece along the ridge of the heavily eroded Taconics just to the west of the Berkshires. They make nice parallel routes.

The end of warm weather, by the way, is no reason to forsake the Greylock area. Many of the trails in the reservation and surrounding areas make fine backcountry ski destinations, and one, the Thunder-bolt Trail, actually began life as a ski slope, hosting the U.S. Eastern Amateur Ski Association Championships in 1935 and 1936. It connects with the AT a half mile or so north of the summit.

After crossing the summit of Mt. Williams and a side spur of Grey-lock, Mt. Fitch, the Trail reaches the summit of Greylock only six miles from the trailhead on Route 2 in North Adams. In addition to fine views of as many as five states, there is also a hundred-foot-high granite mon-ument to veterans who gave their lives for their country, erected in 1933. From there, the Trail weaves down through the woods of the reserva-tion, passing some of the last boreal bogs on the AT and meeting the junctions of some of the many side trails maintained by the reservation staff. It finally bottoms out at about a thousand feet above sea level at Cheshire.

The AT then heads up on some residential roads toward North Mountain, a southern extension of the Hoosac Range. In this section, the Trail is spared much road walking by grants from the Crane family. Based in Dalton, Massachusetts, they print the paper that our money is printed on. Just uphill from Cheshire (where there are some good views), the Trail first goes by the Cobble, then passes through some wooded, ponded country before hitting the road again near Dalton.

After the Trail leaves Dalton, it immediately crosses the Housa-tonic River and, after less than two miles on roads, heads into the woods again. From here, the Trail will be in wilder land—mostly State Forest—all the way to the Connecticut state line.

First comes the entry into October Mountain State Park, eight trail miles south of Dalton. At 14,189 acres, it's the biggest in Massachusetts. The AT keeps to the ridgeline most of the way, across the peaks of several mountains that are all in the neighborhood of 2,000 feet.

After crossing the Massachusetts Turnpike near Stockbridge (where the Mahicans found their refuge from the Mohawks, and Arlo Guthrie spent a fateful Thanksgiving back in the '60s), the Trail heads into a Natural Area protected by the National Park Service. It's a nice place to hike, but no fires or camping are allowed. After several miles of road walking (at least it's not highway walking—all things considered, not that bad), it once again enters the woods.

This section runs through Beartown State Forest and crosses over Mt. Wilcox, which features a fire tower. Here, hikers pass an old charcoal pit, a remnant of the industry that is primarily responsible for deforesting the Northeast. This presages the many charcoal pits the Trail will pass in northern New Jersey and farther south.

After crossing Route 23, the Trail ascends East Mountain, a precipitous escarpment with fine views to the west and rocky scrambles to get up and down the ledges. This section runs through East Mountain State Forest.

After once again crossing the Housatonic River (renowned for its trout fishing), the Trail enters the popular Bash Bish Falls State Forest. The falls for which it is named, while not on the Trail, are well worth the extra time to visit and afford superb swimming. Right on the New York State border, Bash Bish Falls is complemented by another park at Copake Falls on the New York side. From here, the Trail will head up into the Taconic Range.

As it heads from Jug End (a 1,700-foot summit just to the south of South Egremont) and approaches the Connecticut state line, the AT crosses several more peaks: Mt. Bushnell (1,834 feet), Mt. Everett (2,602 feet), and Race Mountain (2,365 feet). The open summit of Mt. Everett affords superb views—on a clear day, you can see the Catskills spread out over the western horizon.

The AT here follows the eastern escarpment of the Taconics. Another trail, the South Taconic Trail, follows the western flank from Mt. Whitbeck in Bash Bish Falls State Forest and ducks back and forth across the state line for over fifteen miles.

This section is one of the best day hiking destinations along the whole route in Massachusetts. The State Forest offers some of the best wild areas on the AT in this region, and the Trail is accessible by side trails that appear on either side of Mt. Everett and near Race Mountain. The latter, which run from Jug End Road (local Route 41) west to near the summit of Race Mountain, pass several waterfalls and make a fine outing.

The Trail leaves Massachusetts at Sages Brook—the border is in the woods.

THE TRAIL IN CONNECTICUT

The Trail route in Connecticut is short (52.3 miles) and runs in and out of civilization. Some of the valley crossings have proven exceptionally difficult for the ATC to protect. However, the woodland areas of the AT in Connecticut offer some of the finest easy walking in the Northeast and have the advantage of being among the most accessible of the Trail miles.

Connecticut is generally lower in elevation than Massachusetts. In fact, the highest point in Connecticut is actually in Massachusetts—it lies exactly on the state line, on the flank of Mt. Frissell, the summit of which is north of the border.

The highest mountain that lies entirely within Connecticut is 2,316-foot Bear Mountain, which the Trail crosses within two miles of entering the Nutmeg State. The approach is made through some especially scenic woodlands, past waterfalls and streams, and over some treacherous (and therefore exciting) rock slabs near the summit. From there, the AT leaves the Taconics and descends into the Housatonic River Valley, passing by Lions Head, the southernmost peak of the Taconics. The Appalachian Trail will not reach 2,000 feet again until Quirauk Mountain in northern Maryland.

One of my favorite walks anywhere is the section around Kent Falls and Macedonia Brook, where the Trail runs for five miles along the banks of the beautiful Housatonic River. Friends of mine have caught brown trout in there that had to have navigated with sonar. The Trail passes sheltered hollows filled with hemlock groves and pine woods planted years ago and grown to impressive size.

In the Housatonic Valley, the AT passes through several State Parks on its way to the New York State line. South of Falls Village, the sections formerly east of the Housatonic (the "Seymour Smith" section, named after the Watertown man who maintained these miles for thirty years in the '50s, '60s, and '70s) are now blue-blazed and known as the Mohawk Trail; they are managed by the Connecticut Forest and Parks Association. In 1988, the Trail was relocated to the Sharon Mountain area in the Housatonic State Forest, on the west bank of the river. Once the relocation was completed, the old route became part of the extensive Connecticut side trail system. By hooking the AT up with the Mohawk Trail, hikers can make a fine backpacking loop of about thirty-five miles.

As it nears the New York State line, the AT continues in a generally southwesterly direction. It actually crosses into New York once but cuts back into Connecticut to hit Bulls Bridge before making its final approach. Just before crossing the line, it also fords the Ten Mile River on a bridge put in just for the Trail a few years back. The Ten Mile, by the way, was one of my favorite trout fishing haunts when I was growing up nearby. One piece of advice: From sad experience over the years, I can warn you to watch out for hornets' nests on Schaghticoke Mountain, which lies on the state border.

Thanks to efforts on the part of many environmental groups and trail clubs, the wilderness spirit of the Appalachian Trail in Connecticut has largely been protected. Don't be surprised if a wild turkey buzzes you as you walk down one of the damp, hemlock-wooded sections of trail in this otherwise developed state. The Connecticut section of the AT contains some of the best recreational walking in the country, and when you consider what trail crews and ATC member organizations are up against, it stands as a tribute to their efforts.

AUTHOR'S CHOICE

I have two favorites here. As I suggested in the text, there is nothing like a jaunt up Mt. Greylock on a crisp fall day when the foliage is at its height. Just remember that there may be crowds during the fall colors season. Check with the Mt. Greylock State Reservation staff for details. It's easy to run a loop combining the AT with one of the many reservation trails, if you object to covering the same ground twice.

Another favorite, and one I did regularly in my youth, is the easy walk down the banks of the Housatonic near Kent Falls in Connecticut. Spot a car on one end and walk point-to-point.

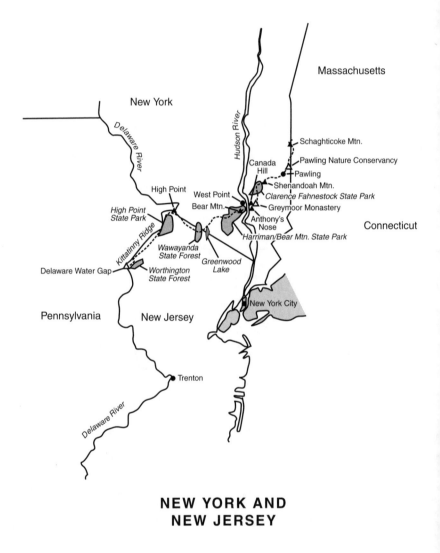

New York

Massachusetts

Delaware River

Hudson River

Schaghticoke Mtn.

Pawling Nature Conservancy

Canada
Hill

Pawling

Shenandoah Mtn.

High Point

West Point

Clarence Fahnestock State Park

High Point
State Park

Bear Mtn.

Greymoor Monastery

Anthony's
Nose

Connecticut

Harriman/Bear Mtn. State Park

Kittatinny Ridge

Wawayanda
State Forest

Greenwood
Lake

Delaware Water Gap

Worthington
State Forest

Pennsylvania

New Jersey

New York City

Trenton

Delaware River

**NEW YORK AND
NEW JERSEY**

New York and New Jersey

Trail Distances:
Connecticut State Line to New Jersey State Line............. 88.5 miles
New York State Line to Delaware Water Gap .... 72.4 miles
Total distance... 160.9 miles

Maintaining Club:
New York–New Jersey Trail Conference and its participating
organizations and individuals

INTRODUCTION
Although, as Appalachian Trail states go, New York and New Jersey
are perhaps less impressive in sheer Trail miles, wildness of the country, and availability of shelters than more remote sections in Maine and
North Carolina, they are nonetheless important. These miles, by their
closeness to the major population centers of the Northeast, represent
better than any other part of the AT Benton MacKaye's vision of a linear park for urban workers.

Even in the early 1920s, nearby New York City was extending its
sphere of influence northward and westward. Westchester County,
which comes as far north as the Trail's Hudson River crossing at the
Bear Mountain Bridge, was fast becoming the bedroom of Manhattan's
white-collar workers. The state of New York eyed a number of sites,
including one at Bear Mountain, for a large prison to shut away human
products of urban blight; Sing Sing Prison was finally built in Ossining, thirty miles north of the city and twenty miles south of the Trail,
and the phrase "sent up the river" was born.

So, the Trail's proximity to Megalopolis is amazing in its way. First,
considering the seemingly invincible juggernaut of development in the
area, it's astonishing that any land has been preserved for the Trail to
cross at all. And second, the trail system created and maintained by
the New York–New Jersey Trail Conference, of which the AT is a part,

offers weary urbanites copious opportunities to "re-create" themselves in precisely the sense in which Benton MacKaye intended when he first conceived the idea of the Trail.

Traffic permitting (which it does, on rare occasion), you can get from Times Square to the Trail in about an hour and a half or less. The areas in which you'll find yourself—the Hudson Highlands, the Reading Prong, and the Kittatinny Ridge—form one of the most spectacular, historically rich, geologically interesting, and scenically beautiful areas in the East.

GEOLOGY ALONG THE TRAIL
New York

Like so many parts of the Trail, the geology of the New York–New Jersey section has one key effect on the hiking: it is rocky. This is one section that need apologize to no other for ruggedness, and the way this happened is interesting.

The Hudson Highlands are actually an extension of the Reading Prong. It was all uplifted as part of the Taconic Orogeny, around 450 million years ago.

So much erosion has gone on since the uplift, including at least two major Ice Ages, that all that is left of what was probably a substantial mountain cordillera is the bones. The rocks of the Highlands are Grenville rocks, many over a billion years old. They are the remnants of the original Appalachians from the dim past, laid down in an episode of mountain-building before life began, and uplifted anew during the formation of the current ranges.

Radioactive dating fixes the Grenville Event at 1,145 million years ago, give or take 50 million years, with another uplift sometime later. The rocks you see in the Highlands are crystalline in nature, ranging from frequent gneisses and schists to granites in the area's many plutons (which formed in the neighborhood of 950 million years ago as the Grenville uplift came to an end). For an example of the latter, visit the Canada Hill Pluton just north of Anthony's Nose.

One of the things for which the Reading Prong has been infamous recently has been radon. The ancient rocks of the Prong contain significant deposits of radioactive elements that emit the dangerous gas as they break down. Radon gas collects in basements of houses and poses a health threat unless the homeowner takes steps to keep it out or vent it away. Anthony's Nose (owned by the military, which takes a dim view of prospectors poking around) has long been rumored to contain uranium deposits.

In the New York area, the various ridges of the Appalachians do continue, but they get compressed quite a bit. In the thirty or so miles from Westchester County to Dutchess County, you'll traverse from the terminal moraine of the Great Ice Age, through the Hudson Highlands' segment of the cordillera, to the rolling hills of upstate New York.

A few dozen miles to the northwest of this narrow band is the next portion of the great range, formed during the later Alleghany Orogeny and consisting of the westernmost ridges of the Appalachians—the Schunemunks and the Shawangunks. Just above that is the Catskill Plateau. The Catskills, geologists are quick to point out, are not really mountains at all, but rather a huge plateau dissected by streams. The plateau was formed by an enormous river delta deposited into the great inland sea off of the eroding Taconic Mountains and uplifted in later rounds of mountain-building. Beginning in North Jersey, the ridges will run almost due east-west until they reach the Mason-Dixon line and head south again.

New Jersey

It is in New Jersey that the Trail finally reaches the long ridge that it will follow with only occasional interruptions all the way to Harrisburg. After crossing the New Jersey state line at Bearfort Mountain (part of the comparatively young, 400-million-year-old Devonian rocks of the Schunemunks), it travels west over the broken country of the New Jersey Highlands. These consist mostly of Precambrian valleys and small ridges and knobs, until the Trail reaches Kittatinny Mountain near High Point, which is naturally the highest point in New Jersey. From there, it heads in a generally southwesterly direction to the Delaware Water Gap, continuing into Pennsylvania as Blue Mountain.

Geologically, Kittatinny is part of an entirely different province than the Highlands. Unlike the older, Precambrian rock found in the Highlands, Kittatinny is made of the same Shawangunk quartzite found in Pennsylvania's Blue Mountain complex. In origin, it is Silurian, deposited as sand on the shores of the great inland sea that formed west of the uplift of the Taconic Orogeny. It was then metamorphosed into quartzite in the various orogenies that uplifted these hills.

HISTORY ALONG THE TRAIL

The river over which the Trail passes was perhaps the most important waterway in colonial America. It was first discovered in 1524 by Florentine navigator Giovanni da Verrazano, but nobody bothered to explore it until nearly a century later, in 1609. Henry Hudson, an English navigator sailing at the time for the Dutch (to this day, he is on occasion remembered in the Valley as "Hendrick" Hudson), arrived in search of a passage to Asia. He became the first to enter the river, sailing upstream about 150 miles, to a point near Albany. His little ship, the *Half Moon*, thus became the first European vessel to pass through the river at Bear Mountain, where the Trail crosses it today. Once at Albany, Hudson determined rightly that the river did not, after all, go all the way through to the Pacific. Forbidden by the English to sail again for other nations, Hudson nevertheless sent his logs to his sponsors in the Netherlands. Based on his information, Dutch settlement of the Valley began in 1629. The Dutch owned the Valley until 1664, when they were forced out by the British.

When Hudson first arrived, he found that like most other places in the New World, it was already inhabited. The people on the east bank north of Manhattan Island were the Wappingers. These Algonkian cousins of the Mahicans lived on the east bank of the Hudson from the Bronx to Poughkeepsie, New York, and all the way east to the Connecticut River Valley. Their name means "Easterners," and they were among the most prolific makers of wampum belts in the country. During the Revolution, perhaps anxious to reverse the British tendency to push them off their lands, the Wappingers sided with the Continentals.

On the west bank were the Lenni Lenape people, who would later be renamed after the Delaware River that ran through their territory, which was in turn named for a family of English nobles. It is not recorded if they were consulted in this renaming. The Lenni Lenape groups that inhabited the southern New York and northern New Jersey woodlands through which the Trail passes were known as the Munsees.

One legacy of Dutch rule was the land ownership system of manor owners ("patroons") supported by the labors of tenant farmers. Huge estates owned by the few were tended by the many, who worked in conditions resembling serfdom. This led to unrest, and there were occasional uprisings, a major one happening in 1754 around Quaker Hill in Wingdale, where the Trail crosses in from Connecticut. This was eventually to be a factor in the Hudson Valley's role as one of the powder kegs of the Revolution.

The instability could not have happened at a worse place, from the British point of view. After Lexington, the hotbeds of the rebel cause were obviously centered in Boston and Virginia. The British moved quickly to isolate the two factions, invading and taking New York City very early on. From there, they attempted a two-prong attack on the Valley, trying to divide the rebellious colonies in half. It was a good idea and a game effort, but it failed.

The two key reasons are well known. First, the Battle of Saratoga in October of 1777, far to the north, is considered by many to be the turning point of the Revolution. An invading army, coming down from Canada under the command of General Burgoyne, was defeated and captured by superior forces under General Horatio Gates.

The second, more infamous episode occurred mere miles north of Bear Mountain Bridge, within sight of the Trail. The other half of the British pincer was trying to push north up the river. The same compressed ridges discussed in Chapter 1 presented the British with a tough choice. They found the way by land barricaded both by colonial forces and by rugged country in which their movements were severely limited. On the east bank, the rocky hills of Putnam and Dutchess Counties (through which the Trail winds) today feature overgrown redoubts thrown up by Patriots worried about a British advance. The rolling hills of northern New Jersey are dotted with the sites of battles and skirmishes where the British tried to cut Patriot lines from the west.

By river, the British were blocked by everything the Patriots could muster, from iron-tipped booms set at angles just below the water's surface, ready to gut any ship that struck them, to enormous iron chains (including one at the site of the Bear Mountain Bridge) strung all the way across, to a string of forts and batteries that controlled key passages. Much of this effort was centered around the more easily defended Highland Narrows from Stony Point, past Bear Mountain and West Point, up to Newburgh. If you'd stood on the banks of the Hudson in 1778, where the Trail crosses today, and looked up and down, you'd be gazing over an armed battle zone.

With their seizure in 1779 of the fort at Stony Point, just south of Bear Mountain, the British almost succeeded. Fortunately, the fort was quickly recaptured by forces under the command of General "Mad" Anthony Wayne, an event commemorated by a historical side trail on the AT that approximates the Patriot route to battle.

After failing to take the river by force, the British tried subterfuge. Opportunity knocked when the British command was approached secretly by the hero of Saratoga, General Benedict Arnold. Passed over for promotion (his occasional rashness tended to alienate his peers), severely wounded and partly disabled at Saratoga, veteran of the grueling and unsuccessful march through Maine to Quebec, and now married to a wealthy Tory from Philadelphia, Arnold offered in 1780 to turn over his new post, the critical fortifications at West Point, to the British. Had he succeeded, this would have effectively eliminated the most powerful batteries overlooking the river, as well as the base for much of the Patriot resistance.

He never got the opportunity. His contact, British major John André, was captured by chance by a group of local ruffians loosely organized into a band of Patriots. They turned the major over to the colonial army, where his papers gave away the planned betrayal. Warned that the jig was up, Arnold quickly crossed the river to the east bank and, after staying a night at the Robinson house (the site is on Route 9D, a few miles north of the bridge), he made his way to Canada, leaving André to hang.

Even as the focus of the war moved to other areas, the tense stand-off continued. However, the actual number of engagements tailed off until the war ended at Yorktown. To this day, though, those of us who grew up in the Valley were brought up feeling that the Revolution may have started in Massachusetts and it may have ended in Virginia, but it was largely fought—and won—by New Yorkers in New York.

The end of Revolution brought change to the river valley. With few exceptions, the manor owners were Tories. As a result, after the war, their seigneurial titles (i.e., those granted by the Crown) to their lands were voided. Their estates were taken from them and were, for the most part, distributed among their former tenants. Most of the dispossessed emigrated. Lord Fairfax's ingenious method of getting around similar seizures will be described in Chapter 9. It was one of the first (and most effective) incidents of land reform in history.

The subsequent history of the Hudson Valley is largely concerned with commerce. River towns served as whaling ports during the War of 1812 as a way of protecting the fleets from British aggression. In 1825 the Erie Canal was completed, making the Hudson the most important waterway to the West. Railroads followed, and with them, names like Vanderbilt and Harriman entered the scene.

Development continued with gusto until late in the nineteenth century, when it turned out that even industrial New York was not immune to nostalgia for the American wilderness. As Benton MacKaye said, industrial lords and workers alike began to wilt under the pressure of life in the Industrial Age. Robber barons like J. P. Morgan built "Great Camps" in the Adirondacks—palatial "cabins" where they would hold court in the wilderness. Morgan named his camp "Uncas," after the renegade leader of the Mohegans we met in Chapter 3. Lesser lords and workers simply blazed trails and hiked.

This wilderness sentiment combined with fortuitous circumstance to ensure a place for the Trail to pass.

Just after World War I, the state of New York had planned to build a prison in the area of the circle just west of Bear Mountain Bridge. That didn't line up very well with the plans of Mary Williams Harriman, widow of railroad tycoon Edward Harriman. It seems that she was in the process of building a park at Bear Mountain. Valley legend says that the Harrimans, snubbed by a downstate country club, had decided to build their own. As so often happens in New York, when the rich dip their oars into the water, the boat snaps to. The plans for a prison magically relocated to Ossining at about the same time a large tract at Bear Mountain was donated to the state as a park. To secure her plans for her own park, Mrs. Harriman and her family built—at their own expense—Bear Mountain Bridge in 1923 and 1924. That fact, combined with generous grants of land to the Palisades Interstate Park, made Bear Mountain the logical place for the Trail to cross the Hudson when planning for the route began in earnest. It was on Harriman-granted land that the first section of the AT was blazed in 1923.

The prominent peak called Anthony's (or Antony's) Nose, which rises above the eastern end of the Bear Mountain Bridge, provokes some historical disagreement. The "Anthony" moniker is said (probably inaccurately) to have been affixed in honor of General "Mad" Anthony Wayne; some hold (probably with more justification) that it was named for the patron of nearby St. Anthonysville (now called Manitou). However, some old maps tend to favor "Antony," and a vocal minority of Valley natives attributes the name to Marc Antony and the hill's resemblance to a good Roman nose.

If you stand on the Bear Mountain Bridge, face downstream, and look south, you'll see Stony Point jutting into the river from the west.

HISTORY OF THE APPALACHIAN TRAIL IN NEW YORK AND NEW JERSEY

That the first tailor-made section of the Trail was blazed in New York State should surprise nobody. Nowhere was the urge for recreation felt more strongly than in its largest metropolis. In fact, the creation of the New York section, along with those in certain parts of New England, was perhaps so easy that the infant Appalachian Trail Conference was, in the end, unprepared for the task of pushing the Trail through in areas where support was not so easy to find

But in New York in 1923, it would have been harder to prevent the blazing of the Trail than it turned out to be to arrange it. Major William Welch and his Palisades Interstate Park had been a force since 1900, hiking clubs had been flourishing in the area for years, and then the Harrimans announced the construction of the Bear Mountain Bridge. It was perfect.

Then, too, there was Raymond Torrey. A journalist in New York, he had already done much to begin the trail system on the west bank of the Hudson, between Bear Mountain and the Delaware River. Benton MacKaye credited Torrey with the first major public relations coup for the infant Appalachian Trail: on April 7, 1922, he published a glowing exposition and endorsement of the whole concept on the outdoor page of the *New York Evening Post*. Two weeks later the New York–New Jersey Trail Conference was officially formed, with Benton MacKaye in attendance at the first meeting.

The blazing of the New York section followed what would become a familiar pattern. The NY-NJTC leadership (formed from the original group that included Welch, Torrey, and Clarence Stein) spent the first year gathering members and mapping out the potential route. Like most areas where the Trail got a quick start (and unlike wilder areas like North Carolina and Maine, where the Trail idea was slower to take hold), New York had a lot to work with. There were already routes crisscrossing the Hudson Highlands on both sides of the river. The route was designed to take advantage of the best topography while utilizing existing trails.

So, it wasn't until more than a year later that the NY-NJTC actually had to blaze a new section. Work parties met on October 7, 1923, at the site of the bridge (under construction at the time) on the west bank and began blazing a sixteen-mile section from the Hudson to the Ramapo River near Arden, New York. It was the first section of Trail blazed especially to link Maine to Georgia. It received an official dedication of sorts on October 26–28, as the new New York–New Jersey Trail Conference met at the Bear Mountain Inn, virtually right beside the Trail. There, a group of Conference members and interested parties, including MacKaye, Welch, Torrey, and Stein, as well as Allen Chamberlain of the New England Trail Conference, met to continue plans for the Trail. It was on the third day that Welch officially introduced his proposal for a Trail logo: the familiar AT with the two letters sharing the crosspiece. It was adopted and immediately put to use on the original square copper marker, which was also designed by Welch.

Over the years, the New York section, like most sections, has had to be rerouted any number of times. One of the most successful instances was in 1981, when the Trail was moved off local roads and onto a beautiful new section obtained by the U.S. Park Service, just off the ridgeline of Hosner Mountain. The first such purchase under the funding of the Scenic Trails Act was at Nuclear Lake near Pawling, on the Connecticut border.

THE TRAIL IN NEW YORK

Contrary to popular belief, there is a wide range of hiking to be had in New York, and not just in the Adirondacks. True, for most of its length it is hard to find a spot where you can pitch a tent with any reasonable expectation of solitude—not in the same sense as, say, up in the White Mountains in New Hampshire.

But that's okay. With so many people living nearby, the proper role of the Appalachian Trail isn't as a high-powered adventure anyway. What people need this close to home is the day-to-day renewal that a pleasant walk in the woods can give. And that's what the AT offers you in New York and New Jersey, while still providing thru-hikers with an unbroken wilderness path.

Starting at the Connecticut border (which is somewhat confused, with the Trail ducking into New York, only to duck right back out again), the Trail route offers splendid day hiking. Coming out of the scenic gorge of the Housatonic River, it enters the eastern hills of the Reading Prong, including Schaghticoke (pronounced "skatticoke") Mountain, Gardner Hill, and Ten Mile Hill. It then loops around the Ten Mile River—long a fine trout stream, and currently the object of volunteer preservation efforts—and up onto the ridges of Leather Hill and Hammersly Ridge.

This is unexpectedly wild country. The valleys are abrupt here, and much of the land is protected by the state, various scout camps, or local preservation groups. The Pawling Nature Preserve, a large tract up on Hammersly Ridge, is simply a superior place for a nature walk—there are flowers there I've seen nowhere else in the state of New York. It's part of the Nature Conservancy, and information and permits can be obtained by contacting the Eastern New York Chapter Office, 19 North Moger Avenue, Mount Kisco, NY 10549, (914) 244-3271.

Once the Trail leaves Hammersly Ridge, it heads down the ridges of the Hudson Highlands along their generally southwest-northeast axis. If you enter the Trail at Route 55, heading southwest onto Depot Hill, you'll find several rock ledges cresting the ridge that offer wonderful views of the rolling hills of the area. Since the lowlands are largely covered by maple and beech mixed deciduous forest, it's a spot to be remembered in the fall.

Crossing the Taconic State Parkway, you reach one of the best opportunities for extended wilderness trekking (in the New York sense), Fahnestock–Hudson Highlands Park. It's an enormous tract of land, and the Trail has for years traveled the length of it.

Ascending from the Taconic Parkway, the Trail reaches the summit of the long ridge of Shenandoah Mountain. (Why this name persists so far north is a mystery to me.) At 1,282 feet it is, according to the guidebook, the highest point in this section. Though it has a rocky summit like its higher northern New England counterparts, I have yet to contract a nosebleed from climbing it. It's a short side hike (a few hundred yards) from the main trunk of the Trail.

From there, the route heads generally south, through some wonderful oak and hickory forest. Keep an eye out for the scrubby shoots of American chestnut sprouting from the route. When I was a kid, you could see large tree trunks lying on the forest floor, the remains of chestnuts that died in the '20s and '30s from the blight. They're mostly gone now, but the shoots, which have long, pointed leaves with hooked serrations, are everywhere. There are several ongoing efforts to restore the chestnut, either through genetic modification or selective breeding of blight-resistant stock.

Fahnestock Park is a good base. You can take day hikes out onto the AT in either direction, or stay around the park and take advantage of the fishing, boating, and camping, which can be had for a reasonable rate (thru-hikers stay free). Of particular interest are the old iron mines that operated here during and after the Revolution. Part of the Trail south of Fahnestock goes along the route of a railroad built to take the ore to the foundry at Cold Spring. Pieces of iron ore can still be found in the area. Just be careful of the mines. The Trail is largely routed away from them, and they have warning signs.

The woodlands in and around Fahnestock Park are riddled with trails, both marked and unmarked. Unmarked trails in the Highlands tend to run along old abandoned carriage roads and railroads and can make for pleasant walks. One interesting side hike in the park goes to Sunk Mine Lake. It's exactly what the name implies—the main iron mine at Fahnestock, filled with water. It was near here that the Wappinger tribes had one of their main villages.

Southwest of Fahnestock Park, the Trail goes through the heart of the area of the east bank contested during the Revolution. Names like Fort Hill and Fort Defiance Hill commemorate the crude, largely earthen redoubts that defended the passes through the Highlands against a British advance. US 9 travels up one pass that was a major worry to Patriot commanders.

At Route 9, the Trail skirts by the monastery of the Friars of the Atonement at Graymoor. A favorite stopping place for thru-hikers, the monastery is also popular with local Catholics looking for an alternative to Sunday services in their home parishes. Graymoor Friars are well known in the area because they frequently help out in local churches. Though the travelers' hostel burned down years ago, thru-hikers can sometimes get meals with the friars.

As the Trail continues southwest, over Canada Hill, it reaches South Mountain Pass at Manitou. From there, it starts to ascend the northern flank of Anthony's Nose. This section was closed during the Second World War because of its proximity to the military facility at Camp Smith. There were once copper mines in this section, but the Trail has been rerouted away from them. Besides being dangerous—they're ugly shafts that go straight down, filled with poisonous gases—they're not really much to see.

After a fairly steep descent down the western side of Anthony's Nose, the Trail finally reaches the river at Bear Mountain Bridge. There is a nominal fee for crossing on foot.

With the exception of the Fahnestock Park trail system and an unmarked loop to the summit of Sugarloaf Hill (it offers a splendid view of the Hudson Valley and West Point and is also the site of a Continental Army encampment and the house where Benedict Arnold took refuge his first night on the lam), there are relatively few side trails on the east bank of the Hudson. This is certainly not the case on the west bank.

As soon as the Trail crosses the Hudson, it enters Harriman and Bear Mountain State Parks. These were gifts of the Harriman family when the first sections of the AT were blazed. With just a few minor relocations, the route is the same one that was blazed back in October of 1923 by Raymond Torrey, Frank Place, and other early Trail luminaries, along with the usual assembly of anonymous workers who have historically shown up at convenient moments.

From a hiker's point of view, the parks constitute a gift of true magnificence. More than twenty miles of Trail pass through some of the last wild land in southern New York. As the Trail winds through—seeming by its circumspect routing to be reluctant to leave the relative solitude of the parks—it skirts ridges, knobs, lakes, and marshes left by the glacier that stopped not far south, the only civilization nearby being the few roads in the parks. The Trail also passes by Hessian Lake, said to be the site of a Continental victory, after which the bodies of Hessian mercenaries were dumped into the lake, giving it its name. There are two shelters conveniently located nearby, among the few in the entire New York section.

Besides the AT, though, the parks are crisscrossed by trails. Many hikers like to climb Bear Mountain itself (the AT goes up there), but that's not all that's available. If you have a historical bent, try the 1777 and 1779 trails. The first follows the route of the British on their 1777 expedition to capture Forts Clinton and Montgomery, which dominated the Hudson from the west bank on either side of the Bear Mountain Bridge site. The second follows the route of Continental general Anthony Wayne and his 1,300 semi-regulars to recapture the fort at Stony Point twelve miles to the south.

Once out of Harriman State Park, the Trail crosses the New York State Thruway—a harsh return to reality. From there, it knob-hops over Precambrian uplands until it reaches the Schunemunk ridge at Bellvale Mountain. It ascends from a low point of around 700 feet at Fitzgerald Falls at the base of Bellvale to over 1,200 feet at its summit. The route then resumes its southwesterly direction down the ridge into New Jersey at Greenwood Lake.

THE TRAIL IN NEW JERSEY

New Jersey has long been a much-maligned state. If the existence of a wilderness trail in New York is surprising to some, the fact of one in New Jersey astonishes most people.

In truth, over the past decade the Trail in New Jersey has become something of a revelation. A major relocation in 2002 routed the Trail through the Pochuck Swamp on nearly a mile of log boardwalks ("puncheons") and across the Pochuck Creek on a fabulous, 146-foot wooden suspension bridge that you have to see to believe. To my mind, the amount of effort that went into just this project is a testament to the importance of the Trail in this part of the country. Though there are no impressive mountains in the Garden State, the Trail nevertheless passes through some pleasant woods and along a wonderful ridge well worth a Saturday stroll or a weekend in a tent.

About halfway down Greenwood Lake, the Trail takes a sharp right, heading in a generally westerly direction. For about twenty-one miles it hops crosslots, off the Schunemunks and over the Vernon Valley (home of New Jersey's only major ski areas), never running more than a mile or so from the New York border. This section has recently undergone several reroutings, most of which have taken the Trail off of secondary roads and into the woods.

Throughout southwestern New York and northern New Jersey, hikers may run across circular depressions in the forest floor. These are the sites of charcoal pits, where local hemlock was burned into the charcoal needed for iron smelting. The charcoal industry denuded the woods from New Jersey to Connecticut.

Charcoal burning wasn't an easy job. To keep the wood from igniting, an elaborate mound was built, with wood carefully stacked inside. Over the wood, the mound's tender put a layer of ferns or wet leaves, covered by a thick layer of sod. Once ignited, he had to watch carefully, daubing any hot spots with a wet charcoal paste to smother any flame.

It was slow, demanding work. A small mound could take a week or two to finish smoldering; a large mound—one around thirty feet in diameter—could take up to a month. The tender had to watch it like a hawk, sleeping in short naps to prevent flame from consuming his work. It was dangerous, too. Tenders often had to climb up onto the mound to smother trouble spots. Occasionally, one would fall through.

The Trail leaves New York near Greenwood Lake and heads in a westerly direction toward Kittatinny Ridge. In the process, it traverses Wawayanda State Park and goes down into Pochuck Swamp and Pochuck Creek, sites of the recent Trail relocation. I can recommend this swamp section for nature watching, especially for birds and wildflowers. It's on my list for some spring day to check out any migrating warblers that might pass through. On a recent August visit, we saw fields of bergamot, ox-eyes, and asters. Around the edges of the swamp, cardinal flowers blazed. A red-headed woodpecker beat his medium-slow rhythm on a dead tree. Painted turtles slid off logs into the water at our approach.

This is New Jersey?

Just be aware in the swampy sections that you may also run into the New Jersey Airlift Wing. This consists of swarms of mosquitoes big enough to show up on radar that arrive *en masse* and try to carry you off. It's another thing for which the Garden State is famous—some say the mosquito is the New Jersey state bird.

After the Trail gets up onto the long Kittatinny Ridge, hikers will find some of the best walking in New Jersey. Starting almost immediately with the short side hike to the top of High Point, and continuing down the ridge toward the Delaware Water Gap, the Trail consists of easy, ridgeline walking. Once again, there are shelters at intervals along the Trail. Elevations, except in the gaps, are consistently in the 1,100- to 1,400-foot range, with occasional points up to 1,600 feet or so.

Because of parallel side trails, day hikers can often set up loop hikes. An example is the series of round trips that can be arranged to the Normanook Lookout Tower (a.k.a. the Culver Fire Tower) overlooking Culvers Gap and Culvers Lake. By starting from the north side of Kittatinny Mountain, at one of a couple of trailheads near the State School of Conservation at Lake Wapalanne, hikers can take trips of eight, ten, or more miles. The hike can even be turned into an overnight, as Gren Anderson Shelter is within easy walking distance. Perhaps the most popular area for day hiking is the series of looping trails on Mt. Tammany, which forms the New Jersey side of the Delaware Water Gap and affords superb views of the Gap. The entire ridge system has dozens of such trails. Take your pick.

An invaluable book for those wishing to hike the ridges of New York and New Jersey is the famous *New York Walk Book,* first published in 1923 by the New York–New Jersey Trail Conference. The first edition was written by AT founding fathers Raymond Torrey, Frank Place, Jr., and Robert L. Dickinson. The authors have changed, but the NY-NJTC still publishes it, and for any hiker living in the New York metropolitan area, it's a work beyond price.

AUTHOR'S CHOICE

My personal favorite is a section of about five miles from Long Mountain Road to Route 301 in Fahnestock Park. It's a section I've literally hiked a hundred times, and it was the site of my first steps on the AT, back when I was about seven. The route travels along a north-south ridge, with a side hike up to the slick, rocky summit of Shenandoah Mountain. As of this writing, there is enough parking for several cars at the trailhead on Long Mountain Road. The old chestnut logs that littered the floor of these woods are mostly gone, but the scraggly survivors of these once-majestic trees remain, a reminder of the wood products industry that thrived in this country as far back as the seventeenth century.

A runner-up for favorite hike is Schaghticoke Mountain, right on the Connecticut border. I used to lead Girl Scout groups from a nearby camp up there in my youth. It's a pleasant day hike, rewarded by vistas of the rolling hills of western Connecticut and eastern New York. Watch for hornets near the top.

Finally, if you're in North Jersey, don't miss the new section at Pochuck Creek. It represents the other side of hiking. Rather than the rough-and-rugged, roots-and-rocks variety you'd find in Maine, it's an easy stroll across boarded walkways over swampy ground, only slightly less easy than walking through oak woods and fields of wildflowers. It's the other form of renewal that Benton MacKaye had in mind, and if you enjoy nature, you can enjoy this. That suspension bridge is worth seeing all by itself.

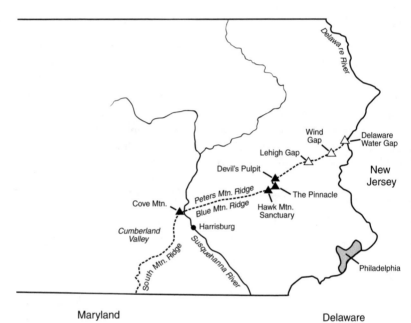

New York

Delaware River

Wind
Gap

Delaware
Water Gap

Lehigh Gap

New
Jersey

Devil's Pulpit

The Pinnacle

Peters Mtn. Ridge

Cove Mtn.

Blue Mtn. Ridge

Hawk Mtn.
Sanctuary

Cumberland
Valley

Harrisburg

South Mtn. Ridge

Susquehanna River

Philadelphia

Maryland

Delaware

PENNSYLVANIA

Pennsylvania

Trail Distance:
Delaware Water Gap to
  Pennsylvania-Maryland State Line.................... 230.1 miles
Maintaining Clubs:
The Keystone Trails Association and its affiliated organizations:
Wilmington Trail Club: Delaware River to Fox Gap........... 7.2 miles
Batona Hiking Club: Fox Gap to Wind Gap ....8.1 miles
Appalachian Mountain Club, Delaware Valley Chapter:
  Wind Gap to Little Gap .... 15.1 miles
Philadelphia Trail Club: Little Gap to Lehigh Furnace Gap.... 10.2 miles
Blue Mountain Eagle Climbing Club:
  Lehigh Furnace Gap to Bake Oven Knob;
  Tri-County Corner to Rausch Creek..................... 65.5 miles
Allentown Hiking Club:
  Bake Oven Knob to Tri-County Corner .... 11.7 miles
Susquehanna Appalachian Trail Club:
  Rausch Creek to PA 225 .... 21.4 miles
York Hiking Club: PA 225 to Susquehanna River .... 7.8 miles
Mountain Club of Maryland: Susquehanna River
  to Darlington Trail; Center Point Knob to
  Pine Grove Furnace State Park .... 29.6 miles
Cumberland Valley A. T. Club: Darlington Trail to
  Center Point Knob................................... 16.9 miles
Potomac Appalachian Trail Club: Pine Grove Furnace
  State Park to Pennsylvania-Maryland State Line.......... 36.6 miles

INTRODUCTION
Pennsylvania shares with New York the distinction of necessity. The
only way for the Trail to go around this state would be over water. For
that reason, Pennsylvania has long been called the "Keystone State,"
staking its claim as the state that held the early Union together. It's a
notion that holds some merit.

Take Pennsylvania's border with Maryland, better known as the Mason-Dixon or Mason and Dixon line. It is named for Charles Mason and Jeremiah Dixon, the two Englishmen who surveyed the line from 1765 to 1768, in large part because the peaceful Quaker, William Penn, had a history of border disputes with his neighbors. Hovering as it does on the edge of two worlds, Pennsylvania has a character that is both northern and southern yet somehow neither. It's a true link.

It's also a link between East and West. The Pennsylvania pioneer routes, linking up as they do with the Ohio River and from there most of North America, were popular in the seventeenth and eighteenth centuries.

If you've never been to Pennsylvania in a warm month, you'll immediately be impressed by its greenness. It's a fertile place, notable for its farmland and wooded ridges. Myron Avery wrote in 1936 that there were more deer killed by hunters in Pennsylvania than in any other state; hunting figures may have changed, but the deer population is still there. Pennsylvania is a deceptively wild state.

GEOLOGY ALONG THE TRAIL

If the Appalachians are the most orderly fold mountains in the world, nowhere are they more perfect than in Pennsylvania. In describing what Myron Avery called a perfect arc, with Washington, D.C., at the axis and the Blue Mountain–South Mountain system and the Alleghenies farther west, the Appalachian cordillera forms row after row of neat, sinuous ridges that cross the state. So neat are they that near Harrisburg, several ridges are known simply as First Mountain, Second Mountain, and Third Mountain. From space, they look like a slightly curved washboard.

Like nearly all Appalachian formations, the ridges of Pennsylvania are underlain by crystalline Grenville rocks. But here, the outer layers haven't been removed yet, as they have been in the Hudson Highlands. Pennsylvania rocks are largely of the Paleozoic Era, between 240 and 570 million years old. They are likely to be of the Silurian, Devonian, Mississippian, and—yes—Pennsylvanian periods. In some of the earlier sediments, hikers may find fossils of trilobites and eurypterids, strange beasties that once lurked in the shallow inland seas before Europe and Africa arrived to hurl the seabeds thousands of feet into the air.

The younger rocks have endured for a very simply reason: the glaciers of the Ice Ages came only as far as northern Pennsylvania, and the ridges of the central and southern parts of the state were never scoured clean by ice. Shortly after the Trail leaves the Delaware Water Gap, it crosses the terminal moraines of the last Ice Age—the sand and gravel around Wolf Rocks.

It was during the Acadian Orogeny, 350 million years ago, and especially during the later Alleghany Orogeny, that the Paleozoic rock strata of Pennsylvania were crushed together like an accordion. As the approaching European and African Plates hit the coast, the millions of years' worth of sediment that had accumulated in the inland sea started bending. Even the most recent deposits—the layers rich in organic material that formed in the marshes surrounding the suture area between the plates—were uplifted even as they were forming. These were crushed by the weight of sediment above and the geologic activity below into some of the largest coal beds in the world. And as the slow-motion continental game of bumper cars squished the rocks, it changed them, creating quartzite where there was once sandstone and anthracite where there was once a thick layer of rotting vegetable matter.

The kind of sediment found in a given area depended on what was going on there at the time. If the deposits were at the edge of the sea, under mountains already uplifted, the layers would probably consist of sand. In the middle of a sea, mud might be deposited, forming shale. A "carbonate bank" in shallow water would form limestone or dolomite. "Dirty sand," a mixture of sand and mud, might form "silt-stone" or "greywacke." Add heat and pressure, and the sediments would be welded into more durable metamorphic quartzites (from sandstone), slate (from shale), marble (from limestone), gneiss, or schist.

The Pennsylvanian ridges are excellent examples of how fold mountains erode into parallel ridge systems. The original mountains formed by the Acadian Orogeny were much, much higher, possibly by tens of thousands of feet. As they eroded down over the 230 million years or so since the mountain-building stopped for good, softer layers wore away quickly, while hard rocks remained to form the new ridgelines. Once the top of a fold ridge was eroded away, the mountain might evolve into twin, parallel ridges further down.

For instance, from the Delaware Water Gap all the way to Indiantown Gap, the Trail follows a ridge made up mostly of Shawangunk Formation quartzite, deposited as sandstone during the Silurian period and since metamorphosed into the harder quartzite. It wore away much more slowly because quartzite is a super-hard, exceedingly durable rock. The softer siltstones, shales, and limestones of the bordering Martinsburg and Bloomsburg Formations wore away, leaving the ridge where the Shawangunk Formation persisted.

Another, more dramatic example is Cove Mountain, on the west side of the Susquehanna River where the Trail crosses. Cove Mountain describes a neat parabola on the earth's surface. I flew over it once and was astounded that such a pronounced and perfect formation could actually exist. It represents the edges of a syncline—a downward fold in the rock strata—that has eroded down to the harder Pocono Formation sandstone. This particular syncline is not parallel to the earth's surface; rather, it is tilted up toward the west-southwest, and Cove Mountain is where the Pocono sandstone from the ridge on either side of the syncline meets up. Farther down the syncline, toward the east-northeast, the center of the syncline is filled with Llewellyn Formation and Pottsville Group sediments—Pennsylvanian period rocks that contain the anthracite coal that hikers keep running into in the DeHart Reservoir and Yellow Springs areas.

One noted (though not universally beloved) characteristic of the Trail in Pennsylvania is the boulder fields. They, too, are peculiar to this area for a reason. Since the glaciers only came down about as far as the very upper part of Pennsylvania, the rest of the state was in what is called a "periglacial" area. This meant that the ground and exposed bedrock were subjected to constant freezing and thawing, as well as substantial meltoff from the foot of the great glaciers. This tended to "seep-freeze" and pry out chunks of bedrock—the water would work its way down into seams in the rock, freeze, and loosen large pieces.

Over more than half of the Trail in Pennsylvania, the bedrock is that bombproof Shawangunk quartzite. The chunks of this hardy stuff, once broken off, tended to roll down the hill a bit and then stay there. Since quartzite weathers slowly, the boulders didn't wear away. Frost and water action rounded them out a bit, but that's all. Hikers' feet probably erode them away as fast as anything else that's working on them these days. They persist through much of Pennsylvania and show up a few times in Maryland as well.

The geology of Pennsylvania is as interesting as any area on the Trail. Just walking down the south slope of Cove Mountain takes you—in the space of six or seven miles—through over 140 million years of geological history. Several places along the Trail are paleontologists' delights, offering fossils of plants and animals extinct for upwards of 400 million years—those Paleozoic seas were trilobite heaven. Perhaps the best place to look is where the Trail passes by Interstate 81 on PA Route 72. The Martinsburg shale in the road cut is full of little critters.

HISTORY ALONG THE TRAIL

When the first Europeans arrived in Pennsylvania, the land along what would become the Trail route was inhabited by two basic groups of people: the Munsee clans of the Lenni Lenapes along the Delaware Valley to the east, and the Susquehannocks, an Iroquoian people, in the central part of the state.

The Munsees followed essentially the same road as their New Jersey neighbors. For the most part peaceably, though inexorably, shoved off their land, they dispersed to the west with the many other groups who fled that way in the eighteenth and nineteenth centuries.

The Susquehannocks' fate was being sealed even as the settlers arrived. At that time they were at war with their cousins, the powerful Iroquois Confederacy to the north. In 1677, they were roundly defeated and forced to move to Oneida, in central New York. There they remained for decades. When their captors finally relaxed their guard, sometime in the middle of the eighteenth century, the battered remnants of the once proud and numerous people gradually drifted back down toward their old haunts near Harrisburg. To their dismay, they found everything changed—the settlers in William Penn's vigorous colony were solidly in control. Over the ensuing years, the Susquehannocks diminished to a ragged band of about twenty souls. These met their end in 1763, when they were massacred by whites in some Indian scare or other.

Generally speaking, though, the history of Pennsylvania following the European settlement was relatively peaceful. This is due in part to a couple of factors.

First, it's undoubtedly true that having the major occupants of the territory you want occupy vacate the premises just as you arrive is quite convenient. The forced removal of the Susquehannocks surely enabled William Penn, who was granted his land in 1681, to insist upon good relations with his Native American neighbors. Why not? Most of them were already out of the way.

Second, though, was Penn's undeniably good administration of his domain. Attempts were made from the outset to parcel the fertile land to settlers fairly, and the colony was governed for the most part in an enlightened manner. Settlers prospered, and more settlers arrived. The Germans and Scots-Irish who arrived in the 1720s and 1730s would a few decades later be the driving force for the settlement of western Virginia and Tennessee, down the long valleys of the Cumberland and the Shenandoah.

HISTORY OF THE APPALACHIAN TRAIL IN PENNSYLVANIA

The Trail in Pennsylvania was blazed by a number of local clubs, some of which were organized in the early days of the AT by the crew of Arthur Perkins, Raymond Torrey, and Myron Avery. It must have been a slick job of organization, because these clubs—a dozen of them—work together to this day within the Keystone Trails Association, and each keeps its section in top shape.

Although it's difficult to single out one club, it seems that there were three prime movers early on: the Blue Mountain Club in the east, organized in Reading in 1926 by a Lafayette College professor, Eugene C. Bingham; the Blue Mountain Eagles Climbing Club in central Pennsylvania; and Myron Avery, Fred Schairer, and the rest of the Potomac Appalachian Trail Club in the southwest. The Blue Mountain Eagles were organized in 1916 and were already a vigorous organization when the AT idea arrived. They were recruited to the task in the fall of 1926 by Professor Bingham, and under the leadership of Dr. Harry F. Rentschler they completed their section from Schuylkill to Swatara Gaps by 1930. Like the Potomac ATC, they also acted as a breeder club, enlisting various other groups to take over neighboring sections.

The Eagles had begun as part of a completely different, largely European tradition. They arose out of an informal group of Pennsylvania Dutch weekend walkers, the "Fussgaengers," who would get together each week to walk, socialize, sing German songs, and tell stories at wine gardens in the area. This is quite reminiscent of the northern European tradition of taking walks with family or friends on weekend afternoons and evenings, and it still can be seen in many German and Dutch villages. (Pennsylvania Dutch are actually of German ancestry—the "Dutch" here is a corruption of *Deutsch,* or "German.")

In 1916, the Fussgaengers went with Dr. Rentschler on a hike to Eagle's Nest, hunting for an actual eagle's nest that Rentschler had seen in the area. The hike, which took place on October 12, is remembered as the official founding of the Blue Mountain Eagles Climbing Club. The Eagle's Nest hike became an annual event, and the club always made one other climb each year to a new peak. In the German tradition, each hike was followed by a feast at a local inn.

It was, therefore, a strong and enthusiastic group that the Blue Mountain Club's Dr. Bingham addressed on October 30, 1926, to recruit them to join in the effort to blaze "The Skyline Trail" as part of Benton MacKaye's Maine-to-Georgia scheme. By May of 1930, their whole 102-mile section, from the Lehigh River to the Susquehanna, was complete.

The Potomac ATC, on the other hand, had a problem on their hands. The route from Blue Mountain west of Harrisburg to South Mountain had to cross the Cumberland Valley as it led into Maryland. In 1930–31, Avery and Schairer finally settled on a route toward Michaux State Forest, where the Trail runs today. But they had to settle for a traverse of the Cumberland Valley, which remains problematic to this day. The valley is largely developed residentially, and the club has been hard-pressed—but not completely unsuccessful—in keeping the Trail off pavement.

Since that time, several newer clubs have taken over responsibility for some of the sections that were originally blazed by the founding organizations. Some of these groups are based miles away from their sections.

The true history of the Trail in Pennsylvania, though, is apparent to anybody who walks it. The trail workers don't erect their monuments to organizations but, rather, to individuals. You'll see a sign to the guy who built the bridge; a plaque to the crew who re-roofed the lean-to; a set of steps named for the lady who sends out the newsletter. There's a lady along the Trail who likes to give ice cream cones to thru-hikers, and a couple who have hikers trained to walk out of their way to get fresh vegetables. It's characteristic Pennsylvania modesty and hospitality. And the recognition is a darned good way to keep volunteers happy and working hard.

Through design or chance, the state itself has also been very helpful in securing the route. From the Delaware Water Gap to the Susquehanna, the Trail route travels mostly State Game Land or State Forest.

THE TRAIL IN PENNSYLVANIA

In New Jersey, the Trail makes a switch from the Reading Prong, the ridge group that it has followed since it crossed into New York from Connecticut, to Kittatinny Mountain, which is the beginning of what will become Blue Mountain when the ridge gets a few miles into Pennsylvania. As the Trail enters Pennsylvania, it's simply a matter of following this same, single ridge system, moving in a generally northeasterly-southwesterly direction from the Delaware Water Gap to the south-central border with Maryland.

The border between New Jersey and Pennsylvania is formed by the Delaware River. Kittatinny has been gashed deeply here by the cutting action of the water. Crossing into Pennsylvania on the I-80 roadway, the Trail quickly ascends the mountain. After it crosses Wind Gap, the name of the ridge will change to Blue Mountain, a designation it will keep all the way to the Susquehanna and beyond. Beginning here, the AT will stay on the ridgeline, descending only to cross gaps or switch to neighboring ridges, all the way to the Cumberland Valley.

The Trail quickly climbs about 1,100 feet to the top of Mt. Minsi, which forms the eastern knob of Kittatinny Mountain in Pennsylvania, or the western escarpment of the Delaware Water Gap.

Soon after leaving Mt. Minsi, the Trail reaches Wolf Rocks, the farthest southern point of the great ice sheet that retreated ten to twelve thousand years ago. The boulders and gravel banks in the vicinity tell the tale of the glacier that stopped here, dumping its load of stone and sand as it melted.

As the Trail leaves Wolf Rocks, it meanders across the wide top of Kittatinny, sidling over to the south onto the beginnings of Blue Mountain. Here, it's just a spur of Kittatinny, going down to Wind Gap to the west.

From this point onward, the Trail traverses the long ridge of Blue Mountain all the way to Swatara Gap, a distance of some one hundred miles. Except for the periodic gaps in the ridgeline, it stays about 1,400 to 1,500 feet above sea level and follows the outcropping of Shawangunk quartzite all the way. At Swatara Gap, the route shifts northward a bit to avoid a military installation, crossing Second Mountain, traveling down Sharp Mountain and Stony Mountain, passing by some old coal mines, and eventually following the parallel ridge of Peters Mountain all the way to the confluence of the Juniata and Susquehanna Rivers at Duncannon.

The Blue Mountain ridge is a narrow, steep-sided finger of wooded and rocky hill that travels nearly due east and west. It separates the Lehigh River to the north from the rich farmlands and rolling hills to the south. On the not-infrequent occasions when rocky knobs top the ridge, Blue Mountain affords splendid views of the surrounding countryside, often in all directions.

One of the more spectacular stretches of Blue Mountain is the exceptionally narrow, steep-sided section west of Lehigh Gap. In addition to Devil's Pulpit (accessed by a side trail just west of Lehigh Gap, it overlooks the Gap and the Lehigh Valley to the north), the ridge offers several other views just as good, including Bake Oven Knob and Bear Rocks (which are reached via a short but difficult side trail) as well as a lookout to the south that the maps refer to as "The Knife Edge" and that the guidebook calls simply "The Cliffs."

West of this section, there is a crimp in the Blue Mountain ridge. Partly due to a complexity in the folding of the strata, and partly due to a series of faults in the rocks, the quartzite layer that the Trail has been following since way up in New Jersey takes a dogleg to the south and continues westward again. The Trail stays right with it.

If you're a dedicated bird watcher, you might someday want to keep on going west, rather than taking the jog to the south. The blue-blazed trail that keeps on going straight ahead leads two miles into the Hawk Mountain Sanctuary, where you'll find a rocky lookout, the sanctuary headquarters, and a small museum. It's one of the finest places in the country to watch birds of prey on their annual migration, which lasts from mid-August to mid-December. In a given year, thirty thousand eagles and hawks of all kinds may pass through. There is a small fee for hiking in the Sanctuary. For more information, write to: Hawk Mountain Sanctuary, Route #2, Kempton, PA 19529.

There are several impressive lookouts in the Hawk Mountain region: Tri-County Corner, where the first blaze in the new Trail went in back in '26; Dan's Pulpit, named for Blue Mountain Eagle founding father Dan Hoch; and the Pinnacle and Pulpit Rock, where the ridge zig-zags around the Eckville Fault before returning to its westward axis. Hikers can also see the remains of more charcoal hearths, much like the ones in New Jersey. This section ends in the steep-sided water gap of the Little Schuylkill at Port Clinton.

Like most narrow ridges, Blue Mountain has short spur trails leading up to the AT from below at frequent intervals. These can be used to gain access to the uplands for short hikes and to form interesting loops from the highway crossings in the gaps. Between Port Clinton and the point at which PA Route 183 crosses the ridge, there are two such trails: Marshall's Path, which runs out of Bellmans Gap off Mountain Road; and the Tom Lowe Trail, which runs a nice loop out of a parking area where Northkill Creek leaves its narrow valley source.

Just west of the Lowe Trail, the Eagle's Nest Trail cuts off to the south. It was the Eagle's Nest knob that became the focal point for the Blue Mountain Eagles Climbing Club when it was founded in 1916.

As the Trail draws closer to Swatara Gap, where it will finally leave Blue Mountain, it passes along a particularly steep section of the ridge. After leaving the parking area at Route 183, it passes the marker for old Fort Dietrich Snyder, built under the direction of Benjamin Franklin in 1756 to protect against Indian attacks. The Trail then keeps close to the steep southern slope of the ridge.

One of the nicest parts about hiking in Pennsylvania is that the blazers of the Trail have taken care to recognize those who have played important roles in the building of the AT. Typical are the Shanaman marker and the Showers steps, which are both found between Route 183 and Swatara Gap. The first recognizes William F. Shanaman, former mayor of Reading and dedicated Trail worker; the latter consists of 500 stone steps leading down to a spring, built by Lloyd Showers, another Trail worker.

When the Trail crosses Swatara Creek it encounters history of another kind. The handsome iron bridge over which the route passes is the old Waterville Bridge, a fine example of a nineteenth-century lenticular structure. (It takes this name from the shape of its trusses: viewed from the side, they bear some resemblance to lentils.) It was built in 1890 over Little Pine Creek and was moved to Swatara Creek in 1985 because it was too narrow for modern automobile traffic. The loss to motorists is a gain for shank's mare travelers.

At Swatara Gap, the Trail takes its leave of Blue Mountain. The ridge continues down toward Harrisburg, while the AT heads northwest over several ridges (Second Mountain, Sharp Mountain–Stony Mountain, and Peters Mountain). It passes several historic sites en route, such as the old Cold Spring Railroad Station at Cold Spring Military Reservation on Dresden Lake (0.9 mile on the Cold Spring Trail, downhill from Sharp Mountain) and the ruins of Yellow Springs Village. It also heads right through St. Anthony's Wilderness, the largest roadless area in eastern Pennsylvania.

As the Trail passes through Rausch Gap, it enters the famous Pennsylvania anthracite coal region. It passes right near old coal beds, and hikers will run into many remnants of the old industry—building foundations, old earthworks for mining operations, and the transportation systems that helped move the coal to market. There are also cemeteries, wells, and a thousand other pieces of debris from once thriving communities that are now ghost towns and ruins. Once the Trail has descended into Clarks Valley, good plant fossils can be found in the old mine dumps near De Hart Reservoir, located about a mile and half up the valley.

Clarks Valley is the bottom of a long syncline—Sharp and Peters Mountains are the two sides, and Cove Mountain, across the Susquehanna, is the end. From the air, the whole complex looks like a huge parabola on the earth's surface.

At the crest of Sharp Mountain, the rocks are Pocono Formation sandstone and siltstone. These are relatively new rocks from the Mississippian period (about 330 million years ago), and they're an indication that these hills could only have formed in the later Alleghany Orogeny. Down in Clarks Valley, the rocks are newer still—Pennsylvanian period (300 million years old) siltstone, sandstone, and shale, with anthracite beds underneath. Then, when the Trail crests Peters Mountain, it will follow the relatively hard Pocono rocks all the way to the Susquehanna, across to Cove Mountain, and leave them only when it turns south toward the Cumberland Valley.

The route down Peters Mountain is much like the rest of eastern Pennsylvania: it runs along the crest of an arrow-straight ridge, maintaining an elevation of around 1,250 feet all the way. There are occasional side trails reaching up to the crest of the ridge from the valleys below, but the AT doesn't turn right or left until it reaches the impressive water gap where the Susquehanna carves its way between Peters and Cove Mountains, which are, with Sharp Mountain, actually part of the same long, U-shaped ridge complex.

The AT crosses the Susquehanna on the Duncannon Bridge, at the confluence of the Juniata, a major tributary. The two rivers are excellent for canoeing, offering easy Class 1 and Class 2 paddling, good fishing, and a fine array of water birds. Paddlers regularly run into huge herons, egrets, and the like—there is a major rookery of these birds on an island in the Susquehanna a few miles downstream, just up from Harrisburg.

Within sight of the Juniata, the Trail once again climbs steeply, this time up Cove Mountain, the first of several mountains of that name the Trail will pass on its way south. It offers splendid views of the water gap and the surrounding countryside before the route goes two-thirds of the way around the huge U of Cove Mountain and descends to the south. Once off of Cove, it isn't long before the AT runs into the northern end of the Tuscarora Trail, the Appalachian Trail's own child. The

Tuscarora and its southern reaches—called "Big Blue" in the Virginias—were blazed starting in the early '60s when the ATC became convinced that it could no longer guarantee an unbroken AT in northern Virginia. So, its members mapped out and blazed a western route along the last of the Appalachian ridges, the Alleghenies.

The Tuscarora–Big Blue system runs around 500 miles until it rejoins the AT in the northern section of Shenandoah National Park. It has been suggested at various times that recognition be given to people who have thru-hiked from Maine to Georgia (or vice versa) using the Tuscarora–Big Blue route instead of the traditional northern Virginia trail.

Upon leaving Blue Mountain (for the last time), the Trail heads into a section of the Cumberland Valley once famous for its road walking. These days, however, things have changed a bit. In the past fifteen years or so, the ATC, in conjunction with the National Park Service, has managed to reroute the Trail through the valley to a low ridge a couple miles west of the former route; the corridor, mostly purchased by the Park Service, is in most places a thousand feet across, with the Trail running down the middle. The route now runs down Stony Ridge toward Boiling Springs, where the ATC keeps an office.

This has made a world of difference. When the first edition of this book was written, much of the walk through the Cumberland Valley in Pennsylvania was along rural and suburban roads. Now, the Trail leaves the woods at the north edge of the Cumberland Valley by switchbacking down Blue Mountain. It then hopscotches across the valley, through fields and woodlots and along a wooded ridge toward Center Point Knob, about fifteen miles away. In the process of rerouting the Trail, the maintaining organization (the Cumberland Valley Appalachian Trail Management Association) has largely managed the delicate task of keeping the path off of the roads and on what they describe in the trail guide as "a mixture of woods, farm paths, and cultivated fields." There is no camping through this section, and you should carry water, but all things considered, the maintainers have done a marvelous job here.

The Cumberland Valley can best be described as a largely rural area that is crisscrossed by two-lane roads, along which homes have been built. This section sees most of its use from thru-hikers. That's not to say that it wouldn't be worth a stroll. If you live in the area, this might be just the right thing for an easy Saturday walk. There is said to be decent bird-watching in the Conodoguinet Creek area in the northern reaches of the valley. The only problem may be that there are not yet parking areas at the road crossings of this section, so you might have some difficulty finding a place to leave the car.

As the Trail reaches the southern edge of the Cumberland Valley, you can get glimpses to the southwest of your next big ridge: South Mountain. At its northern terminus at Mount Holly Springs, it is quite a sight to behold, a narrow tongue of steep highland reaching up to the edge of the Cumberland Valley.

It's in the shadow of South Mountain that the Trail gets back into the woods.

This is precipitous country, full of sharp ridges and sheer cliffs. The Trail hasn't made it into the larger wilderness yet, so there's not much in the way of side trails, but there are again a few access points on the ridgetops from the valleys below. When Pine Grove State Park is reached, on the southeast flank of South Mountain, the Trail finally crosses over into territory maintained and watched over by the formidable Potomac Appalachian Trail Club. Some of the route ahead was blazed under the direct supervision of Myron Avery, Fred Schaier, and the rest of the gang that did so much to put the Trail through back when it was just Benton MacKaye's dream.

The ridges in the southern section of Pennsylvania are littered with the remains of the old iron industry. From Pine Grove Furnace all the way to the Maryland border, there are reminders of the industry that thrived from around the time of the Revolution to about the Civil War. Again, as it has all the way from northern New Jersey, the AT passes the circular clearings that indicate the old sites of more charcoal mounds. At Pine Grove Furnace, the Trail passes old smelters and an ore hole (now Fuller Lake) before passing at last up the slope of South Mountain. Once again, the AT passes largely over public lands, and there are side trails and little-used or unused roads that can be included in day hike loops and exploration routes.

In 1936 in his short work *The Appalachian Trail on Pennsylvania's South Mountain,* Myron Avery wrote, "Not as high as the Blue Ridge, it nowhere exceeds 2,200 feet, yet for expansive outlooks, majesty of forest growth, the excellence of its trails, its peculiar topographic features and its economic and historical background, Pennsylvania's South Mountain Region is a worthy peer of its better-known rival."

The knobs and gullies in this section can be quite steep—the ridges are formed around hard quartzite layers, versus the softer strata in the valleys. In some places, this will be Antietam Formation quartzite, a dull gray variety containing streaks that are actually the holes of the *Skolithos* worm, a sand-dwelling tubeworm that lived 500 million years ago. Cliffs and lookouts are everywhere in these hills; take advantage of the second, and keep an eye out for the first.

As the Trail descends back into Caledonia Gap at Caledonia State Park, it also walks back into history. It was through this gap that Robert E. Lee and his Army of Northern Virginia passed on the way to Gettysburg. According to Myron Avery, the army rested at Travelers Spring, a local water hole in the area. (Perhaps coincidentally, Lee's favorite horse was named Traveler.) It was also near here that Captain John Cook, one of John Brown's aides during his abortive raid on Harpers Ferry, was captured in 1859.

The Trail continues down along South Mountain, which in its northern section is a series of broken ridges and knobs, quite unlike the straight-run escarpment that it will become in Maryland. It makes for some of the most interesting—and pleasant—hiking in Pennsylvania. In most places, you leave behind the knee-popping boulder fields in favor of gentle woods and hills. Lookouts like Chimney Rocks and Buzzard Peak offer fine views at frequent intervals. From here the Trail descends into Antietam Cove and the headwaters of Antietam Creek. It was across this small stream that Lee and McClellan fought the bloodiest battle of the Civil War in 1862, miles to the south near Sharpsburg, Maryland.

In addition to Cove Mountain, Antietam Cove is one of the first appearances of the term "cove" along the Trail. As the AT progresses farther south, it will appear regularly on all the maps, indicating simply a valley that extends into the hills from flatlands lying below.

Having just passed the halfway point of the AT, it's appropriate that another milestone should be passed. As the Trail pulls into Pen-Mar, it passes over the Mason-Dixon line. We have passed from the Keystone of the East into the True South.

AUTHOR'S CHOICE

Pennsylvania is tailor-made for spotting a car and taking a point-to-point hike along one of the ridges. I can recommend two.

Leaving a car at Route 309 and then setting off from the Pennsylvania Turnpike (I-476) will give you a hike of about eleven miles that takes in the lookouts of Bake Oven Knob, Bear Rocks, and the Cliffs. If that's too much for your time or your ambition, start the hike from the dirt road at Bake Oven Road, which cuts off about seven miles.

The section near the Maryland border from Old Forge Road to Old Route 16 near Blue Ridge Summit also makes a good day hike. It's between four and five miles, and you can spot a car at either end.

I'm also fond of the Delaware Water Gap area, simply because it's so scenic. But almost any part of the protected ridgeline in Pennsylvania will give you a pleasant hike.

Pennsylvania

Maryland

Potomac River

South Mountain Ridge

Harman Gap

Turner's Gap

Maryland Heights

Crampton Gap

Harpers Ferry

C & O Canal

Loudoun Heights

West Virginia

Snickers Gap

Devil's Racecourse

Washington, D.C.

Potomac River

Shenandoah Valley

Front Royal

Manassas Gap

Virginia

Chesapeake Bay

MARYLAND AND NORTHERN VIRGINIA

9 Maryland, Northern Virginia, and West Virginia

Trail Distances:
Pennsylvania-Maryland State Line to the Potomac River . . . . . 40.4 miles
Potomac River to Front Royal, Virginia. 58.0 miles
Total Distance . . . . 98.4 miles

Maintaining Club:
Potomac Appalachian Trail Club

INTRODUCTION
The whole feel of the AT changes, as it enters the South in earnest. History, geography, industry, culture—all will be quite different.

This is a haunted land. Great armies passed by here on the way to their destinies, and the story of these hills is written in their blood.

It is also a place where the mountains acted as a true barrier. Settlement to the west could not take place until routes were developed through the seemingly endless line of the Blue Ridge. It is for that reason that the same gaps, the same rivers, and the same towns appear in the history books in the French and Indian War all the way down to the Civil War. Harpers Ferry is among the most contested villages in American history.

So walk, if you will, through the South with John Brown and Stonewall Jackson. In these hills, memories of them are as alive today as they were a century ago.

GEOLOGY ALONG THE TRAIL
In the early Paleozoic Era, 600 million years ago, Maryland lay in a vast sea above the continental shelf, which had yet to be uplifted into the Appalachian Mountains. Later, during the great continental crashes of 450 and 350 million years ago, this area was uplifted to form the eastern border of another inland sea that extended to Minnesota.

When this sea was itself uplifted 250 million years ago, it was drained, with much of the runoff exiting through the Potomac Gorge.

South Mountain, the ridge over which virtually the entire length of the Maryland section travels, is capped mainly by Paleozoic layers like the Weverton and Loudoun Formation metamorphics—sediments laid down in the early Paleozoic Era, at the dawn of life, metamorphosed by the heat and pressure of their uplift. The Weverton Formation is characterized by gray quartzite, a hard, tough rock that tended to prevent erosion of the ridge crest. These rocks remain today in the form of hard boulders along some of the ridgelines that hikers would do well to watch—they can turn an ankle if you're not careful.

Some later Paleozoic fossils can be found in younger layers at the very top of the summits, but in many places the rock has been eroded down to the 870-million-year-old metamorphosed lava flows that once lay under the sediment.

Like the rest of the Blue Ridge, South Mountain's rock strata are tilted upward toward the west. For that reason, the western side is somewhat steeper (although the difference won't be that great in a ridge this old and this weathered) and any cliffs or rock outcroppings will more likely be on the western side. The ridge is divided by major water gaps in four places: Buzzard Knob, Turner's Gap, Crampton Gap, and finally, at the Potomac River.

HISTORY ALONG THE TRAIL
Maryland

The gorges on the Potomac or at Turner's Gap were among the most popular passages through the multi-layered ridges of the Appalachians. Coming up from the current site of Washington, D.C., a settler or explorer would be given a choice of continuing up the Potomac to the northwest or branching off onto the Shenandoah to the southwest, toward the rich inland valleys of Virginia. It was through here that the settlers—largely German and Scots-Irish—passed on their way to settle their dream farms. It was also one of the most important trade routes, linking the Ohio Valley with the East. The main road for a number of years in the early eighteenth century was the "Israel Friend's Mill Road," which ran through Crampton Gap along the route of an old, well-established Indian trail.

It was through Turner's Gap, though, that General Braddock, commander of British colonial forces during the French and Indian War, passed with a young George Washington by his side in 1755, on his way to defeat near what is now Pittsburgh. The retreating Washington, his general dead, may have paused to refresh himself at the South Mountain Tavern. (Abraham Lincoln used to stay there on his way to Congress, and it still stands today.) What is probably the first monument to Washington has stood since 1827 on Monument Knob, just north of the Gap.

On their way through, Braddock and his men created a wagon road that was later to become the famous National Road to the west, today called the Old National Pike. It was through here that most of the early traffic passed from Washington, D.C., to the Ohio Valley and beyond.

Western Maryland was crossroads for more than pioneers and traveling politicians, though. Located as it is, right on the Mason-Dixon line, ideas, runaway slaves, and, finally, armies passed this way as well.

South Mountain was a common avenue for slaves escaping captivity. As they traveled along the present route of the Trail, they lived in constant fear of the slave hunters, who kept careful watch in the mountains farther north, living on the bounties they received for captured escapees.

Abolition made its presence felt in earnest in 1859, when anti-slavery zealot John Brown and a small army of sixteen white and five black followers followed the South Mountain trails and tracks to try to realize Brown's dream of making the area a haven for escaping slaves. Over the summer, they set up a headquarters in a farmhouse in the Maryland hills, waiting. Then, on October 16, the band crossed the Potomac to Harpers Ferry and into history. After their failure to capture a Federal armory located there, Brown and his men were finally cornered by Federal troops under Robert E. Lee. Brown surrendered and was taken to nearby Charles Town, where he was tried, convicted of treason, and hanged. Several of his followers are said to have escaped north over South Mountain.

When the Civil War finally broke out, Maryland found itself in a precarious position. With sympathies that generally ran in favor of the South, they had the ill fortune to be host to the Northern capital. Things around South Mountain quickly came to a head. Situated as it was at the mouth of the Shenandoah, the region was viewed anxiously by the Confederate leaders. It was, after all, the gateway to the rich Shenandoah Valley, breadbasket of the South.

Harpers Ferry in particular was at the crossroads of the Civil War. From the Southern point of view, the site was both a danger and an opportunity. In Federal hands, it lay too close for comfort to the Shenandoah Valley, which the Confederacy hoped to preserve as a safe food supply for the war effort. But effectively neutralized, the great valley system behind Harpers Ferry offered a road to the north.

So, in 1862, Stonewall Jackson and Robert E. Lee took the offensive. The Southern army crossed the Potomac at South Mountain and proceeded north along its eastern flanks. After crossing to the west at Crampton Gap, Lee sent Jackson south again to capture Harpers Ferry while he began maneuvering north toward Hagerstown for a run at Washington, D.C., from the northwest.

Lee was faced by General George McClellan, the Union's Boy Wonder, who marched with his Army of the Potomac to meet the threat. Beyond the fact that he vastly outnumbered his foe, McClellan had an incredible advantage: one of his soldiers had found Lee's marching orders wrapped around three cigars and had actually recognized their importance. The general, however, not only spoke of his find openly—finally alerting Lee to the fact that he had the secret orders—but also diddled away his advantage through endless rehashings of his line of attack.

The first skirmishes occurred at Turner's Gap and Crampton Gap, as the Confederates under A. P. Hill fought to buy Lee time to reassemble his divided army. McClellan's indecision gave them a whole day, and they managed to buy several more hours, just long enough for Jackson to capture Harpers Ferry and get back. The monument to Washington above Turner's Gap served for a time as a Union lookout. It is said to be haunted by the ghosts of a Union deserter and his lady fair, who shriek each year on September 17, anniversary of the battle of Antietam.

The two armies finally met at Sharpsburg, facing off across Antietam Creek a few miles west of Crampton Gap, and they got down to cases. Lee had gone there to gather his scattered army and waited with eighteen thousand men, on a bluff overlooking the creek, for McClellan to arrive with his eighty-one thousand troops.

"Little Mac" did arrive, but then he waited. For a whole day, he pondered his battle plans, until Jackson arrived from Harpers Ferry, doubling the size of Lee's force. Then, cautiously, he engaged the Confederates. He succeeded in pushing them back and was actually on the verge of routing them when his many delays played their final trick, and A. P. Hill's large unit arrived to Lee's aid. McClellan, tired of the fight, let the Confederates get away. But twenty thousand men had died on the field in what was to be the bloodiest battle in a bloody war—the single costliest day in our history, if you count the casualties on both sides.

Later in the war, the huge armies swung to and fro on their way to their last confrontation in the North at Gettysburg, just twenty miles or so from where South Mountain crosses the Pennsylvania line. By and large, the route of the Appalachian Trail stays fairly far from where the action was. Apart from these engagements, the northward progress of the great armies occurred mostly to the east or west.

After the war, Maryland, spared the rigors of Reconstruction, settled back to business as usual. The moonshiners returned to South Mountain, where they had pursued a prosperous antebellum cottage industry. Other forms of commerce, such as the textile industry and the enterprise on the Chesapeake and Ohio Canal that ran past, began to fade away. Floods on the Potomac occasionally washed out the bridges down in Harpers Ferry, and the countryside waited.

It was in the winter of 1931 and spring of 1932 that Myron Avery and his colleagues in the Potomac Appalachian Trail Club really got moving, blazing the trail along South Mountain. Their route was essentially the one we see today, although the PATC is constantly performing small reroutings to improve the experience or to protect the Trail's continuity. The greater part of the Trailway in this region is now protected.

Virginia

If you looked at the Shenandoah Valley from space, you'd see a vast system of valleys running from Vermont and central New York all the way to North Carolina and into Tennessee. This wide, fertile region formed one of the early breadbaskets of the United States.

The river and its valley have borne the name "Shenandoah" for so long that the origins of the word have been lost and can only be guessed at. One tradition has it that it is a local Indian name meaning "beautiful daughter of the stars." It could also have come from an Iroquois chief named "Sherando" who was at war with some of Powhatan's allies about the time of the founding of Jamestown. Then, too, there was a small Algonkian tribe in the lower valley (the northern end—the river flows south to north) called the Senedoes; they were massacred by the Iroquois long before white settlers arrived.

"Shenandoah" is also said to be similar to the Iroquois word meaning "Big Meadow." Take your pick. There are other instances of the word along the Trail, including a rocky ridge in the New York section.

Seeing how far south the valley reaches, it's tempting to assume that settlement moved across the mountain passes in some kind of orderly fashion and that the valley was populated from areas as widely separated as Richmond and Roanoke. And if it were as easily reached through the various gaps via paved highways as it is today, that would certainly be the case.

In the seventeenth and eighteenth centuries, though, things were a bit different. The wall of the Blue Ridge rising in the west was a serious barrier, and the thick Appalachian woods were all but impenetrable; the land beyond unknown. So, after initial exploration in the 1660s and 1670s by John Lederer, a German who was reputedly the first white to see the river (although Captain John Smith is said to have glimpsed the Blue Ridge in the early 1600s), the rich valley lay undisturbed.

It was left for settlement to come instead from the northeast. The clearest shot to the rich farmland was out of central Pennsylvania. In the 1720s, German immigrants made the trip down the Cumberland Valley, through the Potomac Gorge, and up the Shenandoah. They settled up to about halfway into the valley. Once they were established, the way was paved for others to come from the Virginia coast, through the gaps.

The area through which the Trail travels in northern Virginia falls within a land grant made in the seventeenth century by England's Charles II to Lord Fairfax. Fairfax had endeared himself to His Majesty by acting as one of the prime movers in Charles's ascension to the throne of Great Britain after the overthrow of Cromwell in 1660. The grant included all lands between the Potomac and the Rappahannock Rivers. As Virginia at the time had no clearly established western boundary, the grant was huge and went, as far as anybody knew, all the way to the Mississippi.

The typical absentee landlord, Fairfax sold off much of his holdings piecemeal to settlers, and he allowed squatters beyond numbering to ensconce themselves on much of the rest. However, in 1736, one of the lords, Thomas by name, decided to take up residence. He surveyed a tract of nearly 120,000 acres between Hedgeman River and Carters Run and established the famous Manor of Leeds. He became one of the first to do this, building his new home, "Greenway Court," across the ridge in what is now Clarke County, Virginia. He established other manors as well, including a nameless one between the "Upper Thoroughfare of the Blue Ridge" (now Ashby's Gap) and Williams Gap (now Snickers Gap), as well as "Gooney Run Manor" between Gooney Run and Happy Creek (now Chester Gap).

Fairfax was a clever man. In 1767, doubtless foreseeing the upcoming revolution, he signed title of his manors over to his nephew, who immediately gave them back under a private title. After the successful War of Independence, his seignorial title from the King no longer valid, he still held the private title he had obtained from his nephew.

Largely settled by runaway Cavaliers during the Puritan Commonwealth in the mid-seventeenth century, Virginia had thrived in large part thanks to its slave labor force, which equaled the white population in numbers. In spite of the fact that the African slave trade was abolished in Virginia in 1778, the existing slave population was enough to sustain their numbers

Still, when the North-South tensions grew to a fever pitch in the 1850 and 1860s, Virginia nearly did not secede, only doing so after Lincoln called for volunteers to fight the upcoming war.

The secession was a blessing beyond measure for the South. Not only did it get the rich Shenandoah Valley and a base from which to threaten the North, but it also got the landed Virginian gentry and their trained soldiers—men like Robert E. Lee, a skilled army officer and son of a famous Revolutionary War hero, and Thomas J. "Stonewall" Jackson, whose lightning troop movements and diversionary tactics in the valley during the opening years of the war have been stock entries in military textbooks.

After being completely baffled by Jackson in the first months of the war, it wasn't until after Gettysburg that the Union once again turned its attention to the Shenandoah Valley in earnest. By mid-1864, Jubal Early, one of the slickest operators on either side, had repulsed all Northern efforts to penetrate the valley and had driven to within sight of Washington, D.C. Grant responded by sending Phil Sheridan down to settle Early's hash once and for all. Grant's choice was not auspicious for the valley. Sheridan was a bloodthirsty warrior whose best-known legacy was a comment he made in later years during the western Indian Wars: "There is only one good Indian, and that is a dead one."

Grant's orders were perfectly suited to Sheridan's character. Not only did he want him to take possession of the valley, he wanted him to lay it waste—to "eat out Virginia clear and clean as far as they go, so that crows flying over it for the balance of this season will have to carry their provender with them. . . . We want the Shenandoah Valley to remain a barren waste."

Badly outnumbered, Early and his men fought valiantly against this new threat. Narrowly beaten at Winchester and driven from his stand on Fisher's Hill, Early watched as Sheridan put the torch to the northern end of the valley. Taking advantage of his antagonist's short absence at a conference in Washington, Early attacked the Union army again south of Winchester. In a famous incident of the time, Sheridan arrived back just in time, making a celebrated ride from Winchester to rally his men, finally defeating Early. He then completed the scorching of the Shenandoah Valley, which spent the rest of the war as a burnt-over wasteland. Early continued to resist, going down to his last defeat at Waynesboro in March of 1865. For years thereafter, the view west from the Blue Ridge was not a pleasant one.

THE TRAIL IN MARYLAND

The trip through the Free State is without doubt the most straightforward route of the entire AT. For a distance of just under forty miles, it stays within hooting distance of the crest of South Mountain, from Pennsylvania to the Potomac.

Crossing the line at Pen Mar State Park, the Trail continues along the western side of the ridge at about the 1,300-foot level until it turns east to ascend to its highest point in Maryland: 2,000-foot Quirauk Mountain, the first summit to reach 2,000 or higher since northern Connecticut. The Trail then turns south again, passing by Devil's Racecourse, which is named for its large boulders. It's quite similar to the boulder fields you thought you'd left behind up on Blue Mountain in Pennsylvania.

After passing, in rapid succession, three breaks in the ridgeline at Raven Rock Hollow, Warner Gap, and Harman Gap, the Trail again ascends the ridge, which runs unbroken for over thirteen miles. Before reaching Turner's Gap, it passes by the Washington Monument on the crest of the ridge.

Next stop, after a moderate spate of ridge-running, is Crampton Gap, site of the heaviest fighting during the Battle of South Mountain in the Civil War; some earthworks are still preserved. Also of interest is the elaborate gate to the now-defunct Gathland; formerly the estate of war correspondent George Alfred "Gath" Townsend, today it is

Gathland State Park. Gathland's arch, said to be the only war correspondent's memorial in the world, is a study in nineteenth-century
neo-classical allegory. The three smaller arches symbolize "Depiction,"
"Description," and "Photography;" above two shields labeled "Speed"
and "Heed" are carved the heads of "Electricity" and "Poetry." Can't
you just picture the hard-bitten newshounds assembled in a battleside
tavern, discussing the sublime merits of Depiction?

After Crampton Gap, the Trail ascends steeply once again to the
ridge. Six miles later it passes Weverton Cliffs, for which the hard conglomerate quartzite of the ridgetops of South Mountain is named.
Once it reaches the 1,100-foot level, the Trail makes a beeline for the
Potomac. There, it switchbacks down into the gorge and heads up the
canal.

The C & O (Chesapeake and Ohio) Canal runs up the Potomac
River from Washington, D.C., to Cumberland, Maryland, a distance of
185 miles. Begun in 1829, its construction wasn't complete until 1850.
After a storm in 1924, it was put out of service permanently. As the
Trail nears the Potomac, coming down from South Mountain at last,
it crosses the canal and heads west to Harpers Ferry along the towpath, with the Potomac on the left and the abandoned canal on the
right.

The C & O's status as a National Historic Park is due in part to a
publicity walk taken by Supreme Court Justice William O. Douglas.
Always the outdoorsman, Douglas enlisted in efforts in the '50s to save
the abandoned towpath from a plan to put a superhighway along the
route. His celebrated walk from Cumberland to Washington, D.C., in
March of 1954 is credited with raising public awareness of the canal
and aiding its preservation. There were thirty-six other people in his
party, including the renowned environmentalist Olaus Murie, and the
little group was met on the route by delegations of local people offering support.

The Maryland section is maintained in grand style by the Potomac
Appalachian Trail Club, and it shows. The pathway is among the most
solid along the route. That means it's a wilderness trail that somehow
doesn't erode or go off in odd directions. As anyone who has done
trailwork can attest, it takes a lot of work to make a natural-looking
trail that stands up to lots of foot traffic.

Where the PATC really shines in Maryland, though, is in the shelters. These are positively stellar. The Ed Garvey shelter, up between
Brownsville Gap and Weverton Cliffs, is worth the trip all by itself. If

you work in the Capital District, this section of the Trail offers a terrific getaway.

Harpers Ferry, situated on a narrow tongue of land at the confluence of the Shenandoah and Potomac Rivers, presents a spectacular view. Tucked down beneath towering bluffs on all sides, it was described by Thomas Jefferson as "perhaps one of the most stupendous scenes in nature" and "worth a voyage across the Atlantic" just to see it.

Harpers Ferry houses the national headquarters of the Appalachian Trail Conference. In the small building on Washington Avenue, a small band of dedicated people handles virtually all the business of the national organization, and much of the work needed to support the various local clubs.

In addition to being the nerve center for the volunteer and professional efforts to maintain the Trail, the ATC also runs a service center and bookstore on the ground floor. Here, you can find just about any trail guide or map you might want, both for the AT and for many of the major side trails.

The staff of the ATC share a real love for the Trail and for the people who hike it. When you walk in the door, if you get the impression that they're genuinely glad to see you, you're right. They get much of the information they need to improve and maintain the Trail from simple hikers, so don't be surprised if they listen with interest as you tell of your experiences on the Trail.

If you're not a member already, you might consider joining the ATC. It's a great group to be part of.

THE TRAIL IN VIRGINIA

As the Trail winds up out of Harpers Ferry and across the Shenandoah River, it again takes a position astride the great ridge. This is the same Blue Ridge that went all the way through Maryland.

It was this first eighteen-mile section from Harpers Ferry toward the south that the fledgling Potomac Appalachian Trail Club blazed in 1927 as its initial effort on behalf of the AT. Standing atop Loudoun Heights, the hiker can readily see why Harpers Ferry changed hands so often during the Civil War: it is a veritable sitting duck for anybody who can control Loudoun along with Maryland Heights across the Potomac. You'll also find evidence of the Union's recognition of this fact in the form of stone redoubts constructed to aid in the futile (as it turned out) defense of the arsenal.

The Loudoun Heights section is a popular walk. After a brisk 600-foot ascent from the bridge, the walk along the ridge (and the

Virginia–West Virginia border) is easy and pleasant. There is a short, blue-blazed side trail down to the point of Loudoun Heights, which branches off from the AT when it first reaches the crest of the ridge, as well as an orange-blazed route that enters farther down the hill. The two trails have short spurs that lead to good views at Chimney or Split Rocks, and they can easily be linked up into a pleasant loop.

The initial section of the AT between the Shenandoah River Bridge and Snickers Gap is a pretty straightforward run along the ridge. Although the route itself is secure from development, it runs a fairly narrow line between the settled and developed lands below. For that reason, except for a number of side trails coming in on either side, the trail system is somewhat limited. To hike certain sections, you'll have to leave a car at the opposite end of your planned route. Apart from this minor inconvenience, however, this is a fairly easy-going part of the Trail, and its occasional views make it worthwhile.

Twelve miles later you'll run into the PATC's Blackburn Trail Center, which lies down a quarter-mile spur. Not only is the center near a number of fine side routes, but it also marks the beginning of a more rugged part of the Blue Ridge, which will soon enter Shenandoah National Park at Front Royal. Used by the PATC as a work and recreational center, the Blackburn Center was named for longtime PATC stalwarts Ruth and Fred Blackburn. Fred, among other things, was the first chief of the Big Blue–Tuscarora Trail project, and Ruth was a president of the PATC.

The Blackburn Center also offers campsites for PATC members only, though they are said to be hospitable to most hikers. On July 3 the center holds an annual barbeque that is free to thru-hikers (donations are accepted). Water is also available in season.

Another four miles south, the Trail passes through the Raven Rocks area, in the farthest southeast corner of West Virginia. There are more lookouts here, including the third (or is it the fourth?) spot so far bearing the name of "Devil's Racecourse."

South of Snickers Gap, the Trail moves mainly along the ridgeline. The continuous zigging and zagging in and out of the hollows and gullies has prompted the PATC to declare this to be more strenuous than any other section in northern Virginia.

After the Trail passes Ashby's Gap (first known as the "Upper Thoroughfare of the Blue Ridge," and later as "Ashby's Bent," after Thomas Ashby, a contemporary of Thomas, Lord Fairfax), it once again sneaks up to near the ridgeline. As it does, it passes two tracts of public land in rapid succession. First is Meadows State Park; this leads into the G. Richard Thompson Wildlife Management Area, which is part of the Virginia Commission of Game and Inland Fisheries. Although the Trail route is not particularly spectacular (there is an unpaved road that runs right along the ridgeline, reason enough for the Trail to zigzag around on the side slopes), these two parcels of state land do offer access, campsites (at Meadows, for a fee), and a system of trails suitable for creating nice day hike loops.

As a last point of interest in the northern Virginia section, the Trail skirts through the small gap between High Knob and Ravensden Rock. It is here, a few yards down the little valley from the Trail, that the mighty Rappahannock trickles out from among the rocks and roots.

The Trail then crosses Route 55 and heads for the entrance to Shenandoah National Park over some pleasant, unpaved lanes.

AUTHOR'S CHOICE

My favorite is a point-to-point hike down South Mountain from the Ensign Phillip Cowell Shelter to Harpers Ferry. It's a section hike of about thirty miles, easily doable over a long weekend, as long as you can put in ten miles a day. Take four days, and it's a walk in the park. The Trail stays high on the ridgeline, and there are great views most of the way. It crosses by the Washington Monument at Turner's Gap, Gathland State Park, and a number of great cliff-top lookouts.

If you want a shorter hike, you can spot a car at Washington Monument State Park, where there is a hikers' lot.

On the other hand, if you can go the week of July 4, the section from Front Royal to Harpers Ferry sounds like one big party, with festivals, craft fairs, and patriotic celebrations.

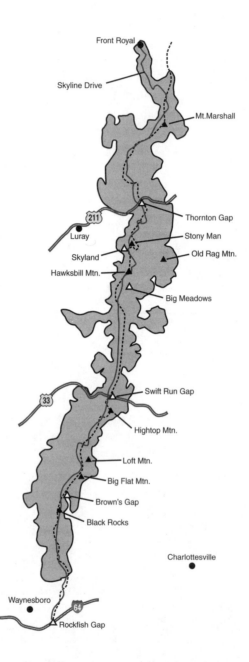

Front Royal

Skyline Drive

Mt.Marshall

211

Luray

Thornton Gap

Stony Man

Skyland

Old Rag Mtn.

Hawksbill Mtn.

Big Meadows

33

Swift Run Gap

Hightop Mtn.

Loft Mtn.

Big Flat Mtn.

Brown's Gap

Black Rocks

Charlottesville

Waynesboro

64

Rockfish Gap

SHENANDOAH NATIONAL PARK

10 Shenandoah National Park

Trail Distance:
Front Royal, Virginia, to Rockfish Gap.....................106.6 miles
Maintaining Club:
Potomac Appalachian Trail Club,
in cooperation with the National Park Service

INTRODUCTION

Shenandoah National Park is the first of several tracts of federal land along the Appalachian ridgeline in the South that protect the route on its way to Springer Mountain. Together, these lands form the heart of the southern Appalachians and do much to give the Trail the feel and spirit that it has today.

Shenandoah Park is where the Blue Ridge really becomes the Blue Ridge. It's the first time since Killington Peak in Vermont that the Trail ascends a ridge that stands over 4,000 feet (and the first trip over 3,000 feet since Greylock in Massachusetts). And because of its protection in the National Park System, it's far more than just a narrow strip of green between housing subdivisions.

The park today has the mixed blessing of the Skyline Drive, which runs at or near the crest of the ridge all the way from end to end. This low-speed, two-lane highway does give hikers easy access to some of the finest hiking trails in the East. The $5 seven-day park pass is the best deal in town, and it hasn't changed in years. But there are other prices. You can never truly get away from the road, and it is often obtrusive to some degree. And Shenandoah's proximity to Washington, Richmond, and the whole populated East Coast makes it the most visited National Park year in and year out.

But the park is large—almost 200,000 acres. Plan right, and you can get a good, long way off the highway. Since the Skyline Drive and the Trail often follow much the same route, this will mean taking advantage of the excellent system of side trails.

GEOLOGY ALONG THE TRAIL

To get a true feel for the geology of Shenandoah, you have to put your mind into geologic time. In the span of a human life, geological processes appear to be very sedate. Substitute, say, ten million years for an hour and then, perhaps, you can get an idea of the violence of geological change. It's an indication of this violence that the rocks along the crest of the Blue Ridge are among the oldest. The area's characteristic greenstone is metamorphosed basalt that was laid down as layers of lava in the distant Precambrian Era. The granodiorite at Mary's Rock and Stony Man and the granite on Old Rag are both far older.

Let's start a billion years or so ago. This was the age of the Grenville Event, that imperfectly understood uplift of the original Appalachians, which were eroded away before the current ones were formed. At the time, the area where Shenandoah Park sits today was being subjected to pluton activity. Huge masses of molten rock were bubbling up from underneath, forming hills and highlands. How high these hills rose is a matter of conjecture. We do know that when volcanic activity started burying the hills nearly half a billion years later, they were still up to a thousand feet tall, so they originally must have been very impressive.

The volcanic activity that occurred 700 million years ago was prolonged and considerable. Oozing up to the surface through dikes in the existing rock (these are clearly visible on the trail to Old Rag, where greenstone dikes have eroded away, leaving narrow corridors in the granite), the lava laid layer upon layer of basalt around the hills. There are up to seven major layers of basalt in many places.

When the volcanism ended, it left an enormously thick layer of banded basalt. Interspersed between layers was a kind of shale—now metamorphosed into slate—that was the result of volcanic ash, mud, and erosion between lava flows. This is clearly visible today as a dark gray to purple slate that lies beneath the greenstone. It's easy to see in such places as the south side of Compton Peak, Swift Run Gap, Smith Roach Gap, and Bearfence Mountain.

Now, remember, this volcanic activity took place on a coastal plain very much like the one to the east of the park today. The lava layer was soon covered by a thin layer of sand that probably eroded off of the basalt and the granite hilltops.

Then the ancient Cambrian sea began to rise, and the coastal plain became a beach. The sediment from the eroding hills accumulated over time to form a deep layer (up to a thousand feet deep) of clean, white sand. Mud and silt built up in places from ocean deposits and from rivers flowing in. Eventually, a layer of limestone may have capped the entire sequence—the resulting limestone is absent from the Blue Ridge but can be seen farther west, where it forms the floor of the Shenandoah Valley. Or it could have been present in the Shenandoahs themselves at one time, only to erode away completely.

Then, in geological terms, all hell broke loose. As plates migrated and continents collided, this enormously thick sequence of layers was crushed together like an accordion, tilted, cracked, and eventually thrust over itself like a rug being shoved along the floor. The layers present in the park have been tilted up and over maybe as much as 110 degrees from where they started. The younger, later rocks are exposed to the west; the older, Precambrian granites are to the east.

Since the uplift ended (perhaps 250 million years ago), erosion has been the name of the game. Where the rocks were tough, mountains remained. The erosion-resistant greenstone and granodiorite form the main ridge in most places. The softer and more water-soluble limestones eroded away.

In places, the Blue Ridge is flanked by boulder fields similar to those throughout Pennsylvania, and they formed for the same reasons. The freezing and thawing that resulted from having a thousand-foot-thick blanket of ice just to the north cracked and split off huge boulders. Those composed of resistant rock types, like the quartzites, have remained.

Another major influence on the present-day shape of the Blue Ridge is water action. The gaps were originally formed by streams and rivers coursing through them. In some gaps, where other streams have pulled the watershed away to one side or the other, "wind gaps" have formed—notches in the ridgeline with no stream. Manassas Gap to the north of the park is a good example.

HISTORY ALONG THE TRAIL

Like the sections to the north of the park, this stretch of the Trail overlooks the rich Shenandoah Valley. It is through the four major gaps in the park that much of the western expansion of the eighteenth century took place.

First Settlers

When the first German settlers arrived from Pennsylvania in the 1720s, the Shenandoah Valley was relatively uninhabited by Native peoples. Nobody knows the reason for this for sure, but the region had been populated prior to then. Perhaps the repeated raids and massacres by the Iroquois Nations from the north had succeeded in exterminating some groups and discouraging others from living out in the open. The Iroquois, who were known locally as the Massawomek, regularly used the ridge and the valley as a route when sending war parties against their favorite enemies, the Catawbas of North Carolina.

The original settlers appeared to have been mainly Algonkians, who were harried by raiding tribes from all sides—not just Iroquois but also Lenni Lenapes, Cherokees, and Susquehannocks. Even when the valley wasn't inhabited, it was used as a key route between places, just as it is today. There was a major trade route along what is now Interstate 81, as well as a ridgetop war route that roughly followed the current route of the AT.

After Lederer's initial explorations in 1669 and 1670 (see page 142), others followed. Some went to trade furs; others to explore as Lederer had done. One expedition organized by the governor of Virginia, dandy Alexander Spotswood, crossed the ridge at Swift Run Gap and went down into the valley below. There, they drank a toast, fired a salute, and claimed it all for their king, George I. Then they drank quite a few more toasts. Real estate matters were simpler then.

Settlement followed quickly. Not long into the eighteenth century, the Great Wagon Road had been established along the route of the Native American trading trail. In addition to the Germans who followed Lederer's lead came Scots-Irish and Swiss. Part of the reason for the speed of the settlement was the fact that unlike other desirable regions, the valley had no native populations already there that had to be dispossessed somehow.

Though the French and Indian War of the 1750s and 1760s forced many settlers back across the Blue Ridge, everybody came back once things were settled. Perhaps unsure of British protection from French and Indian attack, and definitely annoyed by the Crown's interference with westward expansion, the Shendandoah Valley (and indeed, the rest of Virginia) supported the Revolution with vigor.

The Ridge and the Revolution

The Blue Ridge's section in the park was to figure in the Revolution in at least one interesting way. In 1781, with the bulk of the fighting having moved to the coastal plains of Virginia, the British were threatening the state capital at Williamsburg. Thomas Jefferson, then the governor, decided to remove the state archives and seal to prevent their capture or destruction. He entrusted one Bernis Brown with their safety.

Brown was one of the Browns of Brown's Gap, in the southern section of the park. At first, he brought the items to his home below the gap, but when the British started inching closer, he decided to hide them better still.

Loading his cargo onto the backs of mules, Brown and an unidentified "mountaineer" (someone living in the mountains) headed up to Brown's Gap, then turned south toward Black Rocks. There, they hid the Virginia archives and official seal in a cave until the war was over—to this day, no one knows exactly where.

Mary's Rock

Many of the streams and gaps got their names from the families that settled there. Often, they would have a plantation below, and the features on the ridge above would bear some name that they bestowed. The manors were established early on. Gooney Manor, for example, was one of Thomas Lord Fairfax's plantations, which he established in the 1740s. It later passed into the hands of the Marshall family, one of whom (John) became perhaps the finest Chief Justice of the Supreme Court that this country has ever known.

One example of an early family's name enduring is Thornton Gap, which is named for Francis Thornton. In the early eighteenth century, he was given a parcel of land by his father that stretched up from the Piedmont into the Blue Ridge.

Thornton and his wife, Mary, set up housekeeping at his plantation in "F.T. Valley," which runs from near Sperryville south to the foot of Old Rag Mountain. Shortly after they moved there, the two went on a camping trip up into Thornton Gap. They camped at a spring just below the summit of Great Pass Mountain. The next day, Thornton took Mary to the top, where he presented the mountain to her as a wedding gift. Each year thereafter, they would return to the rock and camp at the spring, which became known as "Mary's Spring."

When Francis died, Mary moved up to a cabin in Thornton Gap, from which she could see the mountain. The entire section of the gap became known as "Madame Thornton's Quarter," and in the nineteenth century the rock and spring became a popular courting spot for local couples. An invitation for a private picnic on the rock was usually followed by a proposal of marriage.

AT historian Jean Stephenson, writing in 1945, claimed that the site of the spring was lost sometime in the latter half of the nineteenth century. Perhaps, she speculated, it petered out, or the "roan oak," under whose roots the spring was said to emerge, had died and fallen. Those interested in locating the spring should find the old path that leads uphill from Meadow Spring. Mary's Spring was said to lie between a half and a quarter mile below Mary's Rock, at the spot where the climbing became steep.

The Civil War

The Blue Ridge at Shenandoah Park was witness to much of the same action already described in the chapter on northern Virginia. These hills must have provided shelter and a lookout for Jubal Early's men as they desperately tried to hold on in the waning days of the war. One can almost picture groups of lean, hungry Confederates posted on the western slopes of the ridge, watching ugly columns of black smoke in the valley below—the land they tried so valiantly to defend consumed by flames. They met their final defeat a month before Appomattox, at Waynesboro, near the southern end of the park.

The Coming of the Park

After the war, the land surrounding the Blue Ridge remained rural. Since the farmers of the Shenandoah Valley had never been large-scale slaveowners, little changed in their way of life. They continued to farm and send their products—corn, flour, leather, and fruit, as well as lime that they mined from the bedrock and purified in a kiln—down to market via the C & O Canal at Harpers Ferry. To get their goods that far, they loaded them onto "gundalows," barges up to nine feet wide and seventy-five feet long that were poled down the treacherous bends and shallows of the Shenandoah by fifteen or more men. These would be taken to the canalhead, unloaded, and broken up and sold for timber. The crew would then walk home. This trade went on from 1798, when the fleet was established, into the 1890s.

As the nineteenth century closed and the notion of the romantic wilderness seized the spirits of urbanites, the Blue Ridge caught the attention of people from the lowlands bent on more than exploration and farming. Perhaps the most important of these, from the park's point of view, was George Freeman Pollock, the founder of Skyland. In the early 1890s, he began scouting out the territory in what is now the central section of the park, looking to establish a resort.

The Ridge at the time was inhabited by "mountaineers." These poor, simple folk were the forerunners of the generation that had such trouble with Prohibition enforcement officers. In those days, they also had a sizable cottage distilling operation going. It just wasn't illegal then. Pollock's activities were met with a variety of responses from the locals. In general, they regarded him as somewhat strange—much the way country people have always regarded city people. On occasion, though, they took exception to his alteration of the hills and their way of life.

This led to at least one incident. In 1893, Pollock and a group of friends were hiking around in the area, when they ran into one of Pollock's neighbors, a mountaineer named Fletcher. Relations between the two had never been friendly, but on this occasion, Fletcher took them one step further. While his son held the group at gunpoint, Fletcher proceeded to thrash Pollock, warning him to leave the hills and not to come back upon threat of murder. Pollock, of course, ignored the warning, taking care to avoid running into Fletcher unarmed in the future. He later had friendly relations with the mountaineer's son, Johnny.

Once established, Skyland became a jumping-off point into the Blue Ridge, and especially to Old Rag Mountain, which is one of the most popular hikes even to this day. Pollock became instrumental in the establishment of the park and the section of the Trail running through it. There are newspaper accounts of him entertaining highly placed National Park Service managers as early as 1926, as well as hosting a young man by the name of Myron Avery who had recently moved down from Connecticut.

Pollock's dealings with the Park Service were all part of the beginnings of Shenandoah National Park. The effort began in 1923 with the NPS recommending a park in the southern Appalachians; nearly $3 million had been raised by 1926, and the land purchase began. Some of the mountaineers had no desire to move and had to be wheedled and cajoled out. Many were relocated to the valleys and hollows to the west, bordering the park.

The effort took nearly ten years. In the end, they succeeded in obtaining, through purchase and trade, 176,430 acres. Once the park was dedicated in 1936, the Civilian Conservation Corps (CCC) moved in with their axes and shovels and began building. They would later figure prominently in the history of the Trail in the park.

It was by then apparent what Myron Avery had been doing at Skyland. Since the formation of the Potomac Appalachian Trail Club, the Trail had been blazed over the ridge in what would soon be the National Park. No sooner was it finished, though, than it had to be moved.

This was due to the construction of the Skyline Drive, which was begun in 1931 and completed in 1939. Since the Drive followed the AT route closely, the Trail had to be relocated. (AT trailblazers have always been such skilled routefinders that they have had this problem wherever they go.) This was done in grand style by the CCC.

The Shenandoah National Park section has long reigned as the crown jewel of the Potomac Appalachian Trail Club section of the AT. Right from the very beginning in 1927, their annual get-together (the famous "Midsummer Frolic") was held at Skyland. Use of the park has slowly increased since the '50s, with attendance taking quantum leaps in the late '60s. One problem that arose in those days was abuse of Park facilities by unskilled back-to-the-landers who would take up residence in the shelters and create untold havoc. Current rules against short-term use of shelters except in emergencies and by thru-hikers were prompted by a desire to solve this problem.

THE TRAIL IN SHENANDOAH NATIONAL PARK

Except for a three-mile section in the north and eight miles in the south, the Trail in this section runs entirely through Park land. It quickly ascends to the ridge at Compton Gap at about 2,400 feet and heads in a southwesterly direction, staying very close to the ridgeline all the way to Rockfish Gap.

Two things conspire to make the park a superb site for day hiking and short-term tripping. First is the access made possible by the Skyline Drive. With the Trail never more than a few hundred yards from the Drive, and parking areas appearing every few miles, it is relatively easy to gain access to just about any point within the park.

Then, there is the system of blue-blazed side trails, yellow-blazed horse and foot trails, and assorted nature trails that crisscross everywhere. There are over five hundred miles of these, all maintained by the Potomac Appalachian Trail Club and the NPS. They seem to hit just about every peak, lookout, meadow, and waterfall—of which there are dozens. These side trails offer unparalleled opportunities for side hikes and loops and are too numerous to be covered in detail here. A book called *Circuit Hikes in the Shenandoah National Park*, available from the PATC, outlines thirty-two separate hikes from two to twenty miles long.

Of particular note is the Big Blue Trail, which strikes off to the west from a point just north of Elkwallow Gap in the northern section. This is more than just a side trail. It was begun in the early '60s, when the ATC feared that the route from Shenandoah Park to the Susquehanna River in Pennsylvania couldn't be maintained. As it was blazed with the typical blue blazes denoting a side trail, the PATC members involved began referring to it affectionately as Big Blue. The name stuck.

Unlike Pennsylvania, where the Trail sticks to the 1,400-foot level like glue, the AT in Shenandoah Park goes up and down from peak to valley to knob to gap. In its northern section, for example, it goes in just a three-mile space from Hogback Mountain to Elkwallow Gap, from 3,400 feet all the way down to around 2,400. Then, from nearby Thornton Gap, it's immediately back up to 3,500 feet on Mary's Rock.

Nonetheless, the general condition of the Trail is evidence of the care that the Park Service takes with its property. The grading and footbed of the Trail have eliminated most of the rough edges, and you could practically wheel a shopping cart up most sections. If it can be strenuous going on the many hills, it cannot be said to be rough.

Side hikes in the park are often unique in that you usually start at the high point, dip down into the lowlands, and then have to go up again to get back to the car. This is especially true of hikes to the many waterfalls within the park. Several stand out.

Big Falls, at 93 feet the tallest of the cascades in the park, lies in the northern section about three miles down the Big Blue Trail. It's in the Elkwallow area, which has many side trails even by park standards. You can take the swing down the Big Falls and keep right on going, returning by any of several interesting loops.

Perhaps the best cascade hike, though, is down White Oak Run in the central section. Over a distance of about a mile are a half dozen falls ranging in height from thirty-five to eighty-six feet. They can be reached from Skyland on the White Oak Canyon Trail, which you might want to consider as an alternative route (albeit a lengthy one) either to or from Old Rag Mountain. White Oak Canyon also makes an excellent loop when combined with the Cedar Run Trail, which has falls of its own. These are, however, exceedingly popular day hikes, so expect to run into people unless you're there way out of season.

In the southern section, the best cascades are on Doyles River, just east of Brown's Gap. At twenty-eight and sixty-three feet tall, these are quite worth the trip and have the added advantage of being closer to the road than many other falls. One can imagine Bernis Brown and his mountaineer companion passing by in 1781 on their way to stash the state archives at Black Rocks.

The Popular Central Section

Since the establishment of Skyland late in the nineteenth century, the middle portion of the area covered by the park has been by far the best liked. Not only does it have the best waterfalls; it also has the highest, ruggedest, most spectacular peaks and some of the most interesting terrain.

Hawksbill Mountain is, at 4,050 feet, the highest point in the park. Like most of the other high points, it is made of greenstone, the remains of the lava that flowed 700 million years ago. Just beneath the summit knob, the AT reaches the highest point yet achieved in the park at around 3,600 feet. This will be topped just south of Big Meadows on Hazeltop, which is over 3,800 feet.

Old Rag Mountain lies just off the main ridge to the east of Skyland. Unlike the main summits, it is constructed of the old granite left over from the plutons of 1.1 billion years ago. Especially sought after on this most popular of peaks within the park is the Ridge Trail, which is picked up on the northern approach to the mountain from either the small parking area near the hamlet of Nethers or via the Corbin Hollow or Nicholson Hollow Trails. On this route, the trail passes up through narrow rock-walled corridors that are actually the remains of the dikes through which the lava flowed to form the thick layer of greenstone. The somewhat softer basalt has eroded out of the dike, leaving just the harder granite sidewalls.

Big Meadows are interesting in another way. Composed of plant communities that would be more naturally found several hundred miles to the north, these wide fields are, like the famous balds to the south, most likely the remains of more boreal ecosystems left over from the last Ice Age. If that's the case, then the more typical southern Appalachian forests are slowly encroaching on the meadows. They may last only a few thousand more years, so see them while you can.

The Wild Southern Section

Much of the southern part of the park is designated as federal Wilderness Area. That's not just an honorary title. Only areas that qualify can be so named, and once given this designation, the land has just about as powerful a protection as it can get.

This section of the park is much less developed—and much less visited—than the other two. It is also much wider than some other sections, offering the hiker and backpacker a chance to get a fair piece away from the crowds.

It might surprise some people that the AT doesn't actually pass through the tracts of Wilderness Area, but there's good reason for that. Running as it does along the crest of the Blue Ridge, and accompanied every step of the way by the Skyline Drive, the Trailway is disqualified from being in a Wilderness Area; such lands must be roadless. For that reason, hikers wanting solitude must take to the blue blazes. As elsewhere in the park, the side trails in the southern section go just about everywhere.

AUTHOR'S CHOICE

The name of the game in the Shenandoah is picnicking. Find any part of the Trail you want and take the side trip to one of the dozens of waterfalls.

Second choice: The climb up Rag Mountain is popular for good reason. Take a lunch and enjoy.

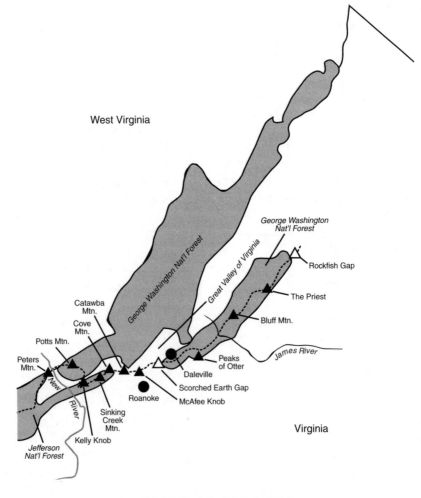

West Virginia

George Washington Nat'l Forest

George Washington Nat'l Forest

Rockfish Gap

Great Valley of Virginia

The Priest

Bluff Mtn.

Catawba Mtn.

Cove Mtn.

James River

Potts Mtn.

Peaks of Otter

Peters Mtn.

Daleville

New River

Scorched Earth Gap

Roanoke

McAfee Knob

Sinking Creek Mtn.

Virginia

Kelly Knob

Jefferson Nat'l Forest

CENTRAL VIRGINIA

▌▌▌ Central Virginia

INTRODUCTION

It is in this section of the Old Dominion that the AT had some of its greatest challenges. Once so remote and wild that it was one of the hardest of the original sections to blaze, the route here was threatened several times by a variety of forces ranging from federal roadbuilding to simple development. The unbroken Trail has in the past been difficult and at times actually impossible to maintain. That it passes through an uninterrupted—and, by now, largely protected—right-of-way is tribute to countless hours on the part of volunteers and professionals alike.

Central Virginia is also where the arrow-straight ridges over which the Trail has passed since near the New York–New Jersey border become much more complicated. They split up, and in places disappear into the flatlands below, only to reappear farther south. The Trail in this section leaves the Blue Ridge, crosses the Great Valley, and passes for a time over the westernmost ranges of the Appalachian system, the Alleghenies.

GEOLOGY ALONG THE TRAIL

As in any part of the Appalachian chain, the ridges and peaks south of Rockfish Gap are a continuation of trends that started far to the north and will continue far to the south. Various rock layers have been shoved up along a line of overthrust faults—sidewise breakages in the rock strata in which layers are shoved up over other layers like playing cards scooped into a pile. The resulting mountains frequently feature older layers lying above younger ones.

Rockfish Gap has given its name to a fault that marks the thrust of one layer, the Lovington Formation, over another, the Pedlar. The Lovington Formation is composed of Precambrian gneisses and granites—the ancient granites that bubbled up through the earth's crust toward the surface. The Pedlar Formation that it climbed over is composed of granodiorites as well as the greenstone and various sedimentary and metamorphic strata that remain from the inland sea of half an aeon ago.

The Rockfish Valley Fault is a scissors-type fault, starting small just south of Old Rag Mountain in Shenandoah National Park and increasing in displacement over the hundred or so miles it travels to the south. The southern reaches appear as though they were swung over each other, with the northern point near Old Rag acting as a pivot.

The Trail in this section comes down off the Blue Ridge and heads over the Valley of Virginia toward the western ranges of the Appalachians, the Alleghenies. The valley is a continuation of the enormous valley system that travels through the Shenandoah River drainage, through Pennsylvania to central New York State, where it passes Albany before heading up to form the Great Valley of Vermont. It is mostly underlain by limestones, indicating its origin in the carbonate banks of the shallow Cambrian and Ordovician inland sea. When the sea was uplifted by the onrushing European and African Plates nearly 300 million years ago, the limestone remained.

Down the center of the valley is a sandstone syncline, a continuation of Massanutten Mountain, the parallel ridge that stands just to the west of Shenandoah National Park. This runs as mountain down to about Harrisonburg—halfway down the park—and continues as a poorly defined syncline all the way to below Waynesboro.

The valley floor is undercut by many caverns that have dissolved their way into the carbonate rock strata. Natural Bridge, to the west of the AT route, is a former cavern that has eroded away except for one part of the roof, which remains as a span.

HISTORY ALONG THE TRAIL

As the Trail leaves the area of Shenandoah National Park, it heads farther west into the more remote reaches of the Appalachians. Under British rule, as we've seen, settlement of these areas was discouraged, and prior to the Revolution, little was known of the area.

When the Europeans arrived in Virginia, finally establishing a permanent presence in Jamestown in 1609, they ran into the numerous Powhatans. These gregarious natives became famous in the annals of American history for the story of John Smith and Pocahontas, which was loosely—very loosely—recounted in the Disney cartoon.

But the Powhatans stayed down in the rivers and the coasts. In the mountains was a confederation of the Monacans and the Mannahoacs, tribes that lived along the Blue Ridge from present-day Roanoke up to the Potomac. They represented yet another linguistic group, distinct from the Algonkians, Iroquoians, and Cherokees, and in fact more closely related to the Lakotas of the northern plains. They lived in palisaded villages containing dome-shaped bark houses, and they pursued typical woodlands agriculture, cutting and burning fields to grow corn, squash, and beans. They traded with the Iroquois to the north and the Cherokee to the south, among whom they were famous for their highly prized beaded necklaces as well as copper, which they mined in their hills. The main route for this trade was east of the ridges, along the Great Trading Road, which ran down what is now Route 29. War parties often used the Warriors Road, which ran down what is now Route 11.

As the white settlers approached from the coast, these people gradually moved inland, back into the hills. Some joined the Tuscaroras of North Carolina and moved north to Pennsylvania and New York. Along the way, some were adopted by the Iroquois Confederacy and moved with them to Canada. Today, some Monacans remain in Amherst County, which the Trail crosses between the Priest Wilderness and the James River.

After the Puritan revolution in Britain in 1649, Virginia became the refuge of outlawed Cavaliers, the nobility that fought against Cromwell and lost. Though Cromwell soon sent a delegation to the colonies to establish Puritan rule across the Atlantic, the change was barely noticeable in a region controlled by the House of Burgesses and an innately independent of the people. The Cavaliers became the first families of Virginia.

Settlement of the lands along the Trail route came slowly. By 1641, white settlement was mainly centered on the James River Valley, and only as far as the first falls. As in other places along the Trail, westward expansion was inhibited in central Virginia by three things. First, the land across the Appalachians was largely controlled by the French and, until the French and Indian War in the 1750s and '60s, crossing the Blue Ridge was also dangerous. Second was the British prohibition in 1763 of settlement west of the ridge. Finally, for most settlers, the wilderness of the Appalachians was just too darned scary.

This changed over time. In the relatively brief period between the French and Indian and the Revolutionary Wars, Britain had taken control of much of the western slopes of the mountains, and Virginia found itself with counties over the mountains, including Kentucky and what would become West Virginia. These were mainly reached through the Ohio or Potomac Valleys.

After the Revolution, western expansion began in earnest. Frontier roads were cut through the passes to connect the western counties with the Piedmont and coastal areas of the state. This was the time and the place of Daniel Boone and the original pioneers.

The plantation system had been established soon after the founding of Jamestown, and slaveholding came along with it. However, the plantations did not extend over the Blue Ridge, and, like Tennessee to the south, the slaveless settlers west of the ridge were not sympathetic to secession once the Civil War came. Even during the Civil War, sentiments in West Virginia were so strong that the Union was able to hold onto the region as a new state. Most of the battles centered on the coastal areas leading to Richmond, and on the battle for the Shenandoah Valley.

HISTORY OF THE APPALACHIAN TRAIL IN CENTRAL VIRGINIA

When the Trail was first blazed in the late '20s and early '30s, it continued southward along the crest of the Blue Ridge as it had done since Pennsylvania. At the time, Roanoke was a Trail town, and the Peaks of Otter section was among the most popular.

In the mid '30s, though, trouble was brewing for the section of the Trail south of Shenandoah National Park. In 1935, the Park Service was proposing an extension of the Skyline Drive farther down the Blue Ridge, all the way into North Carolina and Tennessee. It was a controversial move, and as you'd expect, sides were picked very quickly.

Therein lies one of the great tragedies of the AT. The two luminaries of the entire Trail movement, Benton MacKaye, the spiritual head, and Myron Avery, the administrative head, took opposite sides. Avery favored the extension of the Drive; MacKaye opposed it.

It was probably inevitable. The two men, though equally passionate in their desire to see the Trail completed, were of necessity opposite in their motivations and methods. It has long been an axiom of movements such as this that the idea people tend not to be the best organizers. While the original idea of the Trail and its accompanying parkland was MacKaye's, he never really attempted to coordinate the realization of his dream. Avery, on the other hand, was a goal-oriented man who would let nothing stand in the way once he had decided on a course of action. Energetic beyond belief, inspiring, occasionally abrasive, and psychologically incapable of taking "no" for an answer, he was the perfect choice to head up the Appalachian Trail Conference.

The proposed route of the Drive's extension was virtually identical to that of the Trail for a distance of 202 miles. Avery's point of view was simple: the expanded Skyline Drive (which would be called the Blue Ridge Parkway) would make the new Trail through the southern reaches of the Blue Ridge more accessible, and it would aid maintenance in remote sections. He welcomed the extension, saying, "It is perhaps a great tribute to the original route of The Appalachian Trail that so much of the Blue Ridge Parkway connecting the Shenandoah National Park to the Great Smokies is almost superimposed on the Appalachian Trail in Southern Virginia." Just as the Park Service had done in Shenandoah National Park, so it would here, moving the Trail away from the route.

MacKaye, for his part, felt that the highway would inevitably interfere with the wilderness spirit of the ridge. That, in his mind, was the only important consideration.

Anyway, the two exchanged letters, some of which were reportedly heated. It is said that MacKaye charged Avery with destroying the purpose of the Trail along the Blue Ridge. For his part, Avery supposedly accused MacKaye of insensitivity to the problem of local access. However it played, the result was unfortunate: MacKaye withdrew from most ATC activities. ATC members can console themselves in the thought that this freed MacKaye to devote his energies to helping to found the Wilderness Society. But it would be years before the father of the Appalachian Trail would once again be a close part of the movement he inspired.

The route began running into trouble at this point. Development began encroaching on the wildlands through which it passed, even while the ATC and the Park Service were trying to complete the rerouting made necessary by the Blue Ridge Parkway. In a region where, just a decade before, trailblazing efforts were hampered by remoteness and even by lack of maps, the AT was rapidly reaching the point at which it would have to be put onto roads. When World War II hit, what would today be considered unthinkable happened: gaps appeared in the Trail, and the continuous route was broken. It wasn't until the last 9.5-mile section between the Priest and Three Ridges was completed in 1951 that the route through central Virginia was made whole again.

THE TRAIL IN CENTRAL VIRGINIA

The Trail continues south from Rockfish Gap once it leaves Shenandoah National Park and immediately climbs again to the crest of the Blue Ridge. For the first several miles, the Trailway parallels the Blue Ridge Parkway, although in recent years, trailblazing has moved the path farther from the actual roadway. Though the Trail still parallels the parkway, the re-routing has created a pleasant separation between the two. Now, the Trail runs across the fall line of the ridge, finally ascending to the relatively new Paul C. Wolfe Shelter (built in 1991), which is up about a mile or so short of the Humpback Rocks Visitor's Center. In the process, it quickly ascends to over 3,000 feet and stays there most of the way down the ridge.

After paralleling the Blue Ridge Parkway for about sixteen miles, the Trail branches off to the south, following the Three Ridges (3,970 feet) up into the "Religious Range." Here, on the Priest (other nearby peaks include Little Priest, the Cardinal, and the Friar), it actually crosses over 4,000 feet for the first time since Killington in Vermont. The area alternates between George Washington National Forest and land purchased in the past decade or two by the National Park Service, and it is crisscrossed by trails and unimproved roads that offer access from the paved roads below.

You will run across remnants of the record-breaking rainstorm that hit this section in August of 1969. In places, nearly three feet of rain was said to have fallen in under six hours. There were slides all over the area. Meteorologists theorize that such rainstorms may hit only once in a century—or in a millennium. This one was the result of Hurricane Camille (downgraded to a tropical storm) coming over the ridge from the west and bumping smack into another air mass coming in from the coast.

Staying close to the side ridge along which the route takes it, the AT repeatedly rises above 4,000 feet at Maintop Mountain (4,040 feet),

Rocky Mountain (4,072 feet), Cole Mountain (4,022 feet), and Bald Knob (4,059 feet), before finally crossing Brown Mountain Creek Valley and heading back up to the Blue Ridge Parkway at Little Irish Creek. This has been the route for a number of years, with only minor relocations. It immediately leaves the highway, moving off to the west. At Fuller Rocks, overlooking the James River, it offers one of the finest views anywhere on the whole Trailway. Hikers can see from the Alleghenies to the west all the way across the Piedmont to the east.

Since 2000, the Trail has crossed the James on the James River Foot Bridge, which is named not just for the river but also for Bill Foot of the Natural Bridge Club, who drove the project. The bridge crosses on the piers of an old railroad bridge and spares the hiker the necessity of sharing the Route 501 bridge. At 660 feet, this crossing is the lowest point on the AT in central Virginia.

From there, the Trail quickly climbs into the James River Face Wilderness, topping out on Highcock Knob at around 3,000 feet. This large, roadless area offers acres and acres of wildland, with many trails radiating down into the valleys around it, offering good day hiking from all directions. The James River Face and its contiguous partner, the Thunder Ridge Wilderness Area, make for a five-mile section of Trail that is as primeval and solitary as any in this part of Virginia.

As you'd expect, though, it isn't long before the Trail meets up with the Blue Ridge Parkway again, this time at Petites Gap. It stays with the road closely for about ten miles, then branches off into the Buzzard Ridge–Cove Mountain area. Here again, there are numerous side trails and unimproved roads, giving the day hiker and weekend camper lots to work with.

As the AT winds down off of Cove Mountain (the second of that name on the route so far), it meets up with the parkway again at Bearwallow Gap. For the next seven and a half miles, all the way to Black Horse Gap, you could practically stand in the Trail and spit across the highway. The AT in this area runs through a section of Thomas Jefferson National Forest that is, at its widest, a mere mile and a half across. When it finally leaves the parkway, it heads downhill into the Valley of Virginia in the Daleville-Cloverdale area as it makes its move to the ranges to the west.

Leaving the Blue Ridge

Situated in the Great Valley of the Appalachians that runs all the way down from Vermont in various permutations (the Cumberland Valley in Pennsylvania, the Shenandoah Valley of Virginia), Daleville is popular with thru-hikers in search of mail and ice cream. But for day hikers and short-term campers, it serves mainly as a trailhead for the sections to the east and west.

Heading south (actually west at this particular point), the Trail enters a Trail Corridor, which is just another friendly service of your National Parks and the National Scenic Trails Act of 1968. It consists of a narrow ribbon of protected land over which the Trail passes.

This section of Trail was, as recently as 1978, moved off its traditional route on Catawba Mountain due to landowner troubles. For the better part of a decade, the AT passed instead over the less desirable North Mountain, visible just to the north over the Catawba Creek. Later, the Park Service purchased the land, and the Trail returned to Catawba. Today, the route crosses Tinker Cliffs and the popular (and photogenic) McAfee Knob, with their heart-stopping precipices and splendid views of the Catawba Valley, Carvins Cove, Tinker Mountain, the Peaks of Otter, and—on a clear day—Roanoke.

Out of the valley just south of Daleville, the Trail quickly ascends Tinker Mountain—actually a long ridge—which it follows to the northwest. From there, it descends into Scorched Earth Gap. The gap is named for a 1982 incident in which a hike leader inadvertently led his group through dense thickets. According to another Roanoke ATC luminary, Tom Campbell, who dutifully reported the incident to the *Appalachian Trailway News*, Jim Denton was leading the hike and took the group on a bushwhack off the side of Tinker Mountain. One woman took exception to the routing.

"No one had suspected the wealth of vituperative epithets contained in the vocabulary of one of the women of the group," Campbell reported, "but this soon came to light as the brush thickened. Backlashes from numerous branches encountered her anatomy, and a flow of words directed at our expert increased as we descended.

"By the time the gap was reached, this flow had reached flood stage, and our expert beat a strategic and hasty retreat. It was averred by a number of those present that the very ground was seen to smoke beneath the force of her imprecations." Campbell, ever the gentleman, failed to include the name of Denton's antagonist.

Campbell's own service with the Roanoke ATC wasn't without incident. Once, he and Jim Denton were hard at work negotiating with a landowner as part of efforts to relocate the Trail farther west. He and Denton stood talking with the man for a long while, and when the deal was struck, they left. Only then did Campbell show Denton the bloody chunk that the landowner's dog had bitten out of his leg. Not wanting to spoil the promising business, Tom had decided not to mention that there was a dog taking a piece out of him.

At Scorched Earth Gap, the Trail meets the Andy Lane Trail, which was once the AT when the route passed over to North Mountain at this point. From there, Tinker Mountain turns abruptly southward. This would probably be yet another Cove Mountain were it not for the nearness of another ridge of that name just a few miles down the Trail. At the southwestern end of Tinker Mountain, the Trail climbs up about five hundred feet to MacAfee Knob, long famous in AT literature for the spectacular photos hikers take there of their companions perched on jutting rocks. The Trail then descends to the lower ridge of Catawba Mountain, where it runs for about four miles or so.

Once the Trail has traversed its hard-won (politically, at least) route along Catawba Mountain, it descends into Catawba Valley and heads toward North Mountain and the southern end of the Andy Lane Trail. Passing just west of North, it climbs instead up the eastern flank of yet another Cove Mountain. Like its Pennsylvania counterpart, this cove is also a U-shaped figure on the surface of the planet. The Trail will ascend to its ridge and take the entire ride around the top.

As the AT reaches the southern end of the Cove Mountain ridge, it passes by an impressive standing rock called the Dragon's Tooth. Once called simply Buzzard's Rock, Tom Campbell decided that it needed a better name, so he gave it one. Once around Cove Mountain, the Trail descends into Craig Creek Valley. About 3.5 miles before it reaches the creek, a blue-blazed trail to the right goes 200 yards to the Audie Murphy Monument, site of the plane crash that killed America's most decorated WWII hero.

The trail guide kindly warns hikers that the next section has rocky footing, but except for that, the route is a cakewalk, staying up along the crest of Sinking Creek Mountain, around the 3,200-foot level. In other words, it might kill you, but it won't wear you out. This steep and sometimes narrow ridge offers views into Sinking Creek Valley to the north and Craig Creek Valley to the south. There are a number of good lookouts and ledges.

When it reaches the Sinking Creek Valley at Huffman, Virginia, the AT crosses its first Gulf-bound stream—that is, the first stream that drains into the Mississippi and the Gulf of Mexico. Remember that it was here in the 1950s that the controversial move was made from the Blue Ridge. The route is now getting into the Alleghenies, the westernmost range of the Appalachians. From that point, it's off into the wilderness—Mountain Lake Wilderness Area, that is. At this point, it's again over 4,000 feet at Potts Mountain, including a 2,000-foot ascent out of John's Creek Valley. Throughout this section, which stays for the most part over 3,000 feet, the hiker must be prepared to make rapid ascents and descents.

West of Sinking Creek Gap are two more wilderness areas, Mountain Lake Wilderness and Peters Mountain Wilderness, both of which contain peaks over 4,000 feet. Each offers side trails as well as other routes into the National Forest on either side. At its narrowest point in this section, the forest is two miles wide.

In Peters Mountain Wilderness, the Trail reaches the crest of Pine Swamp Ridge and the Peters Mountain Ridge, which forms the border between Virginia and West Virginia in the area. Staying over 3,000 feet for the next seventeen miles, it heads down the ridge in a west-southwesterly direction. Between Dickinson Gap and Symms Gap, an access trail called the Groundhog Trail has been blazed by the Kanawha Trail Association; it splits off to the northeast. It's the only Trail access from the West Virginia side in this section, and it's accessible from near the Full Gospel Assembly Church on WV Route 219.

Coming down off the ridges into the New River Narrows near the towns of Narrows and Pearisburg, the Trail meets one of the oldest and most interesting rivers in America. The contrarily named New River was actually formed in the Paleozoic Era, before the uplift of much of the Appalachian Range. In point of fact, it is said to be the second oldest river in the world. Geologists claim that the oldest is the Nile, with the third oldest title belonging to the French Broad, farther down the Trail route.

Once a much more forceful stream that cut through over four thousand feet of rock, the New River may in its earliest years have emptied into the forerunner of the St. Lawrence River. When the European and African continents were bashed up against the coast, it in all probability had its mouth in the shallow inland sea that formed so much of the rock that it now cuts through. For a time, during the last Ice Age, it was blocked from its usual destination in the Ohio River by glacial till, and it flowed instead into the Mississippi. It is the only Southern river to flow mostly north, and the only river to traverse the entire Appalachian Range—a feat it accomplished simply by being there before the Appalachians existed, and by cutting through them as they were formed.

AUTHOR'S CHOICE

In a section this long, there are more good day hikes than you can possibly name. One favorite, however, is a point-to-point hike over Tinker and Catawba Mountains near Daleville. You can start near Daleville and hike the entire 19.6 miles to Route 311 near Mason Cove, which makes for a nice two-day outing. For a day hike, cut into the AT at Scorched Earth Gap via the Andy Lane Trail and then hike the 9.6 miles to 311. The Andy Lane access, reached near the intersection of VA Routes 600 and 779, adds a couple of miles. For a long weekend, another alternative is to take a 29.5-mile loop with the AT and the entire Andy Lane Trail across North Mountain.

The section along Tinker and Catawba Mountains has spectacular overlooks at Tinker Cliffs and McAfee Knob. There are several shelters along this stretch as well. Watch your footing, and take water purification.

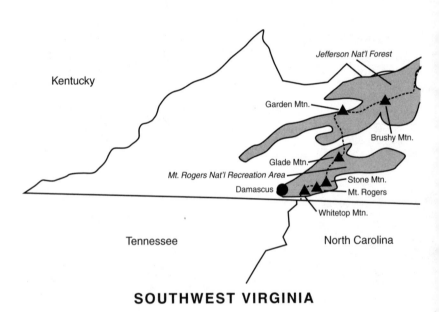

West Virginia

Kentucky

Jefferson Nat'l Forest

Garden Mtn.

Brushy Mtn.

Glade Mtn.

Mt. Rogers Nat'l Recreation Area

Stone Mtn.

Damascus

Mt. Rogers

Whitetop Mtn.

Tennessee

North Carolina

SOUTHWEST VIRGINIA

12 Southwest Virginia

Trail Distance:
New River to Damascus, Virginia . . . . 153.7 miles

Maintaining Clubs:
Roanoke Appalachian Mountain Club:
New River to VA 611 . . . . 34.0 miles
Piedmont Appalachian Trail Hikers:
Bland, Virginia, to the South Fork of the Holsten River . . . . 63.8 miles
Mt. Rogers Appalachian Trail Club:
South Fork of the Holsten River to Damascus . . . . 55.9 miles

INTRODUCTION

The Trail heads south from the New River Valley into the more westerly areas of the Alleghenies. Once a somewhat difficult area in which to maintain a good Trail route, the cooperation between the ATC and federal agencies has now secured virtually all the right-of-way, at least for the foreseeable future.

As the Appalachian Trail heads for Tennessee and North Carolina, it climbs into increasingly tall mountains and passes through more and more federally protected land. By the time it reaches Damascus and the Tennessee border, it will have climbed above 4,000 and even 5,000 feet, staying once again along the crest of a ridge easily as impressive as the Green and White Mountains far to the north. The narrow corridors through which it must pass in the more developed places to the north give way to acres and acres of National Forest and Wilderness Area—fabulous, beautiful, and wild lands that offer in full measure the recreation of the spirit that Benton MacKaye intended his Trail to offer to civilization-weary hikers.

GEOLOGY ALONG THE TRAIL

As the Trail moves farther to the west toward its route in the Alleghenies, it enters the zone of rocks formed in the ancient inland seas 400

175

million years ago. These rocks consist of sandstones, graywackes, and shales that accumulated until they were finally uplifted less than 300 million years ago in the Alleghany Orogeny, when all of Africa collided with North America, buckling the continent all the way to the borders of the Midwest. This was the final crunch, and the heaviest one of all.

West of the Allegheny Mountains lies the Allegheny Plateau, an uplifted area that was too far inland to be folded and faulted, but was raised up just the same. It forms much of the land in central and western New York and Pennsylvania and southward toward the Ohio Valley. Glacial gouges in the Allegheny Plateau, once hundreds and even thousands of feet deep, survive today as the Finger Lakes of New York. The Trail in southwest Virginia travels along this plateau region for much of its route.

HISTORY ALONG THE TRAIL

The early history of this part of southwestern Virginia was most heavily influenced by its remoteness from the coastal settlements. The first forays over the Appalachians tended to take more convenient routes such as those offered by the Potomac River farther north.

In addition to the remoteness, add the fact that over the hills the Shawnees, who controlled the eastern Ohio Valley and the surrounding area, took a dim view of squatters. So settlement proceeded slowly in these parts, accomplished largely by Irish and Scots-Irish who struck off into the wilderness to find a likely-looking spot in a fertile cove or valley.

One such settler was James Burke who, in 1748, led James Patton to a remote valley on the other side of Garden Mountain. Patton was an influential man in Virginia. He surveyed much of the western reaches of the colony, and, if he had not been killed by the Shawnee in the early days of the French and Indian War, he might have cast a shadow in the state's history to rival Washington's. Burke told Patton that he could show him sixteen thousand acres of fertile land to survey, in return for ten pounds and four hundred acres of his own. So Patton headed to the area, guided by the enterprising Burke. The problem was that Burke's ability to estimate acreage was as bad as his ability to recognize desireable land was good. The territory to which he guided Patton was easily as good as advertised but consisted of only about four thousand acres.

Nonetheless, Patton gave Burke the ten pounds and the use of the four hundred acres. Burke took the land he had wanted all along, in a small, extremely fertile valley just west of Garden Mountain; it is known today as Burke's Garden, and can be seen from the Trail off the ridge of Garden Mountain. This tract got its name when Burke, in one of his early trips to the valley, peeled some potatoes next to the fire. When he came back some months later, he found the peelings had grown into a fine patch of potatoes.

There's a footnote to this charming story: fifty years later, when Burke's descendants tried to establish title to Burke's Garden in order to sell it, they found that Patton's legal descendants had not forgotten Burke's failure to come up with sixteen thousand acres. The dispute descended into the typical I-said-he-said legal wrangling that is familiar today.

Around the time of the French and Indian War, efforts continued to purge the Shawnee presence. In 1756, Virginia Governor Dinwiddie ordered Major Andrew Lewis to take up the fight. He wrote to George Washington, "The Cherokees have taken up the Hatchet against the Shawanese and French, and have sent 130 of their warriors into New River, and propose to march immediately to attack and cut off the Shawanese in their towns. I design they shall be joined with three companies of rangers and Capt. Hogg's company, and I propose Colo. Stephens or Major Lewis to be commander of the party on this expedition."

The entire force of some 350 souls crossed via the New River Valley and traveled to the southwest, past the upper reaches of Holsten and Clinch Creeks to head along Sandy Creek for the Ohio Valley. They camped for a few days at Burke's Garden—Burke himself was evidently in the party as well. Their progress was slower than expected as they hacked their way through the forest, suffering hunger and the occasional Shawnee raid. They never were able to carry out the attacks, and they soon abandoned their plans. The party made its way back across the mountains in smaller groups, taking various routes, losing some men, and generally descending into one of the more spectacular screwups of the era. No blame seemed to have been attached to Major Lewis, however, and he later served under Washington during the Revolution as a brigadier general.

Eventually, settler pressure pushed the Shawnee out of the area, and the land rush was on. As the American Revolution made the Proclamation of 1763 less and less of a hindrance to westward expansion, people began moving west in earnest. Perhaps in anticipation of the outcome of the war, Daniel Boone in 1775 blazed the famous

Wilderness Road through the Cumberland Gap in the southwest tip of Virginia.

During the Civil War, the area, still sparsely populated, was something of a hotbed of Union sympathy within the Confederacy. It seems that the hardscrabble farmers in the area tended not to own slaves and didn't care much for fighting a war in support of slavery. Still, Confederate efforts to defend the Shenandoah Valley were successful until very late in the war, effectively keeping major Union pushes away from this part of Virginia, relegating the southwest to a role of mainly hosting Union raids, supported secretly by local sympathizers. And like the hills of Tennessee, this part of Virginia supplied troops to both sides of the conflict.

HISTORY OF THE APPALACHIAN TRAIL IN SOUTHWEST VIRGINIA

The accommodation of the Blue Ridge Parkway in the central section wasn't the end of the trouble with the Trail route. As we have seen, in the years that followed the rerouting around the Parkway, the land south of the James River became increasingly developed. The footpaths over which the Trail passed became roads, and the roads became highways. By the early '40s, it was conceded—even by Myron Avery— that something had to be done about it.

Enter the Roanoke Appalachian Trail Club. Under the guidance of the club's president, Jim Denton, an opportunity was found. The federal government had just purchased more land for the Jefferson National Forest to the west of the existing route, offering a new avenue over the Alleghenies. Denton proposed the change to Myron Avery, still president of the ATC, and Avery reluctantly agreed. First, though, he insisted that they blaze the entire section along the old route, even if most of it had to be on paved roads—which in fact it did. Priority number one was to reestablish the complete 2,000 miles. Denton and the club complied.

The new section, which begins just north of the New River in the central Virginia section, was blazed between 1952 and 1954, with the first blaze made on Sinking Creek Mountain on April 20, 1952. When it was dedicated in May of 1954, the Roanoke Appalachian Trail Club presented the relocation to the ATC, saying, "We, the Roanoke Appalachian Trail Club . . . proudly present to the Appalachian Trail Conference the consummation of a twenty-year dream. It cannot be said to be finished—and a completely finished trail would be one to avoid." It is possibly as eloquent a recognition as there has been in the history of the AT that the Trail is a living, growing thing, subject to constant change and improvement.

THE TRAIL IN SOUTHWEST VIRGINIA

Once across the New River, the Trail climbs steeply for over 2,500 feet to Angels Rest, a fine lookout over the Narrows. It then resumes its ridge-running ways, moving through the thick rhododendron and azalea thickets along the hilltops and down the streambed of Dismal Creek (it's not), passing by a side trail to Dismal Creek Falls. It then travels up high again, cresting Brushy Mountain. Still, that's fortunate. The ridge sides are unusually heavily stream-cut, and any deviation from the ridgeline would be brutal.

The section of Brushy Mountain west of Routes 77 and 52 makes a nice camping destination. It's fairly remote as things go in this narrow strip of protected land, and there are lots of camping areas along the rugged ridgetop. The Trail travels through the Little Wolf Creek Valley just south of the ridgeline (there is a trail along the crest, but due to the woods, no views in the warm months). The route then ascends the ridge again, goes over the other side to the northward-facing escarpment of Garden Mountain, and follows it all the way to Beartown Wilderness. From the top of Garden Mountain, hikers can look to the southwest into Burke's Garden. The Burke's Garden Fall Festival, which takes place in late September, is said to be a great event, with crafts, food, and cultural events.

After crossing 4,000-foot Chestnut Knob, the Trail valley-hops back toward the Blue Ridge, through Poor Valley, Rich Valley, and Crawfish Valley, until it reaches the Mt. Rogers National Recreation Area near Groseclose. This is one of the most popular areas of Trail in Virginia, and it runs almost all the rest of the way to Damascus and the Tennessee–North Carolina border.

Mt. Rogers National Recreation Area

It is here that, for the first time since New Hampshire, the Trail will climb over 5,000 feet, and it's the beginning of more high-elevation hiking to come as the route winds southward. It is named for Dr. William Barton Rogers, who, in 1840 as a University of Virginia professor, was hired by the state to submit reports on resource potential in the region. He later founded the Massachusetts Institute of Technology. Rogers mentions "Balsam" Mountain in his reports, a 5,729-foot peak that would be named for him in 1883.

Many of the trails in the area follow old logging roads and the beds of old railroad routes, placed there just after the turn of the century to haul the timber out of the area (like most areas in the East, the vast majority of the woodlands here are second growth). Where these roadbeds lie—such as in the Iron Mountain area just to the north of Mt. Rogers, on the old roadbed of the "Virginia Creeper Railroad"—the walking can be expected to be fairly uniform and pleasant, if a bit less challenging than an area that hasn't been smoothed over.

The Iron Mountains are a spur of the Alleghenies leading to the summits of Mt. Rogers and Whitetop Mountain, the two highest peaks in Virginia and among the highest in the Allegheny Range. This area is covered with alpine-type meadows as well as rock outcroppings made of sedimentary rocks that were thrust up from the bed of the Paleozoic inland sea. The summit of Mt. Rogers itself is one of the northernmost "balsams," a Southern term for a summit covered by balsam or spruce. The stand on Mt. Rogers is of Fraser fir, the only native Southeastern fir species. It's also known as "balsam" locally, and the smell of it will remind any Northern mountain hiker of home.

The area around Mt. Rogers is laced with fine side trails, including the former route of the AT across Iron Mountain, just to the north of its current route over the shoulder of Mt. Rogers. This trail parallels the current route from Chestnut Flats (just north of Mt. Rogers) almost the entire way to Damascus, Virginia. It can be used as a 50.7-mile circuit hike from either Damascus or VA Route 603 outside the small town of Trout Dale. Other trails loop around on either side of the AT, such as the many side trails on Stone Mountain that lead to several impressive side peaks.

The Mt. Rogers National Recreation Area is bordered to the south by the Grayson Highlands State Park (another area protected from development), which offers campsites and other access routes. Several trails lead from the parking areas at Grayson to the summit of Mt. Rogers and the surrounding area.

Since 1984, there have been two National Wilderness Areas within MRNRA: Lewis Fork Wilderness Area, which covers the immediate surroundings of Mt. Rogers itself; and the Little Wilson Creek Wilderness Area, in the Stone Mountain area. The Trail traverses sections of both.

The ridgeline in the Mt. Rogers area, if it can be called a ridgeline, has been heavily eroded by stream action. This has created countless side valleys and coves, each an environment unto itself. There are many meadows reminiscent of the "balds" so common on the summits to the south, as well as treeless areas covered instead by rhododendron and azalea. Others are simply open meadows, such as the one on Pine Mountain just east of Mt. Rogers.

Even though they're over 5,000 feet high, these peaks aren't truly over treeline the way their northern counterparts are. In spite of their occasional sub-alpine "balds," the summits are likely to be wooded. Some of the higher areas are even grazed—a thing that no northern farmer would even attempt above 4,000 feet.

After passing by Mt. Rogers (the summit is half a mile off the Trail on a blue-blazed route), the AT passes directly over Whitetop Mountain, the second highest in Virginia. It then descends gradually until it hovers around 3,000 feet, finally making the last drop off of the Cuckoo (a knob on Feathercamp Ridge) into Damascus, Virginia.

Damascus, called "Trailtown, U.S.A." by some, is an obligatory stop for thru-hikers. Famous for its hospitality to hikers, it makes a fine jumping-off point for the veritable supermarket of hiking in the Mt. Rogers National Recreation Area.

AUTHOR'S CHOICE

It's a no-brainer here, especially if you're coming from out of the area. The Mt. Rogers National Recreation Area is not only the home of the two tallest peaks in Virginia (Mt. Rogers and Whitetop Mountain); it also contains extensive crossing trails and side trails in addition to the AT. Nearby Balsam Mountain and Grayson Highlands complete a picture of rugged highland walking that offers something for everyone.

Virginia

Damascus

Tennessee

Watauga Lake Dam

North Carolina

Laurel Fork Gorge

Unaka Mtn.

Yellow Mtn. Gap
Roan Mtn.

Shelton Monument

Hot Springs

Snowbird Mtn.

Mt. Cammerer

Mt. Kephart   Mt. Guyot

Max Patch
Mtn.

*Pisgah Nat'l
Forest*

Clingmans Dome

Great Smoky Mtns. Nat'l Park

Thunderhead Mtn.

Bryson City

Asheville

Shuckstack

Nantahala Nat'l Forest

Tennessee

North Carolina

Georgia

South Carolina

TENNESSEE AND
NORTH CAROLINA

13 Tennessee and North Carolina

Trail Distance:
    Damascus, Virginia, to Fontana Dam, North Carolina .... 283.9 miles

Maintaining Clubs:
    Tennessee Eastman Hiking Club:
        Damascus, Virginia, to Spivey Gap .... 125.6 miles
    Carolina Mountain Club:
        Spivey Gap to Pigeon River........................... 87.8 miles
    Smoky Mountains Hiking Club:
        Pigeon River to Fontana Dam .... 70.5 miles

INTRODUCTION

The Appalachian Trail in this section succeeds in making the shift from the Alleghenies back to the western branch of the Blue Ridge Mountain complex. As it does, it enters the southern Appalachian forest in earnest. This area is noted for its almost endless variety of tree and plant types; in its more mountainous regions, it features successive floral types ranging from lowland pine forests, moving up through mixed deciduous forests of incredible vigor and variety, and finally to the boreal fir-spruce forests that look and smell much like their northern counterparts.

This is also a region of incredible topographical variety. The distance from the Great Valley of Tennessee to the Great Smoky Mountain summits just a few miles to the east, for example, constitutes a rise in elevation of over 5,000 feet in places. Summits over 6,000 feet will here be the rule rather than the exception, and the 5,000-foot level will be reached literally dozens of times before the southern terminus at Springer Mountain.

Incidentally, Springer is, by the time you reach Damascus, just 450 miles away. The Trail has reached the quarter pole, and it's heading into the stretch.

GEOLOGY ALONG THE TRAIL

The western reaches of the Blue Ridge complex are largely character-ized by a move to younger, more sedimentary, less metamorphosed bedrock. These are the sediments laid down on what was originally the continental shelf of pre-Appalachian North America's inland sea 600 million years ago.

This is a region characterized by parallel folds and thrust faults—great, thick slabs of bedrock that broke off at low angles and slid to the west over neighboring slabs. As we have seen in other sections, older rocks will sometimes be thrust over younger ones, much like a patio made of flagstones that has been scraped into a pile by a bulldozer. In places, the slabs will be piled up onto each other; in others, they will be jumbled in different directions.

In the more eastern areas, the sediments will be more clastic, like the sandstones and siltstones that eroded out of the old Grenville mountains and, later, from the new mountains formed just to the east by the earlier stages of the Appalachian Revolution. As you travel west, into the Great Valley regions, the bedrock will be even younger limestones, formed closer to the center of the inland sea. In the final episodes of the Appalachian Revolution, 250 to 350 million years ago, the older rocks were pushed to the west, thrusting up and over the younger layers. In the eastern Blue Ridge (which the Trail left north of Roanoke) it is the ancient Grenville gneisses and plutonic granites that have been uplifted. As a general rule, the farther away from the coast you are, the younger the rocks are. Along the ridges of the Unakas and the Smokies, the Trail passes largely over late Precambrian, Cambrian, and Ordovician bedrocks, occasionally (depending on how far east or west the route travels) dropping down to exposed rocks of either earlier or later eras. It is in these erosion-formed "windows" that we can see the configuration of the faults and folds in a given area. Watauga Lake, just south of Damascus, offers such a window to an area of younger rocks. Many of the coves in the various ranges will also offer views of what lies beneath.

NATURAL HISTORY ALONG THE TRAIL

Traveling from the lowlands to the peaks in the southern Appalachi-ans is much like traveling along the coastline from Richmond, Virginia, to somewhere up in Nova Scotia. In the process, you traverse approx-imately the same life zones.

Even here, the Ice Ages had a profound effect. Though the great ice sheets did not come this far south to scrape away topsoil and sculpt the bedrock, their effects are felt in the ecological makeup of this region. For example, the incredible variety of plant species in the mixed, mid-elevation deciduous forests has been attributed to climatic swings caused by the glaciers. In the relatively short warming periods, species from farther south would take hold; the colder times were sufficient to keep them from taking over from the more boreal species.

Some experts theorize that the balds on southern summits (there are said to be somewhere in the neighborhood of eighty of them) are a remnant of a time when these peaks were above the treeline. Just what has kept them clear (they are at present gradually being taken over by the surrounding forests) is a matter of conjecture. Many have been grazed by farmers' livestock for the past several hundred years; they may also have been burned off by Native Americans. Many of the balds may endure; the Forest and Park Services are keeping several clear, to preserve them for posterity.

On the summits and in the areas immediately below, the spruce-fir forest is king. Left there by the retreating glaciers, the conifer-clad highlands form islands of a more typically northern ecosystem. Holding sway as the dominant species down to the 5,000-foot level (though boundaries are never distinct in this mild climate), they are also found mixed in at lower levels, while still containing some of the mighty monarchs that made them such a paradise for loggers—huge, straight giants that three people can't gird with their arms fingertip to fingertip. Southern fir is still written into the beams and studs of northern building codes.

Unfortunately, what the Forest Service and the Park Service now protect from logging may fall before other threats. The ridgelines in the Great Smokies are crested with the dead trunks of trees killed by the balsam woolly aphid, a parasite that bores into the bark and breeds in the delicate cambium layer. Then, too, there is the as-yet-unmeasured damage caused by acid rain; as the political argument plods on, otherwise healthy trees—especially red spruce—wither and die.

On a more pleasant note, the deciduous forests in the middle elevations continue to thrive. These woodlands contain not only species that New Englanders would recognize but also countless others. In one cove, you may find yourself walking through a Southern variety of maple-beech forest; on a nearby ridgeline, it may be oak-hickory. Then, there are the sometimes-huge yellow poplars that Northerners know mostly from cultivated specimens, and which they call tulip trees. At the borders between deciduous and coniferous forests, there will even be the birches so dear to Northeasterners.

The Southern Appalachians are home to many animals (although the elk is gone, remembered mostly in place names), most of which would be recognizable to people in the North. There are, however, a few exceptions. Most noticeable is the European wild boar. Brought over early in the twentieth century for a nearby game park, a number of them escaped around 1909 and took hold in the Great Smoky Mountains area. They are ill-tempered and territorial and revel in rooting up ground cover with their noses. They are beloved only by local hunters, which is perhaps just as well.

The wild turkey has remained strong in the southern ranges, and hikers will hear them—if not see them—often. They are heir to the gobblers that amazed the eyes and delighted the palates of Spanish and English explorers three and four centuries ago, when there were still birds over fifty pounds in these hills. Although mostly smaller, these turkeys are just as wily as their ancestors.

HISTORY ALONG THE TRAIL

These mountains were once (and, in some places, still are) the home of the marvelous Cherokee people. This was the nation that developed a written language (the only Native American people to do so) and that formed a government and a society as well organized as that of the Europeans who conquered them.

The term "Cherokee," like so many other tribal names that have endured, was probably not what they called themselves originally. It may have come from a Chocktaw word meaning "Cave People," or perhaps a Creek word meaning "People of a Different Speech." According to one source, they called themselves "Yunwiya." In any case, the closest relatives of the Cherokees were the various Iroquois nations to the north. The Cherokee language is a very distant relative of Iroquois—truly "different speech."

The first European to meet the Cherokees was Hernando de Soto in 1540 (more about him in a bit). Intent as he was on finding riches, he apparently noticed little about them beyond the fact that they didn't have any gold. Their next contact was with Spanish captain Juan Pardo, who sallied west from his base on Parris Island, following orders to "discover and conquer territory from there to Mexico." He made it about as far as the Blue Ridge in North Carolina, where he established a fort for a couple of years.

In that area, he probably encountered the "Valley Cherokee," who lived in the eastern foothills of the Blue Ridge. Between there and the Smokies lived the "Middle Cherokee," with the "Overhill Cherokee" located west of the Smokies and Unakas. At the time, there were probably somewhere in the neighborhood of twenty-two thousand Cherokees in the area. They had originally come from the Great Lakes region but had been forced south by pressure from the Delawares and their own cousins, the Iroquois.

During the Revolution, the Cherokees supported the British, mainly because the colonists had their usual track record of taking over Native American lands without much attention to legal niceties. Their support, however, was not influential: in their two attempts to aid the Crown—raids on Continental forts at Eaton's Station and Ft. Watauga—they failed badly.

After the Revolution, the Cherokees made the best of the situation, as was their habit. They adopted the colonists' methods of agriculture and architecture. Soon allied with their former enemies, they helped Andrew Jackson in his war against the Creeks.

In fact, the early years of the American Republic were a kind of short-lived Golden Age for the Cherokees. Their culture thrived in this period, as did their fortunes. It was during this time, in 1821, that Sequoyah, a half-Cherokee who had served with Jackson, invented the Cherokee alphabet and written language. So ingenious was this system that virtually the entire tribe became literate within months. In 1828, a Cherokee newspaper was founded, the *Cherokee Phoenix.*

For all these reasons, what was about to happen to this most Europeanized of Native American cultures should have been unthinkable—as if anything that European settlers and their descendants did to the Native peoples can be described as "thinkable."

What happened to them was, however, predictable. Land speculators entered the scene, eager to move the Cherokees off their lands and not too careful about how they went about it. They engaged in constant anti-Cherokee agitation, which bore some tragic results. In 1814, for example, as Chief Junaluska and his warriors fought at Jackson's side against the Creeks, other white soldiers were back in Cherokee villages, raping and pillaging.

Then, in 1827, the speculators discovered that there was gold on Cherokee land in northern Georgia. Whipped up by gold fever, the

Georgia state government immediately declared all Cherokee lands forfeit, treaties be damned. It was a neat package—Native Americans were forbidden to dig for gold on their own land, and they were also forbidden to testify against whites or to resist in any way the seizure of their lands.

By 1836, efforts by the Cherokees themselves—and by sympathetic whites such as Congressmen David Crockett, Henry Clay, Daniel Webster, and Edward Everett—proved to be of no avail. Not even the law could help: informed of a Supreme Court decision in favor of the Cherokees, President Andrew Jackson quipped, "[Chief Justice] John Marshall has made his decision. Now let him enforce it."

In spite of widespread sympathy for the plight of these people (one general, sent in 1836 to prevent a supposed Cherokee uprising, gathered his men together and pointedly informed them that they would instead protect the Cherokees from harm, and that the whites deserved no such protection), General Winfield Scott was sent south in 1838 to relocate them to Oklahoma.

Thus came to pass the Trail of Tears. After gathering seventeen thousand Cherokees, Scott herded them into what amounted to concentration camps. From there, they were marched—as quickly as possible, on starvation rations—all the way to a desolate plain in Oklahoma. Over four thousand died.

Some stayed behind. Anyone who has wandered the Great Smokies and other ranges in Cherokee territory can understand how Winfield Scott couldn't possibly gather them all. Those that remained (some one thousand or so) fought and hid, raided and endured—and somehow survived. They were only allowed to come down from the hilltops years later, when one of their elders, Tsali, agreed to surrender himself with two of his sons. According to the agreement, they would be executed for murder, and the hunt for the rest of the Cherokees would stop. Gallant Tsali, whose only sin was killing one of Scott's men while resisting brutal capture, handed himself over to federal authorities near the present town of Cherokee. The federals, too, kept their part of the bargain, in all its gruesome particulars. Later, the Qualla Indian Reservation was established on the eastern edge of the Great Smokies, largely on land donated by W. H. Thomas, a merchant and philanthropist who had maintained contact with the band during its flight.

One little-known legacy of the Cherokee Nation is the inspiration for the Uncle Remus tales. Apparently great storytellers, they also told of a race of little people who lived in the hills. About the size of children, very pretty, and with long hair down to their ankles, they were said to lead lost children home, and, on occasion, to come in the night to do work for good people.

It's ironic that the people that the settlers forced from the land should view the wilderness as such a friendly place.

At Hot Springs on the French Broad River, the Trail crosses the route of Hernando de Soto, who in 1540 came up out of present-day Asheville via Hickory Nut Pass and crossed over the mountains at Hot Springs on his way to the Knoxville area. From there, he continued to his fateful crossing of the Mississippi, which, promising lots of mud and not much gold, he passed by as though it were of little consequence.

De Soto's must have been a bizarre entourage. He had begun the previous year in Florida with a train of some six hundred iron-clad conquistadors and a herd of a few hundred pigs. These animals were intended for consumption by his men, but for the first year, he refused to allow any to be slaughtered.

Like all the Spanish military leaders in the New World, de Soto was a working, breathing son of a bitch. He regarded the native peoples as something less than human, and torturing a Native to death in response to news he did not wish to hear was as natural to him as eating and sleeping. Small wonder that the Native chiefs learned quickly to tell him exactly what would please him.

News of gold, of course, was what he longed to find. Unfortunately, there really was no gold to be had in the area. (Even the modest Georgia lodes that would come to haunt the Cherokees three centuries hence were unknown then.) So the chiefs devised a method of dealing with their rude, overbearing, overeating, and generally undesirable guest. "Sorry," they would say, "no gold here. But our neighbors, just west of here—they have lots of gold. Just head up through that pass and ask them. They'll be glad to give you a bunch of it."

They might then provide him with a guide, who would stay with de Soto just long enough to see him over the border and then vanish. De Soto, who doubtless caught wise to what was being done to him, really had no choice in the matter. "Oh, sure," he would say. "Well, men, let's go. It's over the next hill for us."

What a sight he must have made—clanking and oinking down the narrow valleys, followed by his men and his swine. The latter had, of course, bred in the interim, and de Soto the conquistador was followed by six hundred disgruntled men and literally thousands of grunting, squealing pigs.

De Soto's legacy, though, remains. Upon sighting the high mountains ahead, he promptly named them the Appalachians, after the Appalache tribe he encountered along the Gulf Coast. But lest this explorer's name be forever besmirched by the fact that he named the great range after the wrong tribe, it should also be mentioned that his estate contained another interesting item. When he died on the banks of the Mississippi the next year, his share of the expedition's pork consisted of over two thousand pigs. And in local terms, that's making good, indeed!

Like the rest of the Appalachians, the southern parts of the range presented a formidable barrier to western expansion for several centuries. For that reason, the lion's share of settlement came not from the east but from the north, as immigrants from Pennsylvania made their way down the Great Valley along the New and Holston Rivers.

It really wasn't until the latter part of the eighteenth century that overland routes were found from the east. This was the era of Daniel Boone, who established several routes to eastern Tennessee and Kentucky. Too footloose to stay still for long, ol' Dan kept moving west, finally hanging up his long rifle near Defiance, Missouri, on the Missouri River.

It should be noted that Boone and his compadres pushed west in defiance of the British edict of 1763 against western expansion. The Tennesseans and Kentuckians paid even less attention (if that was possible) to the prohibition than did their Pennsylvanian and Virginian counterparts.

Those who did settle in the coves and valleys were of necessity an independent breed. Sequestered by geography from their eastern neighbors, they developed ways of their own. Largely too poor to own slaves, the sympathies of these "mountaineers" lay largely with the Union during the Civil War, to whom they sent more volunteer soldiers than they did to the South.

This mountain way of life has been slow to disappear. Famous in literature (especially in the *Foxfire* series, which documented mountain crafts, folk medicines, cooking techniques, and the like, and which I recommend highly), it is also preserved within the Great Smoky Mountains National Park, with a reconstructed mountaineer homestead at the Oconaluftee Ranger Station on the south border of the park, and a more extensive museum of mountain lore and crafts at Cades Cove to the north.

THE TRAIL IN TENNESSEE AND NORTH CAROLINA

Leaving Damascus, Virginia, and crossing into Tennessee, the AT immediately climbs back up to around 4,000 feet. It then heads off in a generally southwesterly direction, along the ridge crest of Holston Mountain.

Holston and its neighboring ridge, the Iron Mountains, look too similar, too parallel, to be together by mere coincidence. They are, as a matter of fact, the two rims of a very regular syncline. The sandstone from which they are constructed has resisted erosion on either side. To the west, Holston is bordered by the Great Appalachian Valley, over which its sandstone was thrust; to the east of Iron Mountain lies a geologic "window" to the younger shales and limestones that lie underneath the overthrust.

The Trail in this area, like most stretches on Forest Service land, is well graded and protected from erosion.

This area is full of side trails. When the Trail leaves Holston Mountain at Double Springs, an old route of the AT (abandoned in 1954) continues south along Holston's ridge for another 13.1 miles to Holston High Knob. Another blue blazer runs from near where the AT reaches the crest of the Iron Mountain ridge after leaving Holston Mountain. This route starts about three miles down a narrow road from there, then runs sixteen miles back northeast, almost all the way to Damascus, before a short side trail hooks it up to the AT again. In addition, there are numerous side trails to both the AT and the Iron Mountains route from the Shady Valley area along Beaverdam Creek.

Once on the Iron Mountains, the Trail once again heads in the same general direction it followed on Holston Mountain. Soon after joining the ridge, it passes near the grave and monument to hermit "Uncle Nick" Grindstaff (the trail guide will tell you exactly where). It then follows the narrow, at times doubled, ridge of Iron Mountain for fifteen miles until it descends again to Watauga Lake.

The lake, a 1949 TVA project, is near the site of Fort Watauga, raided unsuccessfully by the Cherokees in their efforts to aid the British during the Revolution. It is also on the line of the Iron Mountain Fault, the fracture between rock strata where the sandstone of Iron and Holston Mountains slid over the limestones and shales of the lower valleys. The fault is visible on the eastern end of the dam, with the older sandstones clearly visible above the younger limestones.

This next section is especially nice. The Trail crosses Watauga Dam and, after passing by a couple of USFS Recreation Areas, heads up onto Pond Mountain, just to the south of Watauga Lake. Once up on the ridge, it travels through some rugged country and passes a 1.1-mile side trail to the summit of Pond Mountain. In this area, the Trail passes over a succession of knobs, and there are campsites and many side trails in the highlands.

West of the Watauga Lake geologic "window," the Trail goes up onto older, more metamorphosed quartzite formations. On top of the Pond Mountain ridge, the quartzite contains a common AT feature— the *Skolithus* wormholes left by some of the earliest forms of life to exist on earth. These have remained, even though the rocks that formed from the beach sands in which they lived have been crushed into hard quartzite.

The hardness of the rock is also responsible for Laurel Fork Gorge, the narrow, cliff-lined defile through which the Trail passes after descending from the Pond Mountain ridge. This exceedingly rugged stretch of trail covers 2.7 miles, passes by some fine forty-foot waterfalls, and contains a stone shelter. Laurel Fork is a rocky, tumbling stream with its sources in the high country.

After leaving Laurel Fork Gorge, the AT enters Dennis Cove (another geologic window), which is home to yet another Recreation Area. This one has campsites.

Leaving Dennis Cove, the AT once again enters the woods, climbing up onto White Rocks Mountain (named for the white quartzite of which it is composed). Passing by Coon Den Falls, it then quickly ascends to the White Rocks Mountain lookout tower. Perched at over 4,000 feet, the tower offers great views in nice weather.

At the end of the White Rocks Mountain section, the AT meets up once again with several side trails that it crossed or that were connected to it by other side trails back on Pond Mountain. These routes, lined up with the various small roads and jeep trails, offer fine access to this rugged little section of National Forest.

After passing by civilization again at U.S. Route 19E, the AT enters North Carolina and ascends Hump Mountain. From here, it sawtooths over a few knobs until it descends slightly into Yellow Mountain Gap. Since the state border runs along the ridgeline in this area, the Trail will cross back and forth from North Carolina to Tennessee.

It was at Yellow Mountain Gap, in October of 1780, that a strange army passed. The story is a curious one. Up until that time, the mountaineers had done all they could do to withstand the constant barrage of attacks by the Cherokees, who were allied with the British. That they succeeded in defending this part of the struggling Republic is a tribute to their fortitude.

The standoff might have remained until the end of the war if it weren't for the arrogance of one Colonel Patrick Ferguson, a British officer at the head of a force of Tories. He sent word over that unless the mountaineers declared allegiance to George III, he would "march [his] army over the mountains, hang [their] leaders, and lay [their] country waste with fire and sword."

This message wasn't received in quite the way that Ferguson had in mind. Feeling that they had been insulted, the "Overmountain" men gathered at Sycamore Shoals (today Elizabethton, Tennessee), and decided to teach Ferguson a lesson. Gathering 1,000 men, they set out along Bright's Trace through Yellow Mountain Gap to where they heard the British could be found, over in North Carolina. Their little force reportedly expanded to over 1,800 (though the figure has been estimated as low as 800) as they marched, and they caught Ferguson and his 1,125 Tories at Kings Mountain on October 7, 1780. Ninety minutes later, Ferguson lay dead, his men either killed or captured. Nobody escaped. It was a turning point in the Revolution, opening for Cornwallis another front to the south. Their work done and their honor satisfied, the Overmountain boys hurried back home to take up the fight against the Cherokees once again.

The section near Yellow Mountain Gap, which travels along the Tennessee–North Carolina border, lies above Roan Mountain State Park. Day hikers can find several access points from the park.

Passing down the ridge to Roan Mountain, the AT enters the first groves of Fraser fir (apart from an isolated grove in Shenandoah National Park). This is the aromatic tree that will cover the summits of even the highest mountains for the rest of the way to Springer Mountain. Even a Northerner like me can sit beside a grove of these trees, close his eyes, take a deep breath, and imagine he's in the White Mountains of New Hampshire. It's appropriate. Roan Mountain is the first time since the Whites that the Trail has climbed above 6,000 feet.

Roan Mountain is also known for its "Cloudland Rhododendron Gardens." Not actually cultivated, the name refers to the profusion of pink Catawba rhododendrons that blooms there in mid to late June.

There are also patches of Scotch heather, probably transplanted by a homesick Scotsman. The ridge followed by the Trail also features several balds.

After descending Roan Mountain, the Trail crosses Iron Mountain, still following the state line, and enters Iron Mountain Gap. This passage, along with Bright's Trace through Yellow Mountain Gap, offered the most popular overland routes to the west in this part of the Appalachians.

Iron Mountain Gap also marks the beginning of the Unaka Mountains, which is, along with the Great Smokies to the south, one of the western ranges of this split of the Blue Ridge. The ridge has a road across the top. While it might detract from the wild feel of the area, it does make this nice area easily accessible. There are several balds and open summits, and the views are quite good.

After descending the Unaka ridge, the Trail crosses the Nolichucky at the northern end of that river's spectacular gorge. Once on the other side, the Trail climbs rapidly to the crest of Cliff Ridge, where there are fine views of the gorge it just crossed. The roadbuilders have yet to find a way through the gorge; maybe they never will. The AT then proceeds over Temple Ridge and No Business Knob, which is said to be named for an unidentified hiker who got hung up in the thickets and decided that he had no business being there in the first place.

This is an area of laurel, rhododendron, hardwood, and pine. The Trail does a fair amount of zig-zagging about to stay on the crest of the ridge at around the 3,500-foot level and to avoid descending into any of the numerous valleys. When it comes down into Spivey Gap on U.S. Route 19W, it reaches the end of the Tennessee Eastman Hiking Club section and enters the Carolina Mountain Club's area of responsibility.

On the southern side of Spivey Gap, the Trail climbs very steeply up to High Rocks (a vertical grunt of over a thousand feet), then goes over 5,185-foot Little Bald (which isn't a bald) and 5,516-foot Big Bald (which is a rather nice one, as a matter of fact). By the time hikers reach Big Bald, they have ascended over 2,200 feet in 5.1 miles.

Big Bald, by the way, is owned on its south side by a development company that has put in a network of roads and summer homes. The roads are for the most part out of sight of the Trail. Habitation is not new to Big Bald, though. In the early nineteenth century, it hosted a hermit, David Greer, or "Old Hog Greer." He seems mainly to have chosen the solitary life because of a violent temper that rendered him unfit for the company of humans. He was said to live in a hole he dug under Greer Rock, near the summit of Big Bald, though no trace of his den is to be seen today.

Once down from Big Bald, the Trail leaves the Cherokee National Forest for a time, traveling over private land, some of which is open country suitable for farming. This goes on for about ten miles, with the AT traveling along the ridge of the Bald Mountains, keeping close to the boundary of small tracts of forest. It eventually reenters federal land—this time, the Pisgah National Forest—as it crosses deeper into North Carolina east of Hot Springs.

In Pisgah, the Trail stays along the Bald Mountains, ascending to around 4,200 feet for several miles. It gets into serious rhododendron country here, and for those unfamiliar with the frustration of a rhododendron thicket, a quick trip off to the side of the AT in this section will cure their curiosity.

Pisgah is also fairly wide in places, offering day hikers a number of side trails from which to mount loop routes. This is especially true in the long section east of Route 208 in Allen Gap, which has two shelters and a handful of trails leading off to the north. It's noted for its open crests and pleasant campgrounds.

It is in this section that hikers may find the famous twin tombstones just southeast of Big Butt Mountain, familiar to many around the country from pictures in magazines. These mark the graves of William and David Shelton, a nephew and uncle who, like so many around these parts, enlisted with the Union during the Civil War. Returning to attend a family gathering, they were caught and killed by a Confederate force nearby.

South of Allen Gap, the Trail again follows the Bald Mountain ridge. The best views are at the Rich Mountain fire tower, though Lover's Leap has fine views of the scenic French Broad River Valley five hundred feet below. Throughout these sections, backpackers can find good campsites, and there are shelters located at convenient intervals.

Coming down off of the Bald Mountain ridge, the Trail crosses the road that goes into Hot Springs. It's typical of many of the routes in this part of North Carolina: windy enough to twist a mule. Fortunately, the Trail crosses it and makes a scenic climb up Lover's Leap (said to have been named by the Cherokees for a young woman who hurled herself off of it after her lover was killed by a rival) before descending into Hot Springs.

Hot Springs has a long history. As the name suggests, it is the former home of a famous spa, which grew around the waters of the warm springs on the site. It is also where de Soto passed through in 1540. It seems impossible for him to have been disappointed with the magnificent valley of the French Broad, but he was. Who knows what he saw, but perhaps Benton MacKaye could have straightened him out with his advice for hikers: "To walk, to see, and to see what you see."

Beyond Hot Springs, the Trail starts heading south again, in a leisurely fashion at first. It passes right through town (the Trail Register is in the lobby of the Post Office), past a Jesuit monastery that offers a hostel to thru-hikers, and up into the hills again.

Don't be fooled. This easy stuff won't last long. Seven miles out of Hot Springs, with the Trail having climbed only 700 or 800 feet, it's nosebleed time again. Upon reaching the base of Bluff Mountain, the AT goes on to climb 2,000 feet in about three miles.

This entire section goes up and down a lot after that. It eventually climbs Max Patch Mountain, which, like Siler Bald in the Nantahalas and several side peaks in the Smokies, is being cleared to retain its bald character. Chances are that the Max Patch experience had a lot to do with the decision to clear Siler Bald—it makes a fine destination, with excellent views all the way to Mt. Mitchell in the east.

This part of the Trail is in a relatively narrow corridor, making access generally available only along the AT and from narrow roads at two points, Lemon Gap and Garenflo Gap. There is also a dirt road just below Max Patch Mountain.

The last section of the AT before Great Smoky Mountains National Park crosses Snowbird Mountain, a 4,000-foot-high hump in the southernmost reaches of the Pisgah National Forest. Snowbird has given its name to the Snowbird Formation, a group of sandstones and quartzites that are the oldest rocks of those that form the Smokies. The views of the Smokies from the Snowbird fire tower are among the finest to be had.

Great Smoky Mountains National Park

The section of the Appalachian Trail that traverses this park is one of the crown jewels of the entire system. Despite this being a popular, heavily attended National Park, its layout nevertheless allows hikers to get away from civilization at most times of year.

Great Smoky Mountains National Park, unlike some other parks (e.g., Shenandoah), is not a linear, ridgeline affair. The highest mountains are along a cordillera that generally runs, like the Trail in this part, east to west, but there is an average of twelve to fifteen miles to the edge of the park on either side. Also, unlike other federal lands, there are simply no roads in most sections. Except for the major route through the park at Newfound Gap, and a few others that head partway inland at a few points, you really have to work to get to the Trail in most places.

As you'd expect in a National Park, camping in the backcountry requires a permit. And as is the case in other parks, these are free and may be obtained at ranger stations and at self-service stands at several entry points. There are a number of restrictions, mostly intended to reduce the impact on the land, as well as to spread out human activity in order to lessen crowding and, more importantly, the feeling of being crowded.

Like other trails in other National Parks, the Trail through the Great Smokies was built by the Park Service and is maintained in cooperation with the local Appalachian Trail club—in this case, the Smoky Mountains Hiking Club. Like all Park Service trails, the trails in the Smokies were put in with a lot of CCC effort in the '30s.

Geologically, the mountains of the Great Smokies are mostly formed of late Precambrian sediments, rocks laid down on the continental shelf of pre-Appalachian North America. These are mainly sandstones with some siltstones and shales mixed in.

Again, the farther you go toward the western edge of the ridges— in this case, toward the north—the younger the rocks become. In the southern Smokies, there are several earlier Prcambrian granitic domes reminiscent of Old Rag Mountain in the Shenandoahs, as well as stream-cut "windows" (Big Cove is an example) to the older rocks. In the north, on the other hand, the windows are to younger Ordovician limestones and dolomites—examples include Cades Cove and Wear Cove.

These heavily folded and faulted mountains are the result of a monumental shove from, in all probability, the southeast, which both pushed up the older basement rocks under the middle-aged sandstones and pushed the plates of sandstone over the younger rocks to the north and northeast. Erosion did the rest.

The flora and fauna of the park are what you'd expect from an ecosystem that has been carefully protected since 1930: healthy and diverse. With the exception of the balsam woolly aphid problem among the fir trees at high elevation, the tree and plant life can best be described as vigorous.

The park maintains a staff of experts on all aspects of the wilderness to be found within it. They can be contacted at the Park Headquarters on the Gatlinburg end of the Newfound Gap Road.

The park deserves its status as a popular destination for hikers and backpackers. Not only does the AT run along the highest ridges and through some of the wildest sections, but there are side trails aplenty in literally all parts of the Smokies—mostly of the even-footbedded, erosion-protected, National Park Service variety. To enumerate all the loops, side trips, base-camp-and-day-hike venues, and nature walks would take a volume in itself. Get hold of a copy of *Hiking in the Great Smokies* from the Smoky Mountains Hiking Club. It's also available from ATC headquarters.

The names of land features in the park are much more logical than in most areas. In 1929, as the Park Service was preparing to issue the first maps of the soon-to-be National Park, it formed a commission of knowledgeable people to go through the various (and often contradictory or redundant) names and to straighten out any problems. What resulted was the elimination of many of the duplications—there were, for example, a dozen "Mill Creeks," since every body of water with a mill on it was so named. There were also numerous "Indian Creeks" and "Fork Ridges." Sometimes a peak or gap would be known as one thing in North Carolina and another in Tennessee.

One member of the commission even tried to delve into the origin of the term "Smoky Mountains," discovering that the expression was already in use in 1789, when the state of North Carolina ceded its western land to the federal government. It was, coincidentally, similar to the designation used by the Cherokees, which was said to be "Shacona-ga," which meant "blue, like smoke."

Many of the names are merely taken from the people who used to live in the area. Mt. Mingus, for example, probably comes from the same Mingus family that ran a mill near the present-day site of the Oconaluftee Ranger Station.

Another result of the name survey was that where duplications were eliminated, certain land forms were left without names and could be dedicated to whatever the Park Service chose—people, usually. One example is the first peak that the AT crosses once within the park boundary: Mt. Cammerer, named for one-time National Park Service director Arno B. Cammerer.

Cammerer is an ascent you'll pay for—in about four miles, the Trail climbs about 3,000 feet—but there are several rewards: a magnificent view from the lookout tower, and the fact that you've just done the lion's share of the gruntwork for accessing the nearly 6,000-foot ridge that leads to Newfound Gap.

First, though, you have to dip down into Low Gap, just the other side of the 5,000-foot Mt. Cammerer–Sunset Knob hump. Down the northern slope from the gap is the valley of Cosby's Creek. Near the source of the creek is the place called "Cryin' Creek," named for an incident in which a man accidentally shot and killed his brother while the two were bear hunting. After Low Gap, the Trail ascends to the top of 5,145-foot Cosby Knob, then finally makes its way to the elevation level that will be its norm in the Smokies (5,600 to 5,800 feet).

First stop is the Mt. Guyot area. After crossing 6,356-foot Old Black, the AT traverses near the summit of the 6,621-foot peak named after Arnold Guyot, the Swiss-born scientist and explorer who did so much of the early work in the Appalachians. He spent time in the Smokies before 1860, making maps and noting elevations of the mountains. Mt. Guyot is the second highest peak in the Smokies (and the second Mt. Guyot on the AT).

After crossing the virgin fir-spruce forest of Mt. Chapman (named for Colonel David C. Chapman, who was instrumental in the creation of the park) and Mt. Sequoyah (named, of course, for the great inventor of the Cherokee syllabary), the Trail starts down the long, winding ridge of Peck's Corner and Laurel Top, staying within a few feet of the 5,800-foot level for five miles. There are good views from the fairly frequent overlooks.

Once over Laurel Top, the route descends slightly before climbing sharply up 6,150-foot Mt. Kephart (named for the author of *Our Southern Highlanders,* considered one of the most authoritative volumes ever written on the southern mountaineers). A 0.8-mile side trail leads to the summit and the Jumpoff a few feet below; the best views are from the Jumpoff. From there, it's a short trip down to Newfound Gap at 5,045 feet.

From Newfound Gap, the Trail parallels a Park Service road that runs to the top of Clingmans Dome, a distance of 7.5 miles. After passing a side trail to 5,802-foot Mt. Mingus, it reaches Indian Gap, site of the old Cherokee Trail, which ran from the lowlands to the south and east to the Great War Trail, through the Great Valley on the other side of Gatlinburg, Tennessee.

After crossing the wooded summit of Mt. Collins (6,188 feet) and dipping into Collins Gap (5,886 feet), the AT ascends to its highest point in the entire route from Maine to Georgia: 6,643-foot Cling-mans Dome. Formerly called Smoky Dome, it is named for General Thomas L. Clingman, who first measured the peak in 1858. To those familiar with the bare rock summit of Mt. Washington in New Hampshire, which is over a thousand feet above treeline, it will come as something of a surprise that Clingmans' summit is thickly wooded. Only by climbing up the oddly shaped lookout tower can the hiker see the surrounding countryside.

In his excellent contribution to "The Naturalist's America" series, *The Appalachians,* Maurice Brooks takes up the interesting question of how much higher would the southern Appalachians have to be in order to top the treeline. Actually referring to 6,684-foot Mt. Mitchell in the Black Mountains of the eastern Blue Ridge (though noting that the observation tower on Clingmans Dome might just top Mitchell, making observers there "the highest individuals in eastern North America"), he concludes that if "fifteen hundred feet were added to Mitchell's summit, the new mountain would, I believe, reach treeline."

Be that as it may, you will not find solitude on the AT's highest point. A road leads to a parking lot within about a half mile of the spot, and the trail uphill, though a moderately stiff climb, is paved over with macadam. Still, if you close your eyes, the smell of the Fraser fir and spruce lets you imagine you are elsewhere, and as always, it's perfectly permissible to park the car and hike away from the crowds.

One side trail of note leads south from the Forney Ridge parking lot near the summit of Clingmans to Andrew Bald, 2.5 miles away. It's said to be one of the finest balds in the Appalachians.

The Trail, though, strikes out in another direction, still heading west along the North Carolina–Tennessee border. First stop is 6,582-foot Mt. Buckley, named for S. B. Buckley, who climbed with Cling-man. On this end of the park, the Trail is less often graded carefully. It also travels more through typical mixed hardwood forest and less in the fir and spruce that typifies the eastern end of the park.

From Buckley, the route crosses the narrow ridge called the Narrows, leaving the crest only to avoid ledges. It then ascends 5,607-foot Silers Bald.

Silers is interesting for two reasons. First, it was in the early years of AT planning (before 1930) a bone of contention between the Georgia Appalachian Trail Club and the Smoky Mountains Hiking Club. The former wanted the AT to end in the Mt. Oglethorpe–Springer Mountain area; the latter was just as anxious to have it traverse the entire length of the Smoky Mountains. In order for the Trail to reach Springer, rather than heading for the more westerly (and, to the Georgians' minds, inferior) terminus in the Cohuttas, the plan called for the AT to leave the Smokies at Silers Bald and head down into the Nantahalas. A compromise brought the Trail down farther west, first at Cheoah Dam and later, once it was constructed, at Fontana Dam. It would then head back east for a while into the Nantahalas.

The second point of interest surrounding Silers Bald is its name. Memorializing the Siler family, who once grazed cattle on the summit (names like "Sweat Heifer Trail, near Newfound Gap, begin to make sense in that context), it stands as a reminder of what Maurice Brooks called the lifestyle "from cove to bald." The necessity to find lands for grazing drove the lowland cove dwellers far into the hills in search of the precious open land of the balds. Had they not existed, the hill people would, Brooks opines, have been more the stay-at-home low-landers and not the kind of people they were (and are): isolated, rugged, and independent.

From Silers Bald, the AT passes Buckeye Gap on its way to the junction with Miry Ridge Trail. Miry Ridge's name is pretty self-explanatory, especially for hikers who have wandered off the trail into the black muck that has accumulated in the concave depression along its length over the years.

Once past yet another Sams Gap (the last gap of this name lies 125 miles to the north), the AT enters a seventeen-mile stretch—almost the rest of the way in the Smokies—of strenuous up-and-down hiking. Perhaps the steepest section is the short hop up from Beechnut Gap to Thunderhead.

At 5,527 feet, Thunderhead has given its name to the late Precambrian sandstone out of which much of the Great Smoky Range is made. It offers fantastic views as well.

Running north from the Thunderhead–Rocky Top massif is Defeat Ridge. This isn't named for any dire battle, but rather after an exercise in democracy that took place just before the Civil War on the part of some old-time Cherokee trail builders.

Faced with a choice of routes for the Anderson Road, which had been proposed to run from northern Cades Cove to other settlements on the Tuckasegee Creek to the south, the Cherokees put it to a vote. Not having the "V" sound in their language, they designated the ridge that won the vote as "Bote Ridge," and ever after referred to the rejected route as "Defeat Ridge." A mile down the Trail from 5,441-foot

Rocky Top, on the western end of Thunderhead Mountain, you'll pass the head of Bote Ridge. Traces of the old road can be seen down the ridge near Bote Ridge Trail.

Once down off of Thunderhead, past the Spence Field and Russell Field shelters, the Trail comes down to Big Abrams Gap and Little Abrams Gap, which have a rugged knob between them. Old Abram was the Cherokee chief who led the last war parties against the Watauga settlements during the Revolution. His wife, called Kate by the white settlers, was also immortalized by having her name affixed (after being changed) to Cades Cove.

Above Little Abrams Gap, the AT runs for a half mile or so along a grassy ridgeline, crossing Devils Tater Patch. It then descends into Ekaneetlee Gap, formerly Egwanulti Gap, the site of an old Cherokee footpath between the Middle Cherokee towns and the Overhills.

Another mile or so down the ridge, the Trail reaches Doe Knob, the place where it turns south toward Fontana Dam and the Nantahala Mountains. It descends into the valley surrounding 4,020-foot Shuckstack, a singular knob with spectacular views of the entire ridgeline from Clingmans to Gregory Bald, much of which the Trail has just covered. This view is said to be one of the best in the southern Appalachians.

From Shuckstack, it's an easy downhill to Fontana Dam, where the Trail officially leaves the Great Smokies.

AUTHOR'S CHOICE

One of the best trips I've ever made was to Great Smoky Mountains National Park just to go day hiking and check out the cultural and natural opportunities. Check into a campsite, pack a lunch, and go. It's a perfect family excursion.

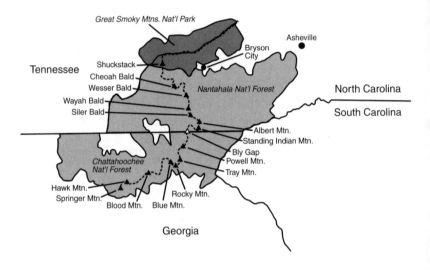

SOUTHERN NORTH CAROLINA
AND GEORGIA

14 North Carolina and Georgia

Trail Distances:
Fontana Dam, N.C., to North Carolina–Georgia State Line... 158.9 miles
North Carolina–Georgia State Line to
    Springer Mountain, Georgia .... 75.6 miles
Total Distance .... 234.5 miles

Maintaining Clubs:
Smoky Mountains Hiking Club:
    Davenport Gap, Tennessee, to Wesser, N.C. .... 100.4 miles
Nantahala Appalachian Trail Club:
    Wesser, N.C., to Bly Gap on the North Carolina–Georgia
    State Line .... 58.5 miles
Georgia Appalachian Trail Club:
    Bly Gap on the North Carolina–Georgia State Line
    to Springer Mountain, Georgia .... 75.6 miles

INTRODUCTION

This entire section of the Trail was almost bypassed when the original route was penciled out. For it was here, back in 1929 and 1930, that the final compromise was made to route the Trail to Mt. Oglethorpe via Springer Mountain.

And what they would have missed! The Nantahala Mountain section has long been touted as the rip-roaringest in the South. In fact, only the Mahoosucs in New Hampshire and Maine claim anywhere near the ruggedness found in the short range between the Great Smokies and Springer Mountain.

This whole area of the South has been undergoing impressive recreational development in recent years. Long famous for whitewater paddling and rafting, there is now also a growing community of rock climbers and other outdoors types assembling in the region.

GEOLOGY ALONG THE TRAIL

As we have seen, when the verdict to take the AT through the Smokies was reached, it complicated the selection of the southern terminus. The logical choice was in the area of Mt. Oglethorpe and Springer Mountain, which are the accepted joining points of the divergent branches of the Appalachian Range. But due to complications in the range, a route had to be found to get there.

Enter the Nantahalas, which are not really part of either branch but are rather a transverse range that crosses between the two. Born of the approach and massive impact of the African Plate over 250 million years ago, the Appalachians in the South seem not to have folded and fractured quite as neatly as they did to the north.

If you want an example of how this happens, lay a few heavy blankets on something slippery like a sheet of plastic. Push the blankets across the plastic and watch how they fold. Then push them from a slightly different direction—rather than pushing perpendicular to the edge of the blanket, push at an angle. What you'll end up with is not a set of parallel accordion folds but rather a wrinkled surface composed of any number of complicated pleats. Somehow, through a quirk of folding, no doubt aided by differences in rock strata, volcanism, and later erosion, the Nantahalas were formed along with other transverse ranges.

Once back onto the Blue Ridge, as the Nantahalas approach Georgia, the Trail joins the same ridgeline that it left near Peaks of Otter north of Roanoke, Virginia. The eastern edge of the Appalachian Ranges, the Blue Ridge is along all its length composed of the older metamorphics and occasional plutons and volcanics that we saw back in Shenandoah National Park. As it moves south, it features a rugged series of balds and knobs that resulted from this moist region's vigorous stream action. This southernmost section, the first part of the Trail covered by the majority of thru-hikers, is a test of strength and fortitude that many do not pass.

HISTORY ALONG THE TRAIL

When the Europeans arrived, the Nantahalas were a kind of border area. Though it was mainly within the Cherokee sphere, there were other tribes in the neighborhood. The Catawbas, who were bounced around by their neighbors quite a bit, occasionally lived in some of the valleys to the east, over by present-day Asheville, North Carolina, and the Cheraws hunted to the eastern borders of the Nantahalas.

Like the mountain areas immediately to the north, the ranges of northern Georgia and adjacent North Carolina were settled fairly late. Early attempts to settle the coastal areas of North Carolina came to grief. For instance, the British settlement on Roanoke Island simply disappeared; recent archaeological evidence suggests a massacre by local tribes.

When settlement finally did come in the mid to late eighteenth century, it followed the age-old pattern of centering on the coastal areas, spreading out over the Piedmont agricultural regions, and moving slowly up into the mountain valleys and coves.

Like the areas around the Smokies, the hills of Georgia and the Nantahalas were populated by independent mountain people. The culture, renowned for its folkways, craftsmanship, and music, is the object of vigorous efforts at preservation. The *Foxfire* series of books, first published in the '70s, was the result of information-gathering efforts by local students in northern Georgia.

Much of the settlement in Georgia and North Carolina was by Irish settlers, as well as poor English. This fact is perhaps best known to music historians, who for years have traced the Celtic origins of traditional mountain music.

HISTORY OF THE APPALACHIAN TRAIL IN NORTH CAROLINA AND GEORGIA

In the early days of the trailblazing efforts of the Appalachian Trail Conference, if mountain lore was rich in this area, mountain hiking was virtually unknown. This would prove to be a problem.

In those days, the ATC hadn't even decided upon the actual southern terminus of the AT. Largely through the efforts of the Smoky Mountains Hiking Club (established in 1924), it had been decided to route the Trail through the Great Smokies. But from there, nobody seemed able to agree on anything.

Enter Roy Ozmer. In 1929, the ATC asked him to scout out sections of the Trail. He started in the South, intending to walk all the way north. A back injury in Virginia prevented him from becoming the first thru-hiker.

According to sources within the Georgia Appalachian Trail Club, Ozmer was not given much to go on and probably felt that the choice of route was up to him. The route he chose started at Mt. Oglethorpe and headed northeast over Springer, Blood, and Tray Mountains, over the Nantahalas, and across to Silers Bald near Clingmans Dome. With the exception of the compromise that routed the Trail's exit from the Great Smokies farther west to Doe Knob, this is basically the route that the AT follows today.

The trouble was, the ATC had in reality decided on a more western terminus, at Cohutta Mountain in the northwest corner of Georgia. The influential Smoky Mountains club much preferred that course, since it would allow the Trail to traverse the Smokies in their entirety.

In his efforts, Ozmer was assisted by two Forest Service men: Everett "Eddy" Stone and his assistant, Charlie Elliott. They were both passionately devoted to the AT. Ozmer reported his suggestions for routing to the ATC and found a supporter in Myron Avery. It was that fact, along with some compromises with the Smoky Mountains club, that established the present route of the AT. The original southern terminus at Mt. Oglethorpe was abandoned in the late '50s in favor of the current site at Springer Mountain, as Oglethorpe's summit area was being heavily developed for chicken farming.

It was Everett Stone who realized that Georgia's opposition to the proposals of the existing Smoky Mountains club wasn't too compelling without a similar Georgia club to carry out the plans. No matter how often they proposed the eastern route, other clubs kept suggesting changes. And that was the main disadvantage the Trail had in this part of the South. Unlike New England, where things had gone so easily, there were no hiking clubs in Georgia, and no blazed hiking trails. They would have to start from scratch.

So Stone simply ordered Charlie Elliott to start the Georgia Appalachian Trail Club. Elliott, in his own fashion, complained vehemently—and comically—about being told to recruit a mountain club among people who had never seen a mountain. Charlie would have made the perfect movie sidekick—ever the Sancho Panza to Stone's Don Quixote.

After several false starts, Elliott finally succeeded, in the fall of 1930, in getting enough people together to form a club, with Eddy Stone as first president. From the start, they tried to keep the GATC as a club for active people—no "dead wood." It's pretty much that way today.

The following year, Myron Avery came south to hike the recently finalized southernmost section. Taking the trek with him was Warner Hall, soon to replace Stone as president of the GATC; he eventually gained immortality as the hiker whose image appears on the plaque marking the southern terminus on Springer Mountain.

The existing route actually became a reality when the Smoky Mountains club got its compromise. Continuing the route through the Great Smokies past Silers Bald to Doe Knob before descending into the valley of the Little Tennessee River, the Smoky Mountains Hiking Club trail crews pushed the route across the river, then back east along Yellow Creek Mountain, until it hit the main line of the Nantahalas at the Nantahala River near Wesser Bald.

The rest of the North Carolina part of this section was and is the responsibility of the Nantahala Appalachian Trail Club. Its most famous founding father, and its guiding light for most of its first fifty years, was the Rev. A. Rufus Morgan, a local minister and longtime resident of the area. He was a descendant of the Siler family, after whom Siler Bald (not to be confused with Silers Bald in the Smokies) is named. A man of immense personal energy, he would singlehandedly walk the Trail in his club's section with great regularity, on into his later years. He ranks among the major luminaries in Trail history.

THE TRAIL IN NORTH CAROLINA

Back in the day, the AT did not cross the Little Tennessee at Fontana Dam. It traveled instead practically the entire length of the Great Smokies, crossing at Tapoco, North Carolina, before coming all the way back east to where the Trail passes today. But that was in the very early days, before the completion of the Trail.

By 1931, the TVA had put in the Fontana Dam (at 480 feet, the biggest in the East), and the Smoky Mountains Hiking Club quickly took advantage of the occasion to divert the Trail to it, creating a more direct crossing to the Nantahalas.

The Nantahalas aren't nearly as tall as the Smokies—in the entire section, the Trail will top 5,000 feet only a few times, and it won't come near 6,000 again—but they are rugged and wild. It's hard to recommend destinations in this section, since in its entirety it makes for such great hiking.

Like many federal lands along the route, the Nantahala and Chattahoochee National Forests, through which much of the AT in this section passes, are laced with gravel and dirt roads. Many of these are open to the public for their use, but some may not exactly be a great avenue for the family's Honda Civic. Check with the ranger stations about road conditions. They'll be glad to tell you which roads are best to use—especially since it'll probably be them you call to pull you out if you go wrong. They can also tell you good spots to leave the car when you set off on the trail, and they'll help you steer clear of areas where active logging is going on. (You don't have to worry about them clear-cutting the Trail route, but a log truck can make a mess of your car if you block the logging road even a little bit when you park.)

After leaving Fontana Dam, the Trail runs along a road for almost a mile, but it then gets serious in a hurry. In a little more than two and a half miles, it climbs over 1,600 feet to the ridge crest in the Yellow Creek and Cheoah Mountains. This is not a ridgeline like the ones in Pennsylvania, and more than one hiker has lamented the absence of those steady, trustworthy Pennsylvanian walks that go for mile after mile at 1,400 feet. Here, it's the yo-yo routine. First, you're up to 3,500 feet on Yellow Creek Mountain, then down 800 feet into Yellow Creek Gap. Then you're back up, then down again, dipping into Cody Gap, Brown Fork Gap, and the knee-busting (or gut-busting, depending on which way you're going) descent into Sweetwater Gap. After a few more drops, its the big grunt up onto Cheoah Bald—at 5,062 feet, one of the big ones. Then, it's a few more knobs, and the big drop to the Nantahala River. And I mean a big, *big* drop—from 5,000 to 1,700 feet in less than eight miles. That's what I'd call in polite society an inexorable descent. Hikers traveling this section in either direction are welcome to use less restrictive language.

The AT crosses the Nantahala at Wesser, North Carolina. This is one of the homes of the Nantahala Outdoor Center, which has its headquarters in nearby Bryson City and an outpost on the Chattooga down on the South Carolina border. The NOC is famous as a whitewater outfitter, and it offers one of the best training courses in the country on all methods of travel on moving water. I took my first kayaking lesson at their outpost and couldn't wait to do it again. Considering the danger of the potholed, undercut rivers down here, I wouldn't paddle one of them without getting the straight story from the NOC gang.

Once across the Nantahala, the Trail gains altitude lost in the descent into the valley. This time, it's up to Wesser Bald—an ascent of nearly 3,000 feet in 5.7 miles. In the process, it passes by Rufus Morgan Shelter, named for the founder and guiding light of the Nantahala Appalachian Trail Club. It's in this section that the Nantahalas get their reputation as one of the ruggedest sections on the entire AT. The Nantahala ATC has in recent years routed this part of the Trail away from a wooded hike on the east side of the ridge to the ridge itself, providing the hiker with great views from time to time all the way to the summit of Wesser Bald. The route to the top is steep and frequently switchbacked. There used to be a fire tower on Wesser Bald, but all that remains are the concrete footings and an old fire road leading down to the highway near Beechertown.

And once again, it's downward. In two miles of walking, it's down a mere 800 feet to Tellico Gap before ascending once again, this time to Copper Ridge Bald—another 5,000-footer. This is a fun section to walk: it never dips below 4,000 feet, and there are several campsites on the shoulder of Wayah Bald (the peak also sports a restored observation tower with views to just about everywhere). Tellico Gap is accessible by car on some gravel roads between U.S. 19 and U.S. 64, as is Wayah Bald itself, but they don't show up very prominently on the guidebook maps. Get the USFS map of the Nantahala National Forest instead, from one of the Forest Service centers. They charge a couple of bucks for postage and handling.

The section from Wayah Bald south goes mostly over Forest Service trails. These are carefully constructed and well graded, making for less rugged—though just as strenuous—hiking.

After descending off of Wayah Bald, the AT drops another thousand feet or so into Wayah Gap. It was here, during the Revolution, that a detachment of North Carolina irregulars, tired of the Cherokees raiding their settlements, fought a fierce, though brief, encounter with a group of Cherokee warriors, defeating them. The gap is accessible on North Carolina Route 1310, which intersects U.S. 19 and U.S. 64 and runs past Nantahala Lake. The Trail then moves back onto the ridgeline and heads toward Wallace Gap, ascending a few hundred feet to top 5,000 feet again on Siler Bald.

At one point, Siler Bald wasn't so bald. The actual "bald" part had dwindled down to a space about one hundred feet long and seventy-five feet wide, crossed by the Trail just below the summit. After much discussion, the Forest Service decided to clear the top and make it a true bald again. When last I saw it, work had progressed to the point where practically the whole north side above the AT crossing was cleared. Whether it stays that way or not is another matter: the tree stumps on the upper slopes had already sprouted again. But if it can be maintained as a bald, it should offer splendid views of the whole range toward Fontana Lake and down into Georgia. It already has a great view of Wayah Bald and Nantahala Lake.

From Siler Bald, it's down a heavily switchbacked trail (with several good campsites) to Winding Stair Gap and U.S. 64. There's a parking area a few hundred feet down the road. Another couple miles or so brings you to Wallace Gap.

After leaving Wallace Gap, the AT heads up over the last section in the Nantahalas. Unlike most sections of the AT through these rugged hills, the route here sports plenty of side trails to the west of Albert Mountain. There is a National Forest Service campground, the Standing Indian site, about one and a half miles south of Wallace Gap via a branch off of Forest Service Road 67, at the headwaters of the Nantahala.

The Trail heads once again steeply uphill. *Do not cut across the switchbacks.* This area, with 5,250-foot Albert Mountain nearby and side trails cutting across the AT in a half dozen locations between Wallace Gap and Standing Indian, makes a great destination for a day hike. There are many popular campsites in many of the high gaps, like Mooney Gap, Carter Gap, and Betty's Creek Gap. The view from Albert Mountain is phenomenal, made all the more so by a tower on top you can climb.

After Betty's Creek Gap, the Trail heads up a long ridge, Little Ridgepole Mountain, at the 4,800-foot level. As it hits its southernmost spot on Ridgepole Mountain, look to the north along the ridge you've just joined, and tip your hat. On the spot where you're standing, the AT rejoins the Blue Ridge proper, the long line that it had been forced to leave up near Peaks of Otter so many miles ago.

In the meantime, head north again—or, more accurately, northwest. The Trail, after coming within about a half mile of the Georgia border, is looping back again for the specific purpose of crossing near the summit of 5,498-foot Standing Indian Mountain. You'll pay a bit to get there: from Beech Gap, you'll climb around 1,000 feet in about three miles. From Deep Gap on the west side, it's even steeper.

The view from Standing Indian, like that from so many peaks around here, is worth the effort. The Tallulah River Gorge, running out of the southern slopes of Standing Indian itself, is especially impressive, as are the views of the mountains of southern Georgia. For a Northerner, there are few better views of the hills of the South.

Which brings us to an important point. Most northerners tend to hold a rather comic-strip view of Southern people. We've been fed in recent years the idea that they're somehow threatening. Movies like *Mississippi Burning* and *Deliverance* (which was filmed a few miles to the south of where you're standing) presented us with the whole myth, all nicely wrapped in a slick, Hollywood package.

The truth is different. Nicer, more helpful folks have never been born. Just don't try to fight the Civil War (known locally as "the War of Northern Aggression") with them all over again.

The Trail comes down off Standing Indian along the Blue Ridge. There are a few ups and downs, and then you'll pass the Chunky Gal Mountain Trail, which branches off to the northwest. It was named for an amorous lass in a Cherokee legend who crossed the ridge in search of her true love.

Then it's a quick, roller-coaster descent to Bly Gap (3,840 feet), and you're in Georgia.

THE TRAIL IN GEORGIA

> *We are sincere in the belief that we have a very desirable section of the Trail down here and dare say that a great many ideas about Georgia will be changed on a hike through its mountainous portion.*
> —*Charlie Elliott*

Though impressive progress has been made all the way down the line from Maine, Georgia still ranks as the only state along the length of the AT wherein the Trailway is completely protected. The whole thing is within the enormous Chattahoochee National Forest.

Bly Gap marks the start of the Georgia section (though it's actually a few yards within North Carolina) and is a great destination all by itself, especially for overnight campers. Remote and consisting of a pleasant clearing, it's perfect for a weekend getaway. From Bly Gap, you can make day hikes up into the Standing Indian Range or back down the lower Blue Ridge in Georgia, with its terrific views of the Nantahalas and the surrounding Georgia peaks.

The trouble is, Bly Gap is a bit difficult to get to. It can be reached from the north either by the Chunky Gal Trail off of U.S. Route 64, seven miles west of Wallace Gap, or by heading straight to Deep Gap on U.S. Forest Service Road 71. From Deep Gap, it's 7.1 miles; via the Chunky Gal and the AT, it's more like 9.5. From the south, it's a bit more complicated. USFS Road 72 goes through Blue Ridge Gap, 3.1 miles south of Bly Gap, but normally a car can't get through the narrow, rough track. There are some trails up from Road 72 on either side of the gap, on which the Forest Service may be able to give you some information. Some years, though, you may be able to get within a mile or so of the gap, depending on road conditions. Ask the Forest Service for conditions and parking possibilities. A four-wheel-drive vehicle might help.

The 8.7-mile stretch of the AT from Bly Gap to U.S. Route 76 at Dick's Gap will give you an idea of the character of the Trail in Georgia. Situated as it is in the Chattahoochee, it's wild and remote. The Trail here doesn't have to parallel highways as far off as possible to preserve the illusion of wilderness. Instead, it freely cuts across the wildlands, and when it cuts across roads, the intersection is usually perpendicular.

Leaving Route 76, the Trail begins to cross the last miles blazed in this region. These were put through in the spring of 1931 by the GATC.

Although this section traverses over sixteen miles of wilderness, it travels much of that distance over abandoned Forest Service roads. These are pleasant to walk, as they have been graded. However, even roadbuilders can't totally overcome their tendency to go up and down.

But the magnitude of the ascents and descents isn't too extreme. In this stretch, the peaks are around 4,000 feet, with the gaps in the 3,500-foot range. You won't hear your ears popping the way you did in the Nantahalas.

Forest Service road approaches are available at Addis Gap, Tray Gap, and Indian Grave Gap. Some of these, especially the Addis Gap road, are rough and not passable to all vehicles. Again, contact the Forest Service for details. They also have a number of good maps, which generally go for a dollar apiece.

From Addis Gap, the route heads up along "The Swag of the Blue Ridge," a stretch along a ridge crest where the Trail changes elevation very little, staying at around 3,400 feet. The best views in the area are to be found on Tray Mountain (4,430 feet), between the Blue Ridge Swag and Indian Grave Gap. After Indian Grave Gap, the Trail descends into Unicoi Gap, where it crosses GA Route 75. Like so many highways in America, Route 75 lies where an old, popular Native American trail once ran.

At Unicoi Gap, the Blue Ridge makes a semi-circular swing to the northwest as it loops around a large cove containing the headwaters of the Chattahoochee River. There is a short side trail leading downhill from Chattahoochee Gap, 4.5 miles from Unicoi Gap, to Chattahoochee Spring, the official source of the river from which the National Forest gets its name. There is also a 5.3-mile blue-blazed side trail that leads north to Brasstown Bald, the highest point in Georgia.

The Trail in this area generally stays level on the ridgeline, going around 4,045-foot Horsetrough Mountain and reaching two knobs just shy of Tesnatee Gap. Both Poplar Stamp and Sheep Rock Top are in the 3,300- to 3,600-foot range and constitute fast climbs of about 500 feet from the ridgeline below.

Tesnatee Gap is the site of the Richard B. Russell Scenic Highway, another route that members of the local hiking clubs tried in vain to prevent. Until it was completed in 1966, this was the longest section in Georgia without a major road crossing.

The ridgeline west of Tesnatee Gap becomes a bit more saw-toothed, crossing Cowrock Mountain (3,842 feet), Levelland Mountain (3,942 feet), and, after crossing Neels (Frogtown) Gap, Blood Mountain (4,461 feet). The last was supposedly named after a battle between the Cherokees and Creeks that took place there.

Just south of Blood Mountain is De Soto Falls, a series of cascades along Frogtown Creek that might be worth a visit. They can be reached from U.S. 19 a few miles south of Neels Gap. Blood Mountain itself has a number of rocks and ledges from which hikers can get splendid views of the surrounding terrain. There is a stone shelter on the summit, refurbished in 1981.

Descending from Blood Mountain, the AT will remain at around the 3,000-foot level all the way to Springer Mountain. As it crosses the peaks of Big Cedar, Justus, Sasafras, and Hawk Mountains, it continues through the gentle, rolling ridges and valleys of the Chattahoochee National Forest. The ridges here are generally laid out on an east-west axis.

The terrain through which the last miles of the AT travel is characterized by the lush, healthy southern Appalachian forest—the growth that has been so prevalent since Virginia. But all is not always as it seems.

In the last miles, between Hightower Gap and Springer Mountain, the army from nearby Ft. Benning is in the habit of running complicated maneuvers. It may sound like World War III, and you need to be careful of imitation booby traps, mines, and the like. This is all simulated, but it can be somewhat disconcerting just the same. The Army, however, knows full well that the Appalachian Trail passes nearby, and its personnel have a reputation for being generally polite and helpful to hikers.

Springer Mountain (3,782 feet) has been the southernmost point on the Trail since 1958, when the ATC and the GATC finally rerouted the AT from its former terminus amid the chicken farms and desolation of Mt. Oglethorpe. As a destination, Springer is greatly superior. Standing amid a protected wilderness, an 8.7-mile hike from the road, it offers views of the surrounding territory from ledges near the summit. There's a bronze plaque of a hiker (Warner Hall) that is set into the rock at its summit that serves as a fitting marker. It bears the following legend:

APPALACHIAN TRAIL
GEORGIA TO MAINE

A Footpath for Those who seek
Fellowship with the Wilderness

THE GEORGIA APPALACHIAN TRAIL CLUB

The plaque pleased Benton MacKaye so much that he wrote to the GATC: "It is seldom that I've been hit between the eyes with utter and instantaneous delight as I was on viewing [a picture of] this real work of art. Here in vigorous embodiment is (to my mind) the spirit of the Appalachian Trail. . . . 'A footpath for those who seek fellowship with the wilderness.' This (to my mind) is a masterful definition of the Appalachian Trail."

MacKaye then went on to invoke the motto of the GATC. "Your words keep coming back to me: 'fellowship with the wilderness.' The last word cannot too often be repeated—wilderness, Wilderness, WILDERNESS! Not man but nature; man's relation not to man but to nature. And thereby—incidentally—the man-to-man relation finds its place."

To those of us who hike the Trail today, this serves as a reminder. Benton MacKaye's idea, so simple, yet so pervasive, caught on for one inexorable reason: people immediately understood it in a fundamental way, perhaps not on an intellectual level, but in their hearts. Just as the folks in Georgia, with their unpretentious inscription at the southern terminus, defined the concept to the delight of its creator, so did the people of Maine—and the hikers and volunteers of every place in between. Each one of them was struck by the simple rightness of it.

And rightness never dies.

AUTHOR'S CHOICE

As mentioned earlier, Bly Gap makes a great destination. It's perfect for one of those weekends when you want to pitch a tent and kick back. Take a day hike through the Standing Indian Range or the lower Blue Ridge, or just camp out and think beautiful thoughts.

As a day hike, Albert Mountain is also perfect. It's a decent trek up and back, with fun trails and great views off the tower on top.

Appendix

LOCALISMS

The Appalachian Trail runs through several different geographic and demographic regions of the United States. What is called one thing in Maine may be called another in North Carolina, and some hikers may occasionally become confused with the terminology used.

A narrow mountain valley that is called a *notch, pass,* or even *col* in the Northeast will be called *gap* by the time the Trail reaches Pennsylvania. Where Northeasterners tend to regard a summit as a *summit,* the farther one travels south, the more differentiation there is, depending on what the summit is like. Beyond the general Southern terms for a peak (*top, knob, high top, high knob*), a rocky summit will be known as a *dome.* A mountain topped with meadows is a *bald,* while one topped with heath is a *slick.* A predominance of balsam or spruce earns the title of *balsam,* while mountain laurel and rhododendron will sit atop a *laurel.*

This only occasionally gets confusing, as it does on Clingmans Dome, which is actually a balsam. It was formerly known as Balsam Mountain. The "dome" designation may prove prophetic, as the balsam woolly aphid and acid rain are conspiring to kill all the trees on the highest summit on the AT.

On the other hand, in his 1943 book *The Great Smokies and the Blue Ridge,* Roderick Peattie said, "A hogback vividly if inelegantly describes a type of mountain so characteristic that it might almost be called an appalachian as one speaks of an alp." He was speaking, of course, of the long, hump-backed, ridgelike mountains so common in all parts of the Appalachians.

In the South, valleys also have specific designations. A big one may just be called a *valley,* while a smaller one might be a *hollow.* A small valley leading up into the mountains is a *cove,* while true bottomland is called a *bottom.*

Streams, too, get special consideration. In Maine, a small one will be a *stream.* By the time the Trail reaches New Hampshire it will be a *brook.* That term will continue through Vermont and upper New England, only to give way (though not entirely) to *creek* in lower New England and New York.

Once down to Pennsylvania, however, use of the term *brook* peters out until it is totally out of use. In the South, the normal usage is *river* for a large stream and *creek* for a smaller one. It's pronounced "creek," too, not "crick," as they do in the Midwest. The only other variation is the use of the term *run* for creek. This happens only in Maryland and Virginia.

According to a 1941 article in the Potomac Appalachian Trail Club's Bulletin, the seemingly incomprehensible system of what trailside shelters are called can be ironed out as follows:

In Maine, they are *lean-tos.*

South of Grafton Notch, they are *shelters.* Closed shelters are *huts,* except those maintained by the Dartmouth Outing Club, which are *cabins.*

In New York, shelters are called *Adirondack lean-tos* (the original inspiration for the design).

On the Blue Ridge, closed shelters are called *shelters,* while open ones are called *lean-tos.* In the Great Smokies, lean-tos are *shelter-cabins.*

Over the years, as the population of the country moves about, names evolve, but for the most part, the regional destinations have remained. Fortunately, a tent is still a *tent.*

Resources

APPALACHIAN TRAIL NATIONAL HEADQUARTERS
Appalachian Trail Conference
799 Washington Street
P.O. Box 807
Harpers Ferry, WV 25425-0807
http://www.appalachiantrail.org/

The ATC website contains lots of useful information, including:
- Frequently updated lists of shuttle providers over most of the Trail route
- Updates on security problems at parking lots over the Trail route
- Tips on planning a hike
- Suggested hike itineraries
- Clothing and equipment checklists
- Maps and guidebooks—suggested and for purchase
- Safety tips
- Lists and locations of shelters and campsites
- Huts, cabins, and hostels in the Trail area
- Public transportation, including air
- Locations and descriptions of water sources
- Weather warnings and data
- All sorts of Trail statistics

You can also get membership information, which is important if you're serious about using the Trail.

REGIONAL OFFICES
New England
Appalachian Trail Conference
18 On the Common, Unit 7
P.O. Box 312
Lyme, NH 03768

phone: (603) 795-4935
fax: (603) 795-4936
atc-nero@appalachiantrail.org
Area covered: Maine, New Hampshire, Vermont, Massachusetts,
and Connecticut.

Mid-Atlantic

Appalachian Trail Conference
4 East First Street
P.O. Box 625
Boiling Springs, PA 17007
phone: (717) 258-5771
fax: (717) 258-1442
atc-maro@appalachiantrail.org
Area covered: New York, New Jersey, Pennsylvania, Maryland,
West Virginia, and Virginia south through Shenandoah National Park
(to Rockfish Gap/U.S. 250).

Central & Southwest Virginia

Appalachian Trail Conference
1280 North Main Street
Blacksburg, VA 24060
phone: (540) 961-5551
fax: (540) 961-5554
atc-varo@appalachiantrail.org
Area covered: Virginia from Rockfish Gap/U.S. 250 south to the
Virginia-Tennessee state line.

Tennessee, North Carolina, and Georgia

Appalachian Trail Conference
c/o U.S. Forest Service
P.O. Box 2750
160A Zillicoa Street
Asheville, NC 28802
phone: (828) 254-3708
fax: (828) 254-3754
atc-gntro@appalachiantrail.org
Area covered: Tennessee, North Carolina, and Georgia.

MAINTAINING CLUBS

Note: The following represents the latest available information at press time and may change as clubs change addresses, website domains, and officers. The final authority for this information is the Appalachian Trail Conference website, which is the most authoritative source available.

Maine Appalachian Trail Club
P.O. Box 283
Augusta, ME 04332-0283
(207) 265-MATC
http://www.matc.org/

Appalachian Mountain Club (AMC) Main Office
5 Joy Street
Boston, MA 02108
(617) 523-0636
http://www.outdoors.org/

AMC Pinkham Notch Visitor Center
Route 16 (P.O. Box 298)
Gorham, NH 03581
(603) 466-2721

Dartmouth College Outing Club
http://www.dartmouth.edu/~doc/
dartmouth.outing.club@dartmouth.edu

Green Mountain Club
4711 Waterbury-Stowe Road
Waterbury Center, VT 05677
(802) 244-7037
http://www.greenmountainclub.org/

AMC—Berkshire Chapter
chapterchair@amcberkshire.org
http://www.amcberkshire.org/

AMC—Connecticut Chapter

secretary@ct-amc.org
http://www.ct-amc.org/

New York—New Jersey Trail Conference

156 Ramapo Valley Road (Route 202)
Mahwah, NJ 07430
(201) 512-9348
http://www.nynjtc.org/

Wilmington Trail Club

P.O. Box 1184
Wilmington, DE 19899
http://www.wilmingtontrailclub.org/

Batona Hiking Club

215 S. Spring Mill Road
Villanova, PA 19085-1409
http://members.aol.com/Batona/

AMC—Delaware Valley Chapter

chair@amcdv.org
http://www.amcdv.org/

Philadelphia Trail Club

741 Golf Road
Warrington, PA 18976
http://m.zanger.tripod.com/index.htm

Allentown Hiking Club

info@allentownhikingclub.org
http://www.allentownhikingclub.org/

Blue Mountain Eagle Climbing Club

P.O. Box 14982
Reading, PA 19612-4982
info@bmecc.org
http://www.bmecc.org/

Susquehanna Appalachian Trail Club
http://www.libertynet.org/susqatc/

York Hiking Club
http://www.angelfire.com/pa2/yorkhikingclub/
MAINPAGE1.html

Cumberland Valley Appalachian Trail Club
P.O. Box 395
Boiling Springs, PA 17007
http://geocities.com/cvatclub/

Mountain Club of Maryland
7923 Galloping Circle
Baltimore, MD 21244-1254
http://www.mcomd.org/

Potomac Appalachian Trail Club
118 Park Street, S.E.
Vienna, VA 22180-4609
(703) 242-0693
http://www.patc.net/index.htm

Old Dominion Appalachian Trail Club
P.O. Box 25283
Richmond, VA 23260-5283
http://members.tripod.com/smsmith11/

Tidewater Appalachian Trail Club
P.O. Box 8246
Norfolk, VA 23503
http://www.tidewateratc.com/

Natural Bridge Appalachian Trail Club
P.O. Box 3012
Lynchburg, VA 24503
http://www.nbatc.org/

Roanoke Appalachian Trail Club
P.O. Box 12282
Roanoke, VA 24024-2282
http://www.ratc.org/

Outdoor Club of Virginia Tech
http://filebox.vt.edu/org/outdoor/

Piedmont Appalachian Trail Hikers
P.O. Box 4423
Greensboro, NC 27404
http://www.path-at.org/

Mt. Rogers Appalachian Trail Club
24198 Green Spring Road
Abington, VA 24211-5320
http://www.geocities.com/Yosemite/Geyser/2539/

Tennessee Eastman Hiking and Canoeing Club
Building 310
Eastman Road
Kingsport, TN 37662
http://www.tehcc.org/

Carolina Mountain Club
cmcinfo@carolinamtnclub.org
http://www.carolinamtnclub.com/

Smoky Mountains Hiking Club
P.O. Box 1454
Knoxville, TN 37901-1454
http://www.smhclub.org/

Nantahala Hiking Club
173 Carl Slagle Road
Franklin, NC, 28734
http://www.maconweb.com/nhc/

Georgia Appalachian Trail Club
P.O. Box 654
Atlanta, GA 30301
http://www.georgia-atclub.org/

OTHER IMPORTANT CONTACTS
Baxter State Park, Maine
64 Balsam Drive
Millinocket, ME 04462
(207) 723-5140
http://www.baxterstateparkauthority.com/

White Mountain National Forest, New Hampshire
http://www.fs.fed.us/r9/white/

White Mountain National Forest Supervisor's Office
719 Main Street
Laconia, NH 03246
(603) 528-8721
(603) 528-8722 TTY

Androscoggin Ranger District
300 Glen Road
Gorham, NH 03581-1399
(603) 466-2713 x 0
(603) 466-2856 TTY

Pemigewasset Ranger District
RFD # 3, Box 15, Route 175
Plymouth, NH 03264
(603) 536-1310
(603) 536-3281 TTY

Saco Ranger District
33 Kancamagus Highway
Conway, NH 03818
(603) 447-5448 x 0
(603) 447-3121 TTY

Ammonoosuc Ranger District
660 Trudeau Road
Bethlehem, NH 03574
(603) 869-2626
(603) 869-0314 TTY

Evans Notch
18 Mayville Rd.
Bethel, ME 04217-4400
(207) 824-2134
(207) 824-3312 TTY

Croatan-Nantahala-Pisgah-Uwharrie National Forests
160-A Zillicoa Street
Asheville, NC 28802
(828) 257-4200
Mailroom_R8_North_Carolina@fs.fed.us

Cheoah Ranger District
Route 1, Box 16A
Robbinsville, NC 28771
(828) 479-6431

Highland Ranger District
2010 Flat Mountain Road
Highlands, NC 28741
(828) 526-3765

Tusquitee Ranger District
123 Woodland Drive
Murphy, NC 28906
(828) 837-5152

Wayah Ranger District
90 Sloan Road
Franklin, NC 28734
(828) 524-6441